The Domestic Life of the Jersey Devil

The Domestic Life of the Jersey Devil

or, BeBop's Miscellany

Bill Sprouse

For MeMom and BeBop

DISCLAIMER

On being related (distantly) to the Jersey Devil, and why this whole thing was probably a mistake

The following is a work of nonfiction on the subject of the Jersey Devil—a kind of winged, fire-breathing monster indigenous to the central and southern parts of the state of New Jersey. It's a distant relative of mine.

Although the Jersey Devil is an important subject, one sadly overlooked by historians and social commentators, I feel I should alert you up front that this is really an excuse for me to write about myself, my family and the place where I grew up. I'm calling it The Domestic Life of the Jersey Devil to emphasize these ordinary, household qualities.

Additionally, this is a *self*-published work of nonfiction. Though my attorney will have examined the document for breaches of privacy and/or local libel statutes, none of the historical claims have been vetted by the standard committees or authorities.

All nonsense expressed herein is purely that of the author.

The Jersey Devil—and there's no pleasant way to put this—is a monster. It has horns, hooves, wings, scales and a tail. Sometimes the wings are bat wings, and sometimes the head is a horse's head. The body is sometimes that of a kangaroo and sometimes this body is striped. It flies, it breathes fire and it lives in New Jersey, in a big forest called the Pine Barrens (but more on this later).

The Jersey Devil is part folklore, part literary amalgamation—meaning it belongs both to a spoken tradition and to a written one. Tracing its history across three centuries requires the skills of both the folklorist and the historian (I claim neither). In physics, it might be called quantum rather than classical Newtonian. It exists in many places simultaneously and you can't observe it without altering it.

In South Jersey, where I grew up, the Jersey Devil was a kind of local celebrity, the central figure in the state's most famous folk story, a sort of regional Santa Claus—except in this case Santa would eat your children, fly off with your livestock and set your crops on fire.

I was about nine years old when my grandmother—my *BeBop*—told me I was related to the beast. She pulled a book down off a shelf somewhere and presented this information to me in the most straightforward manner. I remember yellowed pages and black-and-white photographs and the basic message, which was that a flying kangaroo with the head of a horse and the wings of a bat was somehow the thirteenth child of a distant relative.

She lived in the smallest house you'd ever seen, BeBop did, with a kitchen full of candy-making equipment and a ceiling fan you had to duck under. She could not have had much of a library, but there was room enough for that one important book.

The news that I was related to a regionally famous monster did not make a great impression on me, it must be said, and I promptly forgot the whole incident for the next ten years. It's one of the most important ideas that non-South Jersey persons can be made to understand about the Jersey Devil—lots of us have these funny little connections to the story. Nobody thinks it's all that unusual. It's not until we leave the region that it really becomes a conversation topic even.

My other childhood memory of the Jersey Devil comes from the Chelsea Village Apartments in Atlantic City, where I lived until I was ten. Like a lot of villages, Chelsea Village had a witch. This person lived in a ground-floor apartment that was filled waist-high with stacks of old newspapers. Her windows were perpetually steamed up and covered with black mold because she kept her faucets running hot water at all times. She left her apartment only at night, a program that, along with the steam, kept her skin radiant.

One day, we were sitting in the bushes beneath her window—a few of the other Chelsea Village kids and me probably, probably throwing pieces of wood mulch at each other—when the witch's proximity must have caused our minds to turn toward the occult, because soon we were chattering away about the Jersey Devil.

The Jersey Devil had been born far away, we surmised, maybe in Chelsea Heights or maybe in the Inlet. Its parents had locked it away in the basement and fed it raw meat, until one day, when the parents were too old or too sick to keep it locked up anymore, the Jersey Devil escaped into the wildernesses of Atlantic County, where it lived to this day.

I relate these stories not only because they constitute my sole childhood memories of the Jersey Devil, but also because they underline a certain problem that anyone involved in research of this kind must confront. When I started this project—when I started accosting *strangers* in the *streets* with lists of questions about the Jersey Devil—I would always ask people how they had first learned of the monster. Had they been taught the story in school perhaps? Or seen it on television? Or read about it in a book? Or been told the story by a Girl Scout troop leader or kindly old aunt?

Like a lot of devil hunters, I wanted to isolate the folk story so that I could match it up with a particular history—in my case with the story of a woman named Deborah Leeds, who had lived in Leeds Point in the 1730s, and who BeBop said was the *real* Mother Leeds behind the Jersey Devil folklore.

But the Jersey Devil story has been in the water supply in South Jersey for one hundred and fifty-five years, probably much longer. There is no folk story anymore—no single, informal, spoken tradition that's distinct and separable from the written or professionally produced versions of the story. There's only Wikipedia and *Weird New Jersey* and *MonsterQuest* and NBC 40 Nightly News and the Press of Atlantic City and James McCloy and Ray Miller's books and Leut's Devil Hunters and the countless other vectors by which this story—or

3

any story really—gets passed around. *I* can't remember how I first heard of the Jersey Devil and I'm supposedly related to the thing.

Still, maybe the exercise wasn't wholly without value.

I too might have gone through life thinking that the Jersey Devil was not that unusual, thinking lots of people had grandmothers who told them they were related to fire-breathing monsters. But I left South Jersey. I told my Jersey Devil story. People seemed to like hearing it. I'd never really had a story that people liked before.

I repeated my Jersey Devil story. It became my anecdote of choice. I'd never really had an anecdote before, and I was determined to use this one—in job interviews, at conference luncheons, on long-haul flights, on my personal pub crawls across lower Manhattan. I used it so often that I decided, at some point, I should find out what I meant by it.

Sprouse
Mexico City
October, 2013

ONE

BeBop and I go to Galloway Township

On an afternoon in March, 1999, BeBop and I drove to the Galloway Township Municipal Complex in Galloway Township, New Jersey, a kind of suburb of Atlantic City, to look for the Jersey Devil.

It was a weekday, bland and colorless. I was home from college for spring break. I'd borrowed my mom's car—the green Dodge minivan—and because I knew she would be interested, I drove over to Northfield and picked up BeBop—my blind, eighty-three-year-old grandmother—at my Aunt Maureen's house, and together we rode up the Garden State Parkway (about six miles) to the Galloway exit, then headed east down Jimmie Leeds Road a few miles to the municipal complex, a collection of beige buildings in the middle of a big field. A light rain fell as we sat in the minivan.

And that's how this whole lunatic misadventure began: me and BeBop at the Galloway Township Municipal Complex, looking for the Jersey Devil.

TWO

'Everyone liked being related'

I'm trying to remember what I *knew* about the Jersey Devil at this time, at the beginning. All good South Jerseyans can be counted on to know a few basic facts about the Jersey Devil, but the picture I had in my head of the beast was far too detailed to have arrived via the customary osmotic channels. I had spoken with BeBop, and I'd read the classic book on the subject—James McCloy and Ray Miller Jr.'s magisterial *The Jersey Devil* (1976), a battered, bright-orange copy of which sits next to me as I type this. The cover is delaminating, and from it peers an image of the Jersey Devil itself, floating elk-like and bewinged above some pine trees.

I knew that in the earliest written sources the Jersey Devil wasn't actually the *Jersey* Devil at all but rather the *Leeds* Devil or Leeds's Devil or, my particular favorite, the *Leeds Ghost*. In 1858, when W.F. Mayers went into the Pine Barrens, he emerged with stories about the Leeds Devil. In 1909, when sightings of the monster were reported in many newspapers, the monster on most peoples' minds, apparently, was the Leeds Devil.

But at some point, the old name gradually started to be replaced in the popular consciousness by the now-familiar Jersey Devil, and today that's how most people know the monster. In recent years, as the Jersey Devil had been seen less and less in the Pine Barrens, it seemed to be getting more and more attention in places like Galloway, where there was an effort by some members of the township administration to adopt the creature as the Official Township Mascot. Monster letterhead was circulated. Hats, tee-shirts and sweatshirts were put on sale. A Jersey Devil costume was commissioned. Plans for an annual Jersey Devil Ball were drawn up, "to be the annual social event in Galloway Township," as one official said.[1]

About four miles east of the Galloway Township Municipal Complex, in the woods out near the end of Leeds Point, were the ruins of an old house where people always said that the Jersey Devil had been born. No signs marked the location of these ruins. Their coordinates had been set down on no map, but it was a popular pastime among the local South Jersey youth to drive out to the end of Leeds Point late at night to peer into the woods in the hopes of seeing the ruins.

James McCloy and Ray Miller, in their valuable book, say that the most "widely-held" belief about the Jersey Devil is that it was the thirteenth child of a woman known only as *Mother Leeds*. Mother Leeds had been a Quaker, and she lived in the early decades of the eighteenth century either in Leeds

---

[1] Robert Nigro, "Galloway Township Officially Goes to the Devil," Mainland Journal (don't know the date)

Point or in Burlington. She was old and poor, and she had a large family. In a moment of frustration she said, "If I ever have another child, may it be a devil." And so it was. In 1735, when Mother Leeds gave birth, her thirteenth child was born normal, but as the midwife looked on, it transformed into a monster with a horse's head and bat wings, and it flew out the window into the Pine Barrens.

In BeBop's account, Mother Leeds was a real woman named Deborah Leeds who had lived, with her husband Japhet, in Leeds Point during the first decades of the eighteenth century. Japhet and Deborah were Quakers, apparently, and the local Quaker Meeting was held in their house. And they had a large family.

In 1704 Deborah gave birth to her first child, Mary. This event was followed by the arrival of Robert in 1706. Then came John in 1708, Japhet Jr. in 1710, Nehemiah in 1712 and Sarah in 1713. In 1714 there was James. Then came Daniel in 1716, Deborah in 1720, Dorothy in 1722, Ann in 1724 and Hannah in 1726.

Six boys and six girls.

Both Japhet and Deborah appear to have been alive in 1735, because Japhet's will was written in 1736 and Deborah was named in it. She would have been about fifty years old. Japhet would have been about fifty-two.

Japhet and Deborah's third child, John Leeds, married twice—first to Rebecca Cordery (1737) and then to Sarah Mathis Coate (1751). John and Rebecca's first child was William Leeds (b. 1738). William married Mary Osborne and they had a son, Richard (b. 1771), who in turn married a woman named Sarah (last name unknown) and had a son Joel (b. 1796), who grew up to become a ship's captain.

Captain Joel Leeds married Amy (perhaps Amy Rose) in 1819 and they had a son, Thomas (1826), who married Emaline. And Thomas and Emaline Leeds in turn had a son, Charles Augustus Leeds (about 1853), who grew up to become a Leeds Point bay man, fishing and clamming in the waters around the mouth of the Mullica River.

Charles and his wife, Sarah Kirkbride, had one child, a son,

William Maxwell Leeds, who lived in Leeds Point too.

William Leeds married a woman named Dorothy Holt and they raised a family of nine children, including a daughter (their second child), whom they named Mildred Helen Leeds (b. 1916), and who would come to be known by her own grandchildren as BeBop.

My grandmother, in other words, was a direct, male-line descendant, eight generations removed, from the Mother Leeds of the Jersey Devil legend.

Or so she said, anyway.

BeBop didn't think that Deborah Leeds had really given birth to a winged monster of course, but she did think that Deborah was somehow the inspiration for the story, that she *was* in some sense the real Mother Leeds.

The question was: Why? What had happened in Deborah Leeds' life to make people tell such an outlandish story about her?

BeBop told me that she'd first heard of the family connection from her own grandfather, Charles. It was kind of a family joke, she said. Whenever it snowed, Charles would make tracks on the roof of the house and tell his grandchildren that they'd been put there by the Leeds Devil, a distant relative.

"Everyone in Leeds Point liked being related," she said.

THREE

BeBop's beef with Harry

If the Jersey Devil had an official spokesperson, this title would belong to Harry Leeds. Whenever reporters or camera crews came to South Jersey to do stories about the Jersey Devil, they seemed to be guided, as if by magic, in the direction of Harry.

When I met him, he had been interviewed, by his own account, in The Washington Post, The Boston Globe, The Wall Street Journal, The Philadelphia Inquirer, countless times by reporters from the local papers—the Press of Atlantic City,

The Courier-Post, etc.—in each case emitting his down-home observations on the local monster, to which of course he was distantly related.[2]

There was the story in The New York Times where Harry said that the Jersey Devil exerted a "controlling influence" on South Jersey's youth, "especially for the ones that are considering running away."[3]

There was the *other* story in The New York Times where, after a particularly grisly B-movie about the Jersey Devil, Harry defended the beast against the suggestion that it had killed people.

"I've never heard of the Devil killing people," Harry said. "Of course, there's the movie version and there's the real version."[4]

When a reporter from The London Sunday Times came to Galloway, Harry somehow found out and called *him* on the phone in his hotel room.

"Hi. I'm hearing you want to meet the Jersey Devil," Harry had said. "I think I can help. The name's Leeds."

"Leeds…Leeds. Like old Ma Leeds, beldam of the monster?" the reporter said.

"That's right," Harry said. "Meet me at Oyster Creek tonight at eight."[5]

Such stories tended to depict Harry as an obscure fellow who'd had to be tricked out of the bushes with a tin of cat food, but he was in fact once the mayor of Galloway Township. He was still kind of the unofficial mayor in some circles.

BeBop detested the man.

This is a strong statement, I know, and ideally here I would supply two or three epigrammatic illustrations to support it, but BeBop's *extreme disapprobation* for Harry was of the diffuse, long-suffering kind, nurtured over decades and communicated

---

[2] I was only able to corroborate the NYT, London Times and Star-Ledger

[3] Eric Epstein, "Once Upon a Time, the New Jersey Devil Meant More than Hockey," in The New York Times, April 26, 1998

[4] Margo Nash, "The Devil You Think You Know," in The New York Times, Oct. 13, 2002

[5] Vincent Crump, "Would You Go Down to the Woods Today?" in the Sunday Times, Aug. 24, 2003

mostly indirectly through epithets and hurled cooking equipment. I'm not sure I ever really understood it.

I could say that it was kind of a family joke that BeBop disapproved of Harry, and this would be true. Over the years, I'd personally heard her say that she wanted to "brain" the man (her word). I heard her say that she wanted to "strangle" him. In a life remarkably free of grievance or enmity of any kind, Harry was the only person I'd ever heard BeBop say such things about.

Part of it, I think, was personal. BeBop and Harry had grown up together. They had gone to school together in a one-room schoolhouse in Oceanville back in the 1920s, and Harry'd had a distinct reputation as a hell-raiser. Though BeBop never mentioned any specific incident, I kind of got the feeling there was some ancient grudge left over from childhood.

Part of it might have been, for lack of a better word, *aesthetic*. In a region where lots of people were *related*, however tenuously, to the Jersey Devil, only Harry had succeeded in using this fact to get his name in the pages of The New York Times—twice. Something in his tone seemed wrong to her. He was using the story for his own personal "notoriety," she said.

But most importantly, I think, was a question of basic accuracy. Harry had said that he was related to the Jersey Devil. BeBop said that she was related to it. But BeBop was emphatically *not* related to Harry. This posed a problem.

BeBop's sister—my Great Aunt Dottie, who was, if anything, even more anti-Harry than BeBop—said that their grandfather Charles had been very emphatic on this point, very *particular*. Harry and his family were from a "different branch" of Leedses.

"Them Oceanville Leedses are no relation to us," Charles had said.

"Your great-great grandfather, Charles—two greats— would have rolled over in his grave if he heard you say that name," Aunt Dottie said. "He was very emphatic about this," she said. "Very particular."

Whatever the precise reason, diplomatic relations between the two branches of the Leeds clan were not good. Things seemed to be heading for some kind of showdown. On several occasions, both BeBop and Aunt Dottie had threatened to go down to city hall to confront Harry on certain genealogical claims that he'd made in the press. One incident, in which Harry was seen standing in front of the Leeds Point cemetery, waving around a copy of a family tree, had displeased them extremely. Somehow they could tell (no idea how) that the family tree that Harry waved was their own family tree and not Harry's at all.

BeBop had taken to carrying around a copy of the document on some of our trips, on the off chance that we'd run into Harry. That way she could ask him how he "fit in there" in the genealogy (her words), what obscure agenda he was using those people at The New York Times—those gentle, uninquisitive souls at The New York Times—to promote.

She was looking for answers, she said. Mostly, I think, she was looking for a fight.

FOUR

Harry does something peculiar

On the afternoon in question, BeBop and I had a simple mission. We wanted to learn the ownership history of a particular plot of land. The ruins of the old house in Leeds Point— because they were seldom written about and wholly unofficial, they seemed like one place where the folklore intersected with the actual, physical, corporeal world. We wanted to know who had owned the land and what we could learn about their lives.

At the Municipal Complex, BeBop and I milled around in the lobby for a while until someone came to ask us what we were doing. In research of this kind, there's often a moment when you're required to announce that you're looking for the Jersey Devil with your grandmother, and then you wait to see if the response is simpatico or if someone quietly slips off to phone an ambulance.

By happy coincidence, an old family friend was working

11

that day, Beth Stasuk—I'd played football and baseball with her son—and she wanted to help. She knew just the right person, she said. An old guy. Knew everything there was to know about the Jersey Devil. Great with quotes. In fact, he used to be the mayor of Galloway Township. In fact, he was still kind of the unofficial mayor. She'd give him a call right now. His name was Harry Leeds.

And about forty-five seconds later, in streamed Harry like he'd been waiting for us all morning.

My notes from this initial encounter include an estimate of Harry's age (inaccurate), and the following observations on his physical appearance:

- Stubbly
- Sweatpants during business hours
- Shit-kicker boots
- Shiny, Elks-Lodge-type jacket
- Marine Corps haircut
- Rolling gait

He spoke with a proper, old-timey South Jersey accent,[6] and he carried under one arm a manila folder that contained many documents. In his hand he held a videotape.

Harry introduced himself as a member of the Leeds family and as the proprietor of Muskett's Tavern (a notorious dive bar on the White Horse Pike). He said he had a long-standing interest in the Jersey Devil and in telling its story. Then he put in his tape.

About a year earlier, a documentary film crew had come to the Pine Barrens to do a short film on the Jersey Devil. The footage, which aired semi-regularly on The Discovery Channel, was narrated by an energetic and wholly unironic-sounding Englishman who spoke of the Jersey Devil in the kind of tones usually reserved for conspiracies involving the Kennedy assas-

---

[6] The North Jersey accent may or may not = Tony Soprano, but South Jersey is more like Patti Smith

sination and the aliens at Roswell.

He described the events in 1735 when Mother Leeds, a supposed witch, had given birth to the child that became the Jersey Devil, a kind of serpent with a horse's head, a "long bony structure," bat wings and a forked tail. Upon emerging from its mother's womb, the monster attacked the midwife and several other women in attendance, then flew out the window, and for three centuries this creature ("an evil creature") had terrorized the residents of a remote corner of America known as New Jersey.

Over the years, more than two thousand people claimed to have seen this creature ("one of the most extraordinary creatures ever recorded"). Factories and schools had been closed out of fear of the beast, and although *some* regarded it as folklore, *others* felt the weight of evidence was too great to dismiss.

Considerable data were marshaled in support of these claims, and there, amid much monkish chanting and the flitting of woodland animals, appeared Harry Leeds. He spoke of the nightly prowling and the livestock mutilations. He pointed out the ruins of the house where *they always said that the Jersey Devil had been born* ("Notice the lumber—all deteriorated now"). He described the monster's tendency to appear before terrible events in our nation's history—on the eve of war or natural calamity.

The Jersey Devil was a harbinger of doom, Harry said, and although it wasn't seen for years, there had recently been an uptick in sightings, perhaps a sign of some impending evil.

"It seems the Devil is trying to alert the people that something bad that's going to happen," Harry said. "The Devil is— like I say—he's very knowledgeable. He gets around. He *knows* what's going *on…*"

The tape ended. BeBop and I sat there in a kind of stunned silence. The chances of a genealogical showdown, dwindling rapidly throughout the performance, had evaporated entirely with Harry's last suggestion—that the Jersey Devil was not only *out there* but also that it somehow *knew* what was going on and wished to communicate it to us.

In the stunned silence that continued, Harry moved to collect his belongings, packing up his papers and rewinding his tape. We must have exchanged phone numbers. He must have handed me some press clippings.

And then here something unexpected happened. Maybe Harry felt the moment called for further elaboration. Maybe it was the fact that I was sitting there staring at him with a dumb look on my face. But, like Santa Claus in the goddamn Coca-Cola commercial, Harry Leeds looked at me and he *winked*.

I think I was the only one who saw it. BeBop was blind (macular degeneration). Beth Stasuk had long since continued on with her day. There was no one else present. But with that gesture, further conversation seemed unnecessary, and so, without asking Harry any questions or grilling him on his genealogy, BeBop and I left the Galloway Township Municipal Complex.

On the drive home I wondered how many times Harry had given similar performances without suffixing that wink.

FIVE

I take the casino bus to find the Jersey Devil

So began my extensive travels all over the state of New Jersey, looking for the Jersey Devil. After college I'd moved to New York City to live with some friends in a railroad apartment on East Ninetieth Street, having a grand time of it, ignoring everything. I held temporary positions with prestigious-sounding firms. I slept on the living-room floor.

My worldly possessions consisted of a pillowcase full of blue Oxford shirts and khaki trousers, a set of bocce balls, two Tiki torches and a grass skirt, the disintegrating fronds of which gradually integrated themselves into the apartment's industrial carpeting across the seasons of our occupancy. These objects were stowed each day in a heap behind a green pleather recliner that belonged to no one in particular. When the roommates retired by evening to their respective sections of the sleeping corridor, I had the room to myself.

We drank Schaefer Beer and listened to old country music,

14

but the memory of that ancestral monster and of Harry Leeds' performance that day in Galloway remained with me, and I would head home on weekends sometimes to continue my investigations.

To any other form of highway transport, I soon came to prefer the casino bus, a series of subsidized Greyhounds that departed hourly, sometimes half-hourly, from the basement of the Port Authority Bus Terminal next to Times Square in New York City and that were bound for any one of the five or six participating hotel-casinos on the boardwalk in Atlantic City.

These fine-smelling machines buzzed back and forth across the state seven days a week, including holidays—two and a half hours in each direction, one hundred and twenty-eight miles, thirty-five dollars for a single round-trip ticket, and when you got there you were partially reimbursed in the form of a "casino bonus." This used to be cash in an envelope but later turned into a twenty-dollar credit for "slot play" on a little plastic card. Sometimes you won a few dollars back on the machines.

It was a typical, if rigidly circumscribed, view of the New Jersey countryside, as seen through tinted plastic—the exit through the Lincoln Tunnel, ascending the cliffs of Wee-hawken, the Manhattan skyline opening behind you, dropping west through the roadcuts of Union into the big basin of the meadowlands, the sun setting over Pennsylvania as the airplanes landed.

In the beginning, these trips were part of the usual family round. I'd take the bus down on the weekends to talk with BeBop, or spend the day in the library, or drive around the northeast end of Atlantic City, the Inlet neighborhood, where my family had lived. There were Thanksgiving buses, Easter buses, birthday buses, Sunday morning buses full of senior citizens who were strung-out and grouchy after their weekend sprees, Friday night buses with the prohibition against alcohol consumption being discreetly, but very definitely, violated. The drivers would make colorful speeches asking us please to behave ourselves and be patient and to not smoke in the restrooms, bus travel always a sad trial for smokers.

There were Holy Thursday buses when the trees had no

leaves, late-autumn buses when the marshes had gone brown, Christmas Eve buses with the casino skyline reflected like a spray of outlandish jewels in the bay as you crossed into Atlantic City, big LED snowflakes dancing down the façade of Harrah's, Mötley Crüe and their umlauts coming to the Borgata, Tony Bennett at Caesar's.

There were strange petrochemical effects in the skies above the refineries, and telephone poles, some unusually thick and rusting, rising from the marshes at improbable angles, and smokestacks ejecting little plumes of white cloud into the surrounding, slightly less white cloud, and the majestic superstructure of the Linden Co-generation Plant, like the exoskeleton of some dead city that had been strung with light bulbs, and access roads named IKEA Drive and Daffy's Way, and billboards that read "PREFERRED FREEZER SERVICES" and big stacks of brightly colored shipping containers covered with Chinese characters. And sometimes swans would swim in the drainage ditches beside Newark Airport, mixing haughtiness and sootiness in one gray curve of neck.

Around mile marker eighty-eight of the Parkway, the pine trees would begin in earnest, and by exit seventy-seven, you'd be surrounded by them, the weirdness of the Pine Barrens—fifty miles of infirm pine trees, robust pine trees, pygmy pine trees, pine trees on the medians, charred pine trees where forest fires had swept through, the bleached boles of dead pine trees, white sands through brown pine needles.

Near Barnegat a little piece of suburbia would bump up against the Parkway—a bloom of satellite dishes through the pine branches—but then it was another long jump to New Gretna and the Mullica River, where the salt marshes broke open: flat sky, flat marshes, power lines running across the meadows beside the river, the casino lights reflecting off the low cloud above Atlantic City.

The Jersey Devil is typically associated with the Pine Barrens—the forest of pine and scrub oak that covers roughly 1.1 million acres of central and southern New Jersey—and with a certain class of Pine Barrens resident, these the charmingly dysgenic *Pineys*, about whom more later. But the epicenter of my Jersey

16

Devil story is further south and east of the Pines, in the big suburban townships of Galloway and Egg Harbor, in the mainland suburbs of Northfield, Linwood and Somers Point and in the old beach towns of Atlantic City, Ventnor and Longport.

This isn't really the Pine Barrens. People here didn't work in the traditional Piney industries of charcoal-making, blueberry picking and cranberry cultivation. Life in Leeds Point, at the mouth of the Mullica River, was more oriented toward the sea. People there "went into the bay" to make their livings, it was said.

SIX

BeBop's family arrives in Leeds Point

My grandmother's family first came to this place when Thomas Leeds of England arrived in Shrewsbury, in what was then the colony of East New Jersey, sometime in the 1670s. Thomas was a Quaker, emigrating to avoid religious persecution in his native England. There's a story (uncorroborated) that he had been imprisoned in the Tower of London for his opposition to King Charles I. When Charles was beheaded in 1649, Thomas was released, but his stay in prison had made him cautious. A decade later, with the monarchy restored and Charles II on the throne, he began preparations for the move to the colonies.

Thomas had three adult sons—Daniel, Thomas and William—who followed him to the New World. William, a cooper by trade, settled in Middletown, in present-day Monmouth County, and later bought land from his brother Daniel near Absecon Creek, not far from present-day Leeds Point. Like his father and brothers, William was a Quaker, though he eventually broke with the Society of Friends, returned to the Church of England and was baptized along with his wife at the Anglican Church in Shrewsbury in October 1702.[7] According to

[7] Joyce Kintzel, *Tree of Leeds: A Colonial South Jersey Family* (2005)

17

Joyce Kintzel, an amateur genealogist who put together a very convincing history of the Leeds family in New Jersey, the vestibule at the Anglican Church in Burlington contains a memorial to William Leeds, who is listed alongside George Keith and Governor Lewis Morris as an important early benefactor of the church.

The most important of these early Leedses, to historians, was Daniel—Thomas Sr. had died by 1687, and Thomas Jr. left little trace in the historical record in New Jersey. Daniel wrote an almanac that predated Ben Franklin's, one of the first almanacs in America in fact, and he held several important political positions, including the job of surveyor general of West New Jersey. And he was a controversialist of some renown, having been summoned to appear before the Quaker authorities in Philadelphia to apologize for things he'd written. He eventually left the Society of Friends altogether over his involvement in something called the Keithian controversy. And perhaps because of this, he has from time to time been at the center of speculation about the origins of the Leeds Devil story.

In 1968, a folklorist from Maryland named Fred MacFadden wrote to the Atlantic County Historical Society requesting information on Daniel Leeds and the Jersey Devil. MacFadden's theory seemed to be that Daniel's public quarrels with the Quakers had somehow been at the root of the Jersey Devil story. He hoped the historical society could provide, in his words, "an explanation for the date of 1735 for the Jersey Devil."[8]

MacFadden's letter was addressed to Olive Rundstrom, who was then president of the historical society. A few years later, Rundstrom would compile an extensive genealogy of the Leeds family in South Jersey, including information on Japhet and Deborah Leeds, but at the time she could only give MacFadden a few excerpts from Daniel's writings, a short piece of his poetry, and a letter written about him by William Penn. She couldn't, or didn't, give MacFadden the concrete

---

[8] The letter was in the historical society's file on the Jersey Devil.

link between folklore and history that he was looking for, and for the next thirty years, the Daniel Leeds-Jersey Devil hypothesis basically sat on the shelf. McCloy and Miller, in their 1998 book *Phantom of the Pines*, perhaps alluded to the idea, writing that the Quakers "strongly disapproved" of Daniel Leeds' almanac for "being critical of certain religious practices," and suggesting that this "religious controversy" might have somehow "linked 'the Devil' with Leeds' unpopularity with the Quakers," but they too couldn't, or didn't, push the idea forward.

In 1997 a novelist named Cynthia Lamb published *Brigid's Charge*, her take on the origins of the Jersey Devil story. Lamb's novel was historical fiction, but her research into the early history of the legend was probably the most comprehensive and insightful that's ever been published. Her protagonist was a real, documentable, historical figure—Deborah Leeds, in fact—from whom Lamb said she was directly descended. Cynthia is my second cousin—BeBop and Aunt Dottie's niece.

Lamb said that in all her research she found only one woman whose biographical details matched those suggested by the legend—namely Deborah Leeds—and she did something else. Cynthia Lamb was the first person (and to my knowledge the only person) to point out that Japhet Leeds—the husband of Deborah Leeds and father of the supposed Jersey Devil—was the oldest son of Daniel Leeds, about whom people had been speculating for so long.[9]

Cynthia Lamb matched the Jersey Devil legend with concrete historical names, dates and places, and she did so in a way that suggested it might be possible to ground the legend in historical fact. But her book was historical fiction. One of the reasons it wasn't straightforward history was that Cynthia lacked the documentary evidence to portray Deborah and Japhet in adequate biographical detail. They were an obscure colonial couple living on the edge of a wilderness, and there

---

[9] McCloy and Miller actually mention Japhet by name and point out that he's Daniel's son, but they don't mention the twelve children or that his descendants (my grandmother anyway) still talked about him in connection with the Jersey Devil.

was simply not much known about their lives.[10]

But with Daniel Leeds there were plenty of records, and his story seemed too interesting to simply ignore.

Daniel appears to have arrived in East Jersey not long after his father and to have quickly made the beginnings of a famous career. In early land records he was listed as a "yeoman" but he was later referred to using the more honorific title "gentleman." In March 1681, he was sworn in as surveyor general of West Jersey. The next year he was elected to the colonial assembly. He would go on to serve on the colonial council and in the courts at Burlington. But he was probably best known for the almanac. Daniel published Leeds Almanac for twenty-seven years beginning in 1687, and when he retired in 1714, the franchise was handed down to his son Titan, who continued it into the 1730s.

Almost from the beginning, it seems, the Quakers hated it. All copies of one year's edition were seized by the Philadelphia authorities and destroyed, and Daniel was required to publicly apologize, acknowledging that what he had written was "not suitable for an almanack barely considered" and promising that he would "write more serious" in the future and that he would "publicly signify as much" in his next almanac.[11] When Daniel openly split with the Quakers during the Keithian controversy, the almanac was a platform he used each year to attack his former coreligionists.

Daniel originally settled in Springfield, in West Jersey, not far from Burlington, but in 1694 he carried out a survey of land near Smithville, in present-day Galloway Township. The property was bounded by a number of creeks—Mott's Creek, Wigwam Creek, Holly Swamp Creek—some of which are still identified on topographical maps forming a rough border of present-day Leeds Point.

In 1698, Daniel had these surveys confirmed by the colony's proprietary council, meaning—at least to my understanding of colonial real estate—that he took ownership of the land.

---

[10] Lamb talked to me over the phone.
[11] Quoted in John Pomfret, *Province of West New Jersey* (1976)

The historian John Hall, citing records in the archives of the surveyor general's office, said Daniel brought his family to this place and called it Leeds Point. And by 1702, he was signing his epistles to his various Quaker enemies from "Little-Egg Harbour," an old name for the Mullica River.

In the early 1690s, when the Keithian controversy was at its height, Daniel had six children. By 1700, he would have had two more. He would have been in his mid-to-late-forties, seemingly in the prime of this resplendent career. Yet he'd left Burlington and moved his family across the Pine Barrens to a nondescript swamp on the opposite end of the colony.

Trying to assign a motive to this action three hundred years after the fact seemed an unpromising business, but the publication of a pamphlet, *News of a Trumpet*, in 1697, appeared to set many of the subsequent disasters in motion. The document had been printed not in Philadelphia, where Daniel's early work was published, but in New York, where his longtime printer William Bradford had relocated following the Keithian controversy.

Trumpet was a confession of faith, but it was also a critique of the Quaker faith in which Leeds had been raised and for which he had presumably crossed the ocean, but to which he was now openly hostile. It accused eminent Quakers—William Penn and George Fox—of blind prejudice, of "base temporizing" and of refusal to admit errors. It was meticulous and maybe even petty, but it was also genuinely moving on the subject of Daniel's conversion experiences, including the one that, he said, had led him to renounce Quakerism.

It was difficult reading, both because of the arcane style and subject matter and because of the poor quality of the document—a PDF of a photocopy of a three hundred-year-old broadsheet—but in the parts that were legible, Daniel seemed eminently reasonable, apologetic even, given all the fuss it caused.

But he was unapologetically Keithian, even though the Keithian controversy was supposedly several years in the past and the Keithians themselves apparently in retreat. It was in its way an attack document. And Leeds said he fully expected to be attacked in return.

21

Toward the end, in a section on Quaker name-calling (the use of "hard names" by Friends), Daniel cited a poem allegedly written by Quakers, in which they compared certain enemies, in contradiction to their stated principles, to a group of *devils*. The quality of the copy here was not good, but there seemed to be reference to dark devils, dingy gods, a child of Hell even. And Daniel said he fully expected such language to be used against him as well.

"These five men inserted in the aforesaid Rhymes, they call a Team of Devils," Daniel said, "and here I expect they will put me in for a sixth Devil."

And in fact they would.

SEVEN

BeBop and I go to Bombay

My grandmother was the only one in the family who would go with me for Indian food. From among South Jersey's subcontinental options (all two of them) we preferred the Bombay Indian Restaurant, a narrow storefront in the English Creek Shopping Center between the dollar store and the dry cleaner's, and every few months or so we'd sally forth up the Black Horse Pike to the ten dollar all-you-could-eat lunch buffet.

Of the two of us, she was always the more adventurous, sampling all kinds of samosas and pakoras and chutnies, while I'd generally set out in an attitude of high-minded investigation, then blow through three plates of chicken tikka masala and sink back into food coma.

We would sit there beneath the glittering portrait of Rama, Seventh Avatar of Vishnu, and talk about BeBop's family and her early life in Leeds Point.

She was the second of nine children of William Leeds of Leeds Point and Dorothy Holt of Wynona, and she had grown up in a narrow, three-story house on Leeds Point Road. These Leedses were bay people. Her grandfather Charles fished for clams and oysters in Great Bay, as the Mullica River estuary was called, and in the coastal waterways around Brigantine and

22

Atlantic City. When Leeds Point got electricity and the Leeds family got a telephone, sportsmen from Philadelphia would call to arrange hunting and fishing tours with Charles. He built, or caused to be built, the house on Leeds Point Road where BeBop and Aunt Dottie had been born and where the extended family—brothers and sisters and parents and grandparents—all lived. He owned two boats: a flat-bottomed scow for clamming, and a newer, fancier vessel, the *Dorothy H.*, for the charter fishing and hunting expeditions. And he owned a bicycle. Each day Charles would ride his bicycle down to Oyster Creek to go fishing in the bay, until one day in the winter of 1927 he fell into the bay and got pneumonia and died.

Charles' son William Leeds too was a bay man, though perhaps not as frugal or industrious as his father, and when BeBop and Aunt Dottie talked about him, a hint of sardonicism came into their voices. He was referred to as "William the Famous" and "Our Illustrious Father" by Aunt Dottie, who nevertheless remained strongly impressed by his seamanship. Their childhood memories involve big nautical maps spread out across the dining room table by their father, who would study them.

"He knew the ocean all the way to Florida," Aunt Dottie said. "He knew the water like you would never believe. It was just born naturally in him, I guess."

William Leeds had been certified to operate the largest, most prestigious vessels afloat, the *Queen Elizabeth* and ships of her caliber, but mostly he operated the *Miss Atlantic City*, a speedboat that took tourists on day-trips out of Gardner's Basin at the north end of Absecon Island. The story I'm required to tell at this point concerns the onboard guitar player on one such voyage who was discovered, stone dead, sitting in his little musician's chair, shortly after the boat left the docks. William the Captain famously ordered a blanket thrown over the corpse, so it wouldn't disturb the passengers as he continued with his tour of the inland waterways, since he had no intention of cancelling the trip with paying customers still onboard.

BeBop gave me a photocopy of an old picture of Charles and Sarah Leeds standing in front of their house on Leeds Point

Road. The photo itself was sepia-tinted, undated and visibly disintegrating. Charles was wearing white suspenders and what looked like a skullcap, and was standing proudly, maybe, behind his bicycle. Sarah was standing beside him, leaning toward him, maybe, affectionately. Charles looked tall beside his bike and his wife. Each of them looked tanned and lean, gaunt even. They looked like pioneers.

When I asked BeBop what Charles was like, she said, "He was a typical Leeds—Leeds Point Leeds."

"What do you mean by that?"

"Oh, I don't know," she said. "I don't know now what I meant by that."

He was six-foot-four, she said, with a big mustache, and he had gone to sea as a boy. He was "ruddy" she said, "real *roody*" as all the Leeds Point bay men were from spending so much time on the water.

"He could swear like you can't believe," she said. "No foul language, but just ordinary cuss words. And that's where our brother Bob, that's where he learned to swear."

Behind Charles and Sally, in the picture, the house looked spare and isolated too. The trees that now cover Leeds Point had apparently been cut down, and only one or two pines were visible on the horizon. You could see the window to the attic, which served as a bedroom, where BeBop and Dottie slept. BeBop said she sat as a girl in the window and read *Silas Marner* and looked across the marshes. On the horizon in that direction was visible the skyline of Atlantic City.

EIGHT

BeBop prevents civil war

BeBop first told me about the Jersey Devil sometime in the mid-1980s, but it had been her custom to advertise the family affiliation for some years prior. I know this because she was quoted around the time of my birth in the Press of Atlantic City in connection with an ad hoc South Jersey militia that was planning to invade Texas to retrieve the beast, her "ancestor," as she called it.[12]

This incident had its origins sometime in late 1975 or early 1976, when two Texas law enforcement agents out on routine patrol reported seeing a large birdlike object in the skies above Brownsville.[13] Reports of additional sightings followed and as the story gained traction a minor monster scare ensued.

Radio stations across Texas began offering cash rewards for the object's capture. The Texas Parks and Wildlife Department began issuing related counter-statements to remind residents of the penalties for bothering protected birds. The whole affair was spoofed by Johnny Carson on the *Tonight Show*.[14]

The Texans seemed to believe that the monster in question was the famous *Thunderbird* of Native American folklore, but in New Jersey people naturally thought of the Jersey Devil. In South Jersey, a group calling itself the Concerned Citizens for the Return of the Jersey Devil claimed that the monster in fact *was* the Jersey Devil, and that it had been kidnapped by rogue Texans. The group's chief executive, a public relations guru named Len Sheinkin, sent telegrams to Texas Governor Dolph Briscoe and other senior government officials demanding the beast's peaceful and immediate return. When no monster was produced, he organized his raiding party.[15]

The plan, Sheinkin said, was to fly to Texas in a hot-air balloon carrying an army of "little old ladies from the talk shows." Once there, he and the senior citizens would surround the governor's mansion in the middle of the night, ringing cowbells and making other uncomfortable noises.

"We're pretty sure he'll give us the Devil then," Sheinkin said.

The Texans, meanwhile, contemplated a counterstrike involving Texas chaparral—the so-called *roadrunner* birds of Wile E. Coyote fame. "They've got a beak long enough to drill an oil well, which is what they ought to be doing in New Jersey,"

---

[12] From the Press of Atlantic City, confirmed by BeBop
[13] See McCloy and Miller, Phantom of the Pines
[14] I couldn't find anything to corroborate the Carson Show claim.
[15] McCloy and Miller, Phantom

one Texas congressman said.[16]

By this point Sheinkin had appointed himself Commander-in-Chief of the New Jersey Expeditionary Force to Liberate the Jersey Devil, Generalissimo of the South Jersey Fleet and Admiral of the Armies. He had hired a professional balloonist for transportation purposes. He gathered his supporters in a field in Smithville, and he joined them wearing a cape and tricorn hat, like Lord Nelson.

Amid all this, BeBop intervened in her usual conciliatory way, telling a columnist from the Press of Atlantic City that she was a member of the Leeds family, one of a large number of Leedses born in Leeds Point.

"We all claim to be related to the Jersey Devil," she said.

"I know some very nice people in Abilene, Texas and I'm leaving for there immediately to spend a week with them…I'm certain that if my ancestor's there, either I'll find him, or he'll find me. And once I locate him, I'll immediately notify the rest of the Leeds clan, and they'll fly out to Texas and bring him back to South Jersey where he belongs."[17]

Sheinkin's balloon never got off the ground.[18]

NINE

West Jersey as Quaker utopia

The Province of West New Jersey: South Jersey—itself an informal or even *folk* designation, there are no official boundaries—is said to be roughly contiguous with this initial proprietary. A short summary of its founding as a Quaker colony is probably necessary for context purposes:

Sometime in the early 1660s King Charles II of England decided that the Dutch colonies of the mid-Atlantic seaboard

---

[16] McCloy and Miller, Phantom, quoting *The Austin American-Statesman*; the congressman was J.J. "Jake" Pickle

[17] Press of A.C., confirmed by BeBop

[18] McCloy and Miller, Phantom

could be seized to the benefit of crown and country, and so, in 1664, he granted the territory to his brother, and future successor, James, the Duke of York. James in turn dispatched an armed expedition led by Richard Nicolls to dispossess the Dutch.

On August 27, 1664, four English frigates under Nicolls' command sailed into New York Harbor, and Peter Stuyvesant, Director-General of New Netherlands, surrendered his colony to the English without a fight.

Rather than wait for news of Nicolls' triumph, James granted the lands comprising the future state of New Jersey to two royal favorites—Lord John Berkeley and Sir George Carteret. The place would be known as *Nova Caesarea*, in honor of Jersey, the island in the English Channel where Carteret was born.

Nicolls meanwhile remained in America, unaware of his master's business. Attempting to serve his king and strengthen the colony, he invited settlers from New Haven and Long Island to establish towns to the west and south of Newark Bay. This bipartite arrangement, with the "Nicolls patentees" as they would come to be known on the one hand, and the proprietary successors of Berkeley and Carteret on the other—would become a source of "perpetual dispute between two social classes" (in the historian Donald Kemmerer's words). The details of this fight mattered less, Kemmerer says, than the fact that it was never settled.[19]

Berkeley and Carteret assumed that their land grant gave them rights of government, and they proposed a system of laws—the famous Concessions and Agreements, imported from Carolina—which offered religious liberty and regular elections by an assembly of freemen and proprietary agents.

On March 18, 1674, John Berkeley—losing interest in his colony and sensing perhaps the many obstacles that lay between him and any sort of profit from the venture—sold his stake in the colony to two Quakers, John Fenwyck and Edward Byllynge, for one thousand pounds.

---

[19] Kemmerer, *Path to Freedom: The Struggle for Self-Governance in Colonial New Jersey: 1703 – 1776* (1968)

This "amazing pair" (the historian John Pomfret's words) were either "pious frauds" or "self-deluded innocents." And anyway Byllynge was bankrupt, the purchase being part of some obscure scheme to restore his fortunes.[20] Trustees for the bankrupt Byllynge were three Quakers—Gawen Lawrie, Nicholas Lucas and William Penn. They took over Byllynge's stake and began selling shares. The Dutch re-conquest complicated proceedings, but the deal was still a fantastic one for the Quakers.

At some point it was decided that Carteret would not be able to agree on methods of governance with his funny new neighbors and that the colony should be divided. Thus, on July 1, 1676—nearly five years *before* Penn was granted his charter for Pennsylvania—the partition document was signed creating the sister provinces of East and West New Jersey, with West Jersey designed as a haven for displaced Quakers.

As the historian Edwin Tanner puts it, "Here, rather than in Pennsylvania, are seen the applications of the teachings of Fox [Quaker founder George Fox], unmixed with the ideas of feudal proprietorship."[21] The boundary ran diagonally across the colony from a point just north of Leeds Point.

And it was to this initial Quaker utopia—this perhaps fatally contrived Quaker utopia—that Daniel Leeds and George Keith came at the end of the seventeenth century.

TEN

Keith's beef with the Public Friends

George Keith was a surveyor and a writer and a Quaker and a Scot, and in 1690 he began a very public critique of the social and religious establishment in the Delaware Valley that shook the Quaker political project there to its foundations.

Keith had been born about 1638 on the Aberdeenshire coast of Scotland at Peterhead to Presbyterian parents who

---

[20] John Pomfret, *Colonial New Jersey: A History* (1973)
[21] Edwin Tanner, *The Province of New Jersey: 1664-1738* (1908)

disowned him when they learned of his Quakerism. He studied philosophy, math and ancient languages at Marischal College in the 1650s (the historian Jon Butler calls him "the most urbane and sophisticated of the Public Friends to emigrate to America") but he would later denounce the university as the "stews of Anti-Christ."[22]

He was evidently a charismatic fellow, with a naturally odd speaking voice that combined with his thick Scots accent to make him unintelligible to many persons, yet he remained in demand as a preacher.[23] He joined the Aberdeen Meeting of the Society of Friends sometime in the 1660s (Butler puts his "convincement" in 1664) and was thus subject to the many imprisonments, stonings, beatings, etc. that made up the life of a seventeenth-century English Quaker, all of which enhanced his reputation among his coreligionists. In the 1670s he toured Europe with leading Quaker figures, including George Fox and William Penn. His travelling companions would later call him moody, brooding, tempestuous, possibly deranged.[24]

In 1685, following a year at Newgate Prison, he was offered the job as surveyor general of the Province of East New Jersey by his friend, the governor, Robert Barclay. He accepted and sailed for Perth Amboy with his wife, two daughters, an apprentice and two servants. One of his first jobs was to survey the boundary between East and West Jersey.

Not long after his arrival in the colonies Keith began to observe, and to note in letters to his superiors, that not all his fellow émigrés shared his understanding of basic Christian doctrine. There were many "Ranters and airy Notionists" among the colonists who needed remedial training. When Keith appealed to local leadership for support in this matter, he found, to his dismay, that they were ranters and airy notionists too.

---

[22] Butler, "Power, Authority, and the Origins of the American Denominational Order: The English Churches in the Delaware Valley, 1680 – 1730," in *The Transactions of the American Philosophical Society* (1978)
[23] Ethyn Williams Kirby, *George Keith: 1638-1716* (1942); she cites George Whitehead on the voice thing.
[24] Gary Nash, *Quakers and Politics* (1968)

In 1689, Keith left his estate in East Jersey to take a job as head of the Latin school in Philadelphia (his biographer, Ethyn Kirby, suggests he was ready to leave the colonies altogether), and not long after this move, the festivities began in earnest. In March 1690, he presented a paper titled *Gospel Order Improved* to the Philadelphia Meeting of Ministers, a group of influential Quakers who traveled around evangelizing, dispensing advice and generally "offering their Light" to the ordinary, workaday Quakers who made up most of the rest of West Jersey and Pennsylvania society.

The Quakers were theoretically an egalitarian group, but in practice they had developed their own hierarchies, with certain members serving as de facto ministers. These *Public Friends*, as they were called, delivered introductions and conclusions to meetings, and sat in special seats, sometimes up in the balconies, from which they could look down on their humbler brethren, the "gathering of the simple-hearted ones," as they were sometimes called.

Keith's Gospel Order Improved was either read to or circulated among the Public Friends, who were also the target of its reform proposals. It was, historians seem to agree, an extraordinary document.[25] At once conservative and forward-looking, it claimed that the Pennsylvania and New Jersey Quakers had drifted from the standards of the society's founders. Imperfect elements had crept in, and antiseptic measures were needed. Keith said that a creed should be drawn up and new members should be required to give their assent. He said converts should be required to give an account of their *convincements* as a way of demonstrating their commitment to basic Christian doctrine. But Gospel Order Improved was also a critique of the Quaker system of church governance, and here Keith entered into an elaborate back-and-forth with the Quaker leadership.

Keith had raised some important questions, the Public Friends said, but time was needed to think. They would discuss his proposals when they met again in one week. When a week had passed, the Public Friends said more time was need-

---

[25] Butler, Kirby and Nash all seem to agree on this.

ed and pushed the discussion back six months to September 1690. As September approached, the Quakers punted again, this time pushing the discussion back a full year. Gospel Order Improved, they said, would be taken up by the Yearly Meeting in September 1691.[26]

In the meantime, relations between Keith and the Public Friends were "generally harmonious" (Butler's words). Keith kept his job at the Latin school. He went on preaching expeditions to Maryland and Virginia. He merrily launched a theological attack on Cotton Mather. And so forth.

But sometime in the spring or early summer of 1691 the hammer fell when William Stockdale, a Public Friend, accused Keith of preaching the existence of *two Christs*—one Christ who was divine and lived in heaven and a second, disturbingly separate Jesus Christ who was a human being and lived on earth. Moreover, Stockdale said, Keith placed an undue emphasis on this second, terrestrial Jesus and on his role in salvation, thus denying the *sufficiency* of the *Inner Light*, a central tenet of Quaker belief.

The accusation was, in Keith's view, not only heretical but also nonsensical. The "mystery" of Christ's dual nature as man-god (the "hypostatic union") had been a favorite subject of Christian philosophers since the earliest days of the church. Stockdale's accusations simply exposed his ignorance of a doctrinal debate that had been going on for more than a thousand years. When influential Quakers made noises that seemed to support Stockdale, Keith realized the extent of their ignorance too.

The relationship seemed to fall apart quickly after that. Keith's reforms were not adopted by the 1691 Yearly Meeting. As the months passed, factions formed and hardened. On one side were the orthodox Quakers—led by a mix of wealthy men and political elites—and on the other were the Keithian *separates*, including men like Thomas Budd, William Bradford, the

---

[26] Butler, "Gospel Order Improved: The Keithian Schism and the Exercise of Quaker Ministerial Authority in Pennsylvania," in *The William and Mary Quarterly* (July, 1974)

printer, and Daniel Leeds.[27] At some point the Keithians began holding separate religious services. Keith said orthodox
Quakers would follow him from meeting to meeting to "violently oppose" his testimony, using their "Magistratical Power"
to obstruct his work.[28] Thomas Budd described one scene
where he intervened to protect Keith from Arthur Cooke, a
Public Friend who tried to intimidate him as he spoke. Budd
said he stepped between Keith and a furious Cooke, trying to
calm Cooke down by, "stroking his face… Gently…as a
Nurse would do a sucking Child, and as one will do another
that is familiar to him, intending no hurt, not doing no hurt in
the least, more than a Nurse will do to a child."[29]

A delegation was sent by the Public Friends to make peace
with Keith, but he insulted the men. "Openly and in a wrathful
and bitter Spirit he reviled and abused the said Meeting," the
Quakers wrote. "He denied our Authority. He denied [our]
Judgment. He did not value it a pin. He would trample upon it
as dirt under his feet…there was not any one of us all that did
Preach Christ rightly."[30]

As Keith continued to preach in defiance of the Quaker
leadership, an atmosphere of bitterness and recrimination pre-
vailed.[31] The peace of the Quaker meeting system was essentially shattered, Butler says. According to the historian Gary
Nash, by the spring of 1692, the Secretary of the Philadelphia
Meeting declared religious observances impossible, "by reason
of a turbulent and unsubdued spirit, which has much disquiet-
ed us."[32]

That June, the Philadelphia Meeting of Ministers formally
condemned Keith and expelled him from the Society (his Gift
was no longer needed, they said). The Public Friends warned
local meetings across Pennsylvania and West Jersey against
entertaining Keith or giving countenance to his views. In But-

---

[27] Budd owned many thousands of acres of land between the Mullica and
Great Egg Harbor Rivers and some, if not all, of Absecon Island
[28] Keith, *New-England's Spirit of Persecution Transmitted to Pennsylvania* (1693)
[29] Budd, *A Just Rebuke to Several Calumnies, Lyes & Slanders* (1692)
[30] Quoted in Butler's Gospel Ord., citing the minutes of the Philly Meeting
[31] Butler, Gospel Order
[32] Quoted in Nash, Quakers and Politics

ler's telling, the Public Friends would sometimes travel to these meetings to read out the condemnation in person, and as their warning passed from village to village, "ministerial authority" passed with it.[33]

If the Keithians were intimidated, they didn't act that way. As the summer of 1692 drew on, Keith expanded his critique to include a challenge to Quaker political authority, arguing that it was improper for ministers (the Public Friends) to serve simultaneously as magistrates in civil government, and asking if there were "any example or precedent for it in Scripture, or in all Christendom, that Ministers should engage in worldly government, as they do here." As Butler points out, this was less a speculative musing on political theory than a direct attack on a government whose membership contained, at that time, five serving magistrates who doubled as Public Friends.

Facing threats on a number of fronts—a tax revolt and a rejection of their authority in the counties along the lower Delaware—the Public Friends ordered Keith to stop writing criticisms of the government, and they ordered Bradford to stop printing them.[34] When the Keithians disregarded these directions, the Public Friends moved decisively to suppress the upstart rebellion.

ELEVEN

The libel trial of the Keithians

On August 24, 1692, a court in Philadelphia indicted William Bradford and John MacComb, two Keithian Quakers, on charges of sedition, disturbing the peace and subversion of the government. Bradford, the colony's official printer, was accused of sedition for publishing a pamphlet called *An Appeal from the Twenty Eight Judges to the Spirit of Truth and True Judgment*, which addressed the crisis precipitated by Keith. MacComb, an

[33] Butler, Gospel Order
[34] Butler, Gospel Order

innkeeper, was accused of distribution. Depending on whom you believe, he either nailed a copy of the pamphlet to his door or left copies in the open where they were read by patrons. The case against the two men was based on an arcane law that forbid *slighting* speech against government magistrates.

The next day the court met again (in Keith's telling) and convicted him in absentia on essentially the same charges, sentencing him to punishment in the form of a public denunciation to be read by the town crier in the marketplace.[35] The Public Friends also issued a warning, to all those "well affected to the Security, Peace and Legal Administration of Justice in this place," that such citizens give "no countenance to any Revilers and Contemners of Authority, Magistrates or Magistracy." Furthermore, all others should "forbear the future publishing and spreading of the said Pamphlet, as they will answer the contrary at their peril."

In October, a second round of indictments was handed down. This time the arrests included Peter Boss, a seemingly ordinary citizen who'd had nothing to do with the original Appeal but who had read it and been inspired to write a personal letter to Samuel Jennings—a Public Friend and magistrate—notifying Jennings that he *lay under* several scandals. Jennings was an unjust judge, Boss said. He'd once bet on a horse race with a certain John Slocum. He'd "wickedly" surveyed a tract of land belonging to another man. And he'd once had to be carried home and put to bed when he was too drunk to do so himself.

"For this," the Keithians said, the Public Friends, "issued a Warrant against him [Boss], and put him into Prison, without ever dealing with him in a Church method."

Also indicted were Keith and Thomas Budd, each accused of defamation for remarks they made about Samuel Jennings and Thomas Lloyd in a new pamphlet, *The Plea of the Innocent*, wherein they said that Jennings was "too High and Imperious in Worldly Courts" and that he was an "Ignorant, Presumptuous and Insolent Man." Keith and Budd also said that Lloyd,

---

[35] The Keithian account of events is in New-England's Spirit of Persecution.

the lieutenant governor, was unfit to govern and that his name, one day, would "stink."

On December 9, 1692, at the Court of Quarter-Sessions in Philadelphia, the trial of the Keithians went down. The defendants were Keith, Bradford, Budd, Boss and MacComb. In the Keithians' version of events, Bradford and MacComb had spent the weeks between their arrest and the trial in prison. According to Samuel Jennings, who wrote for the Public Friends' side, this was nonsense. Not only had Bradford and MacComb been regularly let out of jail, they had in fact *snuck back in* so that they could continue their public relations campaign from prison, the better to drum up public sympathy.[36] Keith would later admit that MacComb, through the kindness of the jailer, had been allowed home in the evenings to tend to his wife (his sick wife) but noted that "hot spur'd Justices," determined to ruin him, had revoked MacComb's shopkeeper's license. Bradford, in a similar spirit, had had his printing tools (his "letters") confiscated, which tended "to the disabling of him to work for his Wife and Children" (the Keithians' words). Bradford's wife was sick too, naturally.

During the trial itself, Keith assumed the role of ringleader, continually interrupting proceedings, interjecting himself into his comrades' speeches and generally seeking to undermine the credibility of the court—a task that doesn't seem overly daunting. Among the trial's many farces, at least five of the eight justices on the bench were the same Public Friends whose fitness to serve as magistrates Keith had presumed to question. The prosecutor—a last-minute substitute—was David Lloyd, the brother of Thomas Lloyd, himself the lieutenant governor of the colony and one of the alleged victims of Keith's slighting speech.

When the accused were brought before the court wearing their hats, Arthur Cooke (he of Thomas Budd cheek-stroking fame) addressed them, saying, "What Bold, Impudent and Confident Fellows are these to stand thus confidently before the Court?"

---

[36] Jennings' account is *The State of the Case* (1694)

"You may cause our hats to be taken off, if you please," MacComb said.

"We are hear [sic] only to desire that which is the Right of every Freeborn English Subject, which is *Speedy Justice*," Bradford said, "and it's strange that that should be accounted Impudence, and we Impudent Fellows therefore."[37]

With these preliminaries out of the way, the trials began in earnest. First up was Peter Boss who pled not guilty and took the opportunity to remark upon the presence of so many orthodox Quakers on the jury, since they were known to be "deeply prejudiced" against Keith and "all that favour him."

Boss's attorney acknowledged that his client had written the offending letter to Samuel Jennings but said it had been a personal communication with Jennings in his capacity as a private citizen rather than a public communication with Jennings as a public magistrate.

This was nonsense, Lloyd replied. "That what was spoke against Samuel Jennings, must needs relate to him as Magistrate, for take away Samuel Jennings, and where will the Magistrate be?" (Jennings himself would later call Boss's argument a "device" and dismiss the whole Keithian appeal to justice as a dirty trick).

Next up were Keith and Budd, accused of co-writing Plea of the Innocent, in which Jennings was allegedly defamed. Budd, though he admitted to writing the pamphlet, pled not guilty. When the jury was brought in, he too objected to the presence of so many orthodox Quakers, "because I perceive they are them that are parties against me." This objection was not recognized by the court.

Keith too objected to the Quaker jurists and magistrates and said they repeatedly menaced him throughout the trial. He did some decent counter-menacing too, at one point reminding the court that, "both ye and we are as Beacon set on a Hill, and the Eyes of God, Angels and Men are upon us, and if ye do any thing against us that is not fair and just, not only these parts hereaway will hear of it, but Europe also; for if we be wronged (if God permit) we think to make it known to the

---

[37] Keith, New-England's Spirit of Persecution

World."

The Quakers told him: watch it—you're getting yourself in more trouble.

When Keith's trial started finally, he argued protractedly over his plea, asking how he could confess guilt to something that was not a crime in the first place. The offenses he was charged with were not criminal, he said, since "to call a man Proud and Imperious is not Actionable."

"Though not Actionable, yet Presentable," the prosecutor responded.

At one point an onlooker, Ralph Ward, spoke up from the gallery in support of the Keithians, asking why it was a crime merely to criticize Jennings. "May not sin be reproved in a Bishop or Magistrate?" Ward said.

Jennings ordered Ward removed from the court and would later call him "rabble."[38]

Finally, after much back and forth, an audibly exasperated Lloyd directed the clerk to record Keith's plea as *nihil dicit*— 'Said nothing.'

"Why should he record me *nihil dicit*?" Keith said. "I think I have said a great deal."

The next morning, a verdict was returned: Budd and Keith guilty of speaking defamingly against a magistrate and fined five pounds each. Boss, also guilty, was fined six pounds. Jennings sat on the bench and eyed the accused as the sentences were read, "which was judged most unreasonable and illegal by those present," the Keithians said. Jennings would later admit he attended the sentencing but deny that there was anything untoward in his behavior.

The trial of the most significance to historians has probably been Bradford's. On December 10, Bradford too appeared before the court and, after considerable wrangling, offered a plea of not guilty. The prosecutor, Lloyd, began by instructing the jury to consider only the question of whether Bradford had printed the Appeal, since its seditious contents, he said, had already been demonstrated.

"This is wrong," Bradford objected. "I desire you of the

---

[38] In his own account, State of the Case

37

Jury, and all here present, to take notice, that what is here contained in this Paper is not Seditious, but wholly relating to a Religious Difference."

Lloyd answered that the pamphlet had encouraged "Wickedness" and was self-evidently seditious.

Bradford objected to the presence of two jurors on grounds that they had been overheard speaking out against Keithians and were therefore prejudiced against the case. When one of the men, Joseph Kirk, said Bradford was correct and asked to be dismissed, Justice Cooke told him to stay seated.

The prosecution's case against Bradford seemed to be: Of course he printed the Appeal—he's the printer. When Bradford said that the printing press, or "frame" that he'd used to print this allegedly seditious document should be shown into evidence at least, Jennings told him to stop playing "tricks" that wasted the time of the jury, endangered everybody's health and made them all sit in the cold.

In the end, the jury deliberated forty-eight hours. When they emerged without a verdict, Jennings was "furious" (Butler's word) and ordered them to be kept without "Meat, Drink, Fire or Tobacco," (the Keithians' account) until they did their duty. Maybe they were finally shown the printing press, because a story has survived that a sympathetic juror hit the machine with his cane and it fell apart.

In the Keithians' telling, Bradford spent a total of six months in prison and had his printing tools confiscated. His contract as official printer for the colony of Pennsylvania, on whose patronage he depended, had been terminated the previous April in retribution for his support of Keith (though he had offered to print the Public Friends' pamphlets too, he said).

Other Keithians fared better, but the fines imposed, while not large, were important, they said, because they implied a crime where none had been committed. Jennings, who complained openly of Bradford's "baseness" and "treachery" to his benefactors, said the fines were nominal and would not have been collected at all if there hadn't been a change in government.

Daniel Leeds appeared only once in the trial record, when he was called in to testify about whether Jennings had improperly surveyed another man's land (Leeds said he had) but his associates and friends are all through the trial. Keith was a spiritual mentor, probably. Bradford was his longtime printer and business partner, and a veteran of other fights with the Quaker authorities. I wonder if Daniel, as a professional writer, was not an un-credited author of some of the Keithian pamphlets.

Years later, when he gave an account of his decision to leave the Quakers, he would certainly identify as a Keithian and with the defendants in these judicial comedies.

TWELVE

Daniel's relationship with the Quakers at this time

By 1694, both Keith and Jennings had returned to England to argue their cases before the Quaker leadership in London, but these talks were not going well for Jennings. In fact he was "beset" (Daniel Leeds' word). Back in the colonies, Jennings' allies tried to rally support for him, and a document was drafted by the Chesterfield Meeting, reiterating Jennings' case against the Keithians and placing the blame for the "unfair managing" of the crisis on Keith.

In Leeds' telling, these "Chesterfield Certificates" had been written at the urging of Ann Jennings, Samuel's wife, and Leeds said he didn't blame Ann for trying to help her husband (though the document itself of course was "stuft full of Lyes and Slanders"). Ann Jennings got the Chesterfield Meeting to approve the statement, and then a copy was carried to the Burlington Meeting to secure the endorsement of its members.[39]

In Burlington, some Quakers readily signed the document, but others, "more willing to see with their own Eyes" (Daniel's words) "questioned the truth of what was written about D. Leeds," and still others "refused wholly to set hand to it and

---

[39] This is from Leeds' account, which is *The Innocent Vindicated* (1695). He doesn't claim to have been present at this first meeting.

shewed their Reasons."[40]

At this point, an argument broke out. Francis Davenport, a member of the delegation from Chesterfield, stood up to address the meeting and said that Daniel Leeds had long ago split with the Quakers, in spirit if not in actual practice. Davenport said Daniel "had not been in Unity with the Quakers since he came into the Country," citing remarks Leeds had made at a monthly meeting almost a decade earlier, and these words Davenport had "kept it seems, as a Weapon under his smooth Coat, near ten Years, to strike me with at this opportunity," Daniel said.

In Leeds' telling, two-thirds of the Burlington Meeting agreed to sign the document in support of Jennings, a solid majority, but the number of holdouts was high enough to make things awkward for the Quakers, preoccupied as they were with *Unity*. The solution was to rewrite the document and have one man sign for the entire group ("A notable way to force a Unity," Leeds said). The usual clerk—a man "given to drinking and Company keeping"—was indisposed, so a substitute clerk was appointed, and he drafted the document and the next morning it was sent down the river to England.

Now it was Leeds' turn to claim defamation. Daniel traveled to the September 1694 Burlington Meeting to request a copy of the Certificates, wherein, he understood, he'd been defamed. He'd even pay for the copy, he said.

The Quakers answered that, "They had not defamed me, nor wrote any untruth of me," Daniel said. "To which I replyed, If you have not wronged me, I hope you will be the more willing to do me justice, in granting me a Copy."

The Quakers told Daniel that none of their ministers were present, but if he came back in one month, he would have his answer.

At the October meeting, Daniel said, he was again denied a copy of the document, but this time one of the Quakers—J. Wilsford—stood up and gave him a more complete explanation.

"G. Keith and a Company of you have printed and ex-

[40] Leeds, Innocent Vindicated

posed us so shamefully to the World, until you condemn that, thou shalt have no Copy by my Consent."[41]

Leeds said he responded angrily, accusing the meeting of hypocrisy and of preaching eye-for-an-eye justice.

"People behold your Preacher!" he said, "Revenge is his Christian Doctrine, he will not do Justice, because others have done unjustly, as he alleges."

"With that, two of the Meeting rose up and faced me with a fierce Countenance, mixt part with Revenge, and part with Scorn, uttering bitter words, and one of them I remember rendered me as a Jesuit. And this was all the Justice I could obtain from them."

Leeds had not been arrested at the height of the Keithian controversy. He had played only a minor role in the libel trials, but, in his telling anyway, the Burlington Meeting regarded him, alongside Keith, Boss, Budd, Bradford and MacComb, as sharing responsibility for the bitterness and discord of that season.

There are no Keithians today of course. At its peak, the movement only attracted a few hundred followers, and it has been seen largely as a failure. Ethyn Kirby, Keith's lone biographer, calls the Keithians "malcontents" of a type bound to exist in even the most well ordered societies. Keith himself she says was choleric and ambitious. "Bitterly disappointed at his failure to effect those changes which he felt would strengthen Quakerism," she writes, Keith "laid the blame on the shoulders of the Friends in the Ministry [Public Friends] who dominated the Philadelphia 'meeting' and the political affairs of the colony."

Jon Butler, the historian, says the libel trials can only be seen as "an exercise in personal retribution" by the Public Friends against the Keithians, an exercise which he calls a "lapse in ministerial judgment" that came too late to help Keith. Leonard Levy, the First Amendment scholar, says the case was probably the first in America to involve freedom of the press, and that Bradford, though he would later prove in-

---

[41] Leeds, Innocent Vindicated

consistent in his principles, was "the first American martyr to the cause of a free press and the earliest advocate of the jury's power to decide the law in libel cases."[42]

But for Daniel the trial had less grandiose consequences— it deprived him of his printer. By the mid 1690s, his friends and religious allies were defeated or in retreat. He himself was an outcast in his own meeting, suspected if not of outright sedition then at least of consorting with seditious elements. George Keith had returned to England. William Bradford had decamped for New York. Leeds' father, whom he'd followed to New Jersey, was dead. After all this, why would Daniel have stayed in Burlington?

THIRTEEN

The Kingdom of Lucerne, and a sharpshooter

June 2010 – Heritage Day. I took the casino bus down on Saturday morning to attend celebrations marking the tercentennial of the founding of Egg Harbor Township. "Heritage Day," they were calling it.

Apparently, big crowds were expected. Marilyn Gallagher, Chairwoman of the Egg Harbor Township Three-Hundredth Committee, was quoted in the paper saying, "The entire day is expected to be the largest event that was ever held in Egg Harbor Township during our entire three hundred years of history."[43]

Heritage Day was being held in the parking lot of the H. Russell Swift Elementary School, just off Ocean Heights Avenue, a little over two miles from my childhood home. You weren't supposed to drive your car. You were supposed to drive to some other township middle school and then take a school bus back to Russell Swift. The idea of parking being a problem in Egg Harbor Township seemed ludicrous on its

---

[42] Levy, *Legacy of Suppression* (1960)
[43] Jordan Wompierski, "Heritage Day Promises to be a Record-Breaker," in *The Current*, June 22, 2010

face, but I'd been away for a while.

I drove up Ocean Heights Avenue and parked my mom's white Hyundai Sonata beside a vacant lot in a half-finished housing development ("Equestrian Estates") and walked back down Ocean Heights toward the Heritage Day site, reflecting upon heritage. I passed a new golf course (Twisted Dunes) that had been built after the Scottish fashion. There was a loud boom that sounded like artillery fire.

"What examples of our collective history, what treasured objects and customs from our past would be presented to us at this event?" I wondered. I passed a dozen sun-struck houses. I passed an old Chinese man sitting on a footstool in his garage with his tee-shirt pulled up over his head, fanning his belly. Another boom. Surely that was artillery fire. The Chinese man waved as I walked past.

According to its official website, Egg Harbor Township (*EHT: A great place to be*) got its name from the Dutch explorer Cornelius Jacobsen Mey, an agent of the New Netherlands Company, who sailed up the east coast of North America and reached the mouth of what is now the Great Egg Harbor River in 1614, where he found that the "meadows" (salt marshes) were "so covered with shorebirds and waterfowl eggs" that he designated the spot "Eyren Haven" or *Egg Harbor* in consequence.

At one time, Great Egg Harbor had encompassed all of present-day Atlantic County, but over the years various municipalities had broken off and gone it alone, and today the township comprised only the old villages of Bargaintown, English Creek, Scullville, Steelmanville, McKee City, Cardiff, Farmington and West Atlantic City. Some of these places had stronger identities than others. West Atlantic City, for instance, was merely the ass-end of Pleasantville that had been left unclaimed either by Pleasantville or Atlantic City. Cardiff I knew only as a stop on the school bus en route to the C.J. Davenport Middle School, where I went to sixth grade. Scullville on the other hand had its own volunteer fire department, and there were still a few Sculls running around Atlantic County, so that felt more legit.

43

I have no idea where Farmington is.

My family moved to Egg Harbor Township from Atlantic City in 1987. In the maritime vocabulary of coastal South Jersey, a migration of this kind was known as moving *offshore*—like you were taking up residence on a barge or incorporating in the Cayman Islands. To live in the beach towns of Absecon Island—Atlantic City, Ventnor, Margate or Longport—was to live *onshore*, a charming life indeed with its walking-distance proximity to the beach and to the grocery store and beloved family and friends. *Offshore* was the suburbs.

My parents had been *onshore* people their whole lives, having grown up on the same block (beach block) of Vermont Avenue in Atlantic City's Inlet neighborhood in the Fifties and Sixties. Their childhoods coincided neatly with the twilight of Atlantic City's reign as Queen of Resorts. They witnessed the last days of the town's shipwrecked Victorian hotels and expiring entertainment piers. My mom saw the actual Rolling Stones perform live (for a dollar fifty) at the Steel Pier on Fourth of July weekend 1966. Security had to stop the show at one point because the kids were throwing flashbulbs at Mick Jagger. My dad saw Sam the Sham and the Pharaohs play Steel Pier under similarly informal circumstances. They still talk about these events when they try to describe to me what the city had been like at midcentury, before everything went so spectacularly to shit.

They witnessed the dynamiting of the Marlborough-Blenheim Hotel, the Traymore Hotel, the Breakers. Each of them witnessed the demolition of their own neighborhood in the 1960s when the boarding houses and row houses and churches and schools were knocked down, scraped to grade and carted off in pieces to make way for a utopian community of garden-style apartments that never materialized. Decades later you could drive through the Inlet and survey the acres of grassland where a community had once existed, a faintly undulating prairie sitting placidly in the middle of the city, where generations had once lived and died and raised their children. The telephone poles were still standing, though there was nothing left to connect. They listed this way and that, like the masts of a ghostly armada swallowed up by the earth. I once tried to interview an old man who used to hit golf balls out there all the time, but he didn't really want to talk to me.

I was born in Atlantic City the same year casino gambling was legalized, 1976. By this time my parents had left the Inlet for the city's Chelsea district, roughly two miles south, a decidedly upscale neighborhood by Atlantic City standards, certainly by Inlet standards, meaning it wasn't actively burning to the ground.

We lived on the top floor of a three-story apartment complex, the Chelsea Village Apartments, a big red-brick compound populated mostly by civil servants and senior citizens. Our neighbors were firemen and policemen, a future sheriff of Atlantic County, one lifeguard-schoolteacher (a classic Atlantic City career combination), a city engineer, a de-wimpled nun and assorted holdouts from the town's glory days. Some of the apartments were rented as summer homes by Pennsylvanians who occupied them only three months of the year. From our living room window you could see the penthouse façade of Steve Wynn's Golden Nugget Hotel & Casino—big yellow letters, absurd cowboy font—but in fact the casinos impinged very little on the life of the city, on the life of this particular Atlantic City youth anyway. You could grow up on Absecon Island and forget they were even there.

Life in Chelsea Village revolved around a communal central courtyard of cool grass and mature trees and lovingly tended shrubbery. On summer days the Chelsea Village mothers would trundle us children four blocks up Boston Avenue to the beach to spend the day roiling in the surf, making mud pies and throwing clam shells at one another. In the evenings, the senior citizen ladies, of whom my other grandmother (MeMom not BeBop) was one, would array their beach chairs in a semicircle in the courtyard and sit and gossip late into the night.

Atlantic City in the late 1970s and early 1980s was a city in the depths of a profound economic malaise, but as a place that had always existed in part through a tacit partnership with the vice industries, this period may have represented a shining efflorescence from a morals standpoint. When the actual Beach

45

Boys played a free public concert on the beach beside the Million Dollar Pier in the summer of 1983—having been kicked off the National Mall in Washington D.C. for attracting "the wrong element"—it felt like (it still feels like) a high point of Western Civilization. The Chelsea Village Parents Association (an informal group) attended the concert while the kids were left at home under the supervision of a collective babysitter. One forward-thinking parent had consulted the tide charts and walked down to the concert site in the afternoon to set up camp out in the surf, in several feet of water. As show time approached and the waters receded, the campsite dried out, and they had the best seats in the house.

Why my parents elected to abandon this Edenic island of delights and how the move was effectuated are things I understood only in the most superficial terms. Planning and staging were carried out over several years, starting probably around 1984. Offshore living required one—more typically two—working automobiles. We owned but one, alas, a charming 1970-something station wagon with ersatz wood paneling and headrests that had been eaten by the family Springer Spaniel, but the car erupted in big clouds of gray steam each time it was driven across the Black Horse Pike (i.e. off the island) so it was considered unsatisfactory for offshore living. Eventually a more reliable car was substituted. Eventually a second car was added. A loan was secured for residential real estate purposes and a house was chosen—probably not in that order, but you get the point. And so on.

It probably didn't hurt that everyone else seemed to be leaving town too. The population of Atlantic City in 1970 had been 47,859, but by the 1980 census it was down to 40,199, and by 1990 it would be down to 37,986—a twenty percent drop in twenty years.[44] The Chelsea Village Parents Association gradually dissolved due to lack of members. It felt like we were among the last holdouts.

My dad borrowed a friend's truck and we made the move in stages over the course of one sunny spring weekend. I don't even remember leaving the old apartment.

---

[44] U.S. Census figures

When we arrived in the township in the spring of 1987, it seemed that a state of universal construction obtained. Houses were being built at a tremendous rate. The legislation that had underwritten the survival of the Pine Barrens as a national reserve had limited the authority of the townships on the woods' periphery to control real estate development, funneling growth to places like Egg Harbor and Galloway. At the same time, the growth of the casino industry was helping to pull the region out of the profound economic depression of the 1970s and into the more comfortable mild economic melancholy of the 1980s. Egg Harbor Township's population grew more than twenty-six percent between 1980 and 1990. It would grow another twenty-five percent between 1990 and 2000. There were classic suburban housing developments with names like "Beaver Lakes" and "Northfield Estates" and (the one my family moved to) "Brookside Farms." Even in those neighborhoods that had been built out, there was construction everywhere. People's lawns were torn up as they got *city water*—i.e. were hooked up to the county sewage and water systems. Everywhere people's septic tanks were dug up and new pipes laid down.

Egg Harbor Township, to me, was the suburbs, but with retained elements of the rural, pre-suburban past out of which the suburban condition was emerging. When we first moved, there was a working pig farm that could be smelled from our front porch when the wind was right, and the regional landfill was still in operation (it has since been converted into a golf course) and there were stretches of unbroken, secondary-growth forest to run around in and here and there were houses of an older, pre-suburban vintage, sometimes unpainted, sometimes inhabited by sprawling families and surrounded by generations of their own defunct automobiles.

At Heritage Day, a makeshift promenade had been set up in the H. Russell Swift parking lot. It was lined on either side with booths—lots of people looking more or less bored as they hawked articles or propagandized for one or another cause. The local lite-rock radio station was there playing inoffensive music at offensive volume. The local Boy Scouts were selling a revolutionary tick-removal system. "Painless! Fantastic! Hygienic! Unique!" the sign said. "*Five dollars.*" At another booth, a woman was handing out pamphlets advertising New Jersey's official tall ship, the *A.J. Meerwald*, a Delaware Bay oyster schooner, listed on the National Register of Historic Places.

"Meerwald, is that Dutch?"

"*Um.* Yes?"

The Atlantic County Mosquito Control Commission had a booth and the County Mosquito Superintendant, Bill Reinert, (an acquaintance from a previous, similarly misguided reporting project) was manning it. We chatted for a bit. The Cardiff Volunteer Fire Department had sent a delegation. On the side of their truck was an image of a small green lizard, which turned out to be the Jersey Devil. In the outfield where EHT kids played Babe Ruth League baseball, a hovercraft from the Scullville Volunteer Fire Department was doing donuts. A squad of portly, middle-aged G.I.s marched by chanting family-friendly marching cadences. The sun beat violently down. A small child rode past on a tractor.

On an earlier circuit of the grounds, I'd passed a group of Union soldiers beside a small campfire, a nine-foot-tall inflatable Reserve Officers' Training Corps cadet and a squad of World War II infantrymen working a howitzer. It was their booms I'd heard walking up Ocean Heights.

Under a big tent there were also a group of men and women dressed in medieval costume and doing arts and crafts—the Kingdom of Lucerne. As they seemed less heavily armed than some of their colleagues, I resolved to approach them.

At one end of the tent was a big man with a beard, Joe Fulginiti, I later learned. He was explaining to a mother and child the mechanics of a game called "Shut the Box."

"What did people do to waste time?" Joe said. "What do you do when you just, like, hangout? Do you have a Nintendo or a Wii or anything like that? Would you like to see a seventeenth-century Wii game?"

He showed the mother and child a seventeenth-century Wii, which involved rolling dice and flipping over tiles. The winner was the first person to roll the right numbers and then triumphantly shut the box.

"That's awesome," the mom said. "Five and two!"

"Today, schools in America are using the same game to teach small children how to add," Joe said.

At the other end of the tent, a Lucernian was talking shop with a Confederate soldier who had wandered into the sixteenth century.

"The big thing was the Civil War," he was saying, "but they had everything from me up through Desert Storm."

"Ah," the Rebel said, "because I do a couple of time periods in addition to Civil War."

The Lucernian was wearing a tunic, and he kind of looked like the actor Martin Clunes. He handed me a business card: Donn Shearer, it said.

"We actually cover time periods from 1000 to 1700," Donn was saying. "We do school demonstrations. We do public demonstrations, when we're asked."

"Last year, we started a reenactors' flea market!" someone said.

Other Lucernians were seated beneath the tent doing various medieval chores—polishing muskets maybe, stretching leather. Someone was carving a bowl out of a piece of wood, I want to say. A big, barrel-chested fellow named Mike was doing some fine needlework on what looked like a piece of stretched canvas—practicing "the fabric arts" someone said.

It was clear that such people would have known all about the Jersey Devil, so I opted to forgo the usual formalities and simply ask them *where* they thought they thought such a story might have come from.

"Oh, who knows," Donn said. "My guess is somebody was probably mad at the Leeds family and made it up. That would be my guess.

"In Scouts they used to scare us with Jersey Devil stories. There's a camp we used to go to—Camp Edge—we went to every year. And one of the lean-tos there has a crack in the cement that's circular. It has cracks radiating out from it. And the story of course is that the Jersey Devil was traveling underground and picked that spot to come up through the cement.

So that's my big Jersey Devil story."

"Do you think someone really had thirteen children?" I said.

"Oh, it's entirely possible."

"There's a woman on TV who's got nineteen," a Lucernian said from beneath the tent.

"It probably has its roots in a stillbirth," Donn said.

"Or a deformation."

"Probably."

"One or the other."

"Or both?"

"*Or both.*"

"See, I like what you're doing," Donn said, "for the simple reason—you've probably heard of Weird New Jersey Magazine? My problem with it is everything—ninety percent of the stuff in there—is from North Jersey. And my contention is that South Jersey is *much* weirder."

Here followed an involved discussion about South Jersey—its boundaries, its characteristics, differences from North Jersey, presumed superiority in terms of both culture, quality of life and general sexiness, etc.

But, define South Jersey, I said.

"Officially, South Jersey is the lower eight counties," Donn said.

That set people off.

"Everybody north of Atlantic City is north," someone said.

"Everything north of Marlton is North Jersey," someone else said.

"Actually, anything north of me is North Jersey, 'cause I take South Jersey with me everywhere I go." There was an implied *BOOM* at the end of this last one, I think.

Reflections on Central Jersey were also offered here. Reflections on the shameful, Laodicean qualities of individuals who would presume to self-identify as Central Jersey.

"There's no such place as Central Jersey.

"The phone company invented it."

"I truly believe that it's because they don't want to believe they're from North Jersey."

"See, I go by the original dividing line," Donn said. "New

Jersey is properly divided into East and West."

"Some people think the North-South Jersey dividing line runs roughly along the same line as the old East-West dividing line," I said.

"It does not," Donn said. "It's similar but they're not exact."

"The shame of New Jersey is that one half is oriented to New York and the other to Philly," someone said.

"But being between New York and Philadelphia actually made the fortune of the state in the later colonial period, because everything traveled through New Jersey," Donn said.

I said I liked the idea, often expressed, that South Jersey was oriented to Philadelphia and North Jersey to New York. All my friends growing up rooted for Philadelphia sports teams, I said, since we had no sports teams of our own to speak of.

"We've got sports teams!" someone said. "The New York Jets, the New York Giants—they play in New Jersey."

"Actually, it's the Jersey Jets, but nobody wants to say that," Joe said.

"As far as I'm concerned, they can both go scratch," Donn said. "Although, if I'm going to visit a city, I'd rather go to Philadelphia."

Much was made of South Jersey's pastoral character compared with the North. There was space to move down here, it was agreed. People from North Jersey couldn't get over how big people's properties were. We also possessed a "rather unique brand" of humor, Donn said, though I'm not sure I really understood what he meant.

As it often does in such cases, the subject of the Pine Barrens came up, and I said it was hard to imagine that the Jersey Devil could have survived without the accompanying, and improbable, survival of the Pine Barrens, but Mike, the big guy doing the fiber arts, noted that in Millville, where he was from, there was a small pond. It was almost downtown Millville, he said, but not quite, and in this pond there was a kind of cave or hollow along the banks. From time to time, people would find the remains of animals in the cave, and they would tell stories about the Jersey Devil. People would find bones, and say,

"Oh, the Jersey Devil lives there," Mike said.

You didn't need an entire forest, in other words. You could take any little space and fill it with monsters.

Back toward the left-field fence the Civil War reenactors were encamped: soldiers from the United States Colored Troop, Sixth Regiment out of Camp William Penn in Philadelphia.

"We're the United States Colored Troop, Sixth Regiment out of Camp William Penn in Philadelphia," the commanding officer said as I approached.

"Camp William Penn raised eleven regiments of black soldiers that served in the American Civil War," he continued.

"New Jersey doesn't raise a regiment of black soldiers because Joel Parker was the governor, and he was a Democrat. So he won't raise a regiment.

"But he is *smart*. When the government says you have to have a quota, he will go back and have each black soldier—twenty-nine hundred of them from New Jersey—counted. And he gets the quota and gets the money from the government for him fulfilling the quota, but he didn't raise…

"There's one hundred and sixty-six regiments of black soldiers that served in the Civil War. They fight in four hundred and forty-nine battles—thirty-nine major battles. They have seven thousand white officers.

"White officers receive thirteen medals of honor while serving with black soldiers. Black soldiers receive twenty-four medals while serving—eight in the army, sixteen in the navy.

"New Market Heights is a battle where black soldiers get fourteen medals of honor—on New Market Heights battlefield, Virginia, in one day."

Have you ever heard of the Jersey Devil, I asked?

"The Jersey Devil, yeah. How can you be from New Jersey and not hear about the Jersey Devil?" he said. "I know two or three Jersey Devils personally."

"Have you ever met anyone who's related to the Jersey Devil?" I said.

"Now, I ain't going to tell you no lies. Because all those people I know? They're good with secrets. Everything they know on their *self* and they don't tell. See, I'm surprised that you told," he said, and he laughed.

"Do you remember any specifics of the legend?"

"Not really. Just that this is a mysterious person everybody's trying to locate. You know what I mean? And no mystical magical power that follows it, but I hear about it.

"In fact, I'm a trap shooter. And down in the Pine Belt in Medford we have a Jersey Devil shoot every year, and last year I won my class in the Jersey Devil shoot. So that's the best thing I can tell you."

The Sixth Regiment had a table with rifles spread out on it. We spent some time talking about effective ranges, the number of shots a well-trained soldier could fire in a minute and whether there had been any famous Black marksmen during the Civil War.

"Did you use one of those rifles at the Jersey Devil shoot?"

"I have a shotgun," he said. "I would hate to use one of those in competition."

FOURTEEN

I go to Wawa

Some weeks or months after that, I first went to Wawa to look for the Jersey Devil. I would go to many Wawas in South Jersey looking for the Jersey Devil.

So much Jersey Devil research was conducted in the Pine Barrens, but growing up in South Jersey, I'd spent very little time in the Pine Barrens, and I'd never met an actual Piney. To me, the suburbanite perspective was woefully underrepresented in this narrative.

In the parking lot outside the Wawa on Ocean Heights and English Creek Avenues, three bikers were yelling at each other, having an impromptu party.

"I'm just as fucked up as you are!" one of the bikers said into her cell phone, as I approached.

Hello. I'm interested in the Jersey Devil, I announced.

Have you heard of it? And what can you tell me about it? (approx.)

"Best [unintelligible] New Jersey has!" one of the bikers yelled back without missing a beat.

The other began pointing enthusiastically at his bicep, where there was a tattoo of the monster.

"You need to go talk to Harry Leeds's family," the first biker said.

Harry's my cousin, he said (but maybe he meant this figuratively). They seemed to be about forty years apart in age.

I grinned. Several eternities lapsed.

I could feel the opportunity slipping away. In a last-ditch effort to make friends, I announced that my grandmother was a Leeds.

"I guess you're affiliated with the Barbers too, and the Friedlanders," the first biker said.

No, I said. "I don't think I have any…"

"You should, if you're a Leeds," he said.

I grinned at them again.

To change the subject I asked, "What version of the story were you told?"

"That's why I said—you better go talk to Harry. Because I don't know nothing. Haa ha hah! *Honestly*…"

I had better luck inside the Wawa. I would go late at night, when the managers had gone home and the staff were bored. A few people thought it strange that I should conduct this type of folklore quasi-research in a convenience store, but most Wawa people understood the rationale instantly, I think.

An off-duty staff member at the Wawa in Northfield— he'd returned to do some shopping and shoot the shit with colleagues—congratulated me on my wisdom in choosing not just Wawa but his *particular* Wawa for my research.

"You bringing it up wasn't, like, strange," he said. "Anybody's ever been in New Jersey asked about it. Anybody's ever lived in New Jersey's talked about it."

These Wawas of which I speak are a kind of convenience store whose name is said to derive from an Ojibwa word meaning "Canada goose." They sell mediocre sandwiches—

which they call, paradoxically, *hoagies*—and big sugary beverages and tobacco products, under heavily air-conditioned circumstances. Wawas exist in Delaware, Maryland, Pennsylvania, Virginia and now, tellingly, in the greater Orlando, Florida, region, but they achieve a pitch of intensity in South Jersey that is equaled nowhere else. Over the years, some Wawas have been turned into Super Wawas, i.e. have been torn down and rebuilt on the same spots, only bigger, sleeker and with gas stations out front, but they remain the quintessential South Jersey environment. There were nine of them within five miles of my childhood home.

Like the Jersey Devil itself, Wawa is so engrained in South Jersey culture that it's not until you leave the region—or have friends who visit you from out of state and can't get over the name—that you come to understand that not everyone buys big sugary beverages in intensely cold surroundings beneath a big sign emblazoned with the Ojibwa word for Canada goose.

I hoped that by speaking with people in Wawa parking lots and other essential South Jersey settings I might begin to understand the true folklore—what people actually *said* when they talked about the Jersey Devil rather than what I read over and over in the same six written sources.

I carried with me on these excursions a little Olympus digital voice recorder and a sheet of paper, folded up in my wallet, containing a list of all-purpose questions. It was entirely consistent with my experience growing up in South Jersey that I should need a list of prepared questions to interact with the neighbors.

- What does the Jersey Devil look like?
- How did you hear about it?
- Are you married?
- Kids?
- What is your social class?
- Why are you talking to me?
- Have you ever met a Piney?
- Do you think there's a factual basis for this story?
- Do we live in a rational society?

- Is New Jersey a cultural wasteland?
- What kinds of things in New Jersey are culturally valid?

I discovered early on that it was unwise to ask my interview subjects—unless they were obvious tourists—if they'd ever *heard* of the Jersey Devil. *Everyone* in South Jersey has heard of the Jersey Devil. Asking the question suggested that I was either an outsider myself or an idiot, and either way it cast an unfortunate pall on any ensuing conversation, so it was struck from the litany. Thus the whole subject of the regionality of the Jersey Devil story was not rigorously tested.

My working assumption was that the Jersey Devil *was* whatever people said that it was—as long as they seemed to be talking in good faith and not obviously messing around with me. By this standard, we had:

"A creature that popped up—God knows when—in the woods."

"Somebody's son—or something—that was deformed."

"A hoofed guy or something."

"Whatever you see drawn. Or whatever you see on TV. That's what you kind of picture."

"Someone told me it was a mix between a pig and a deer."

"Somebody just told me it was a hobbit."

"Half horse, half devil. It's all open to interpretation. Whoever wants to throw it up there."

"In New York, they think the Jersey Devil is a hockey player."

"Yeah, it's supposed to be the thirteenth child or something. I don't know. They threw it out the window or some shit. Something crazy like that. They threw it out the window and it flew away. I've heard *that* story."

"Something about the Light Tower—this guy built it for his wife, and it's haunted."

"To me it's an urban legend, of the guy who runs through the woods and kills people and they never find the bodies—up in the Tuckerton area, in the Pinelands, which is exit fifty-three on the Parkway."

"My dad used to scare the shit out of me telling stories

about it."

"It scared the hell out of me when I was five."

"Sixth child—he was born with, ah, what ya call it. All messed up."

"This woman had a baby, and when it came out of her it, like, killed everyone in the room, I think. That's what I remember. It like came out and it was like this devil. And now it roams the woods of New Jersey."

"No offense, but that's like White-people stuff."

"Yeah, I'm not going to comment on that."

"Well, I'm open-minded, so like every myth is pretty awesome to me."

"I read about it in a book somewhere that was a folklore book."

"They just did a MonsterQuest on it."

"I just watched a myth-or-reality thing on Discovery Channel."

"New Yorker all my life. I don't watch sports."

"You should write to the History Detectives."

"Yeah, I have no comment on that."

Etc.

When I started this project, I never expected to meet anyone who believed in the Jersey Devil. I operated on the assumption set forth by Cornelius Weygandt that the Jersey Devil was "believed in by nobody at all" but "accepted by all as a succulent subject of conversation."[45]

This was madness of course. The world is full of people who think that the Jersey Devil is a real creature and that it haunts the forests of the central and southern parts of New Jersey.

At one of the first Wawas I walked into, I met two such people working either side of the same checkout counter.

"Oh you asked the wrong person about that," the one cashier said, when I launched into my list of questions.

"I know for a fact I seen it and no one believes me," the other cashier said. "Only person that believes me is my daugh-

---

[45] Weygandt, *Down Jersey* (1940)

ter's god-dad."

"My sister-in-law saw it. I seen it. My brother's seen it. I think I saw it but I'm not sure," the first cashier said.

"I seen it on The History Channel," the second cashier said. "Basically this woman, she was giving birth in the forest—I forget where it was—but her baby came out the devil, and she abandoned him and he was like all bitched—all *messed up*—and crazy."

"See I live up in New Gretna," the first cashier said. "The Batsto area. So the stories, *all* the stories, come through my neck of the woods."

"I kept quiet about it for at least, like, two years before I even told anyone, because it scared the crap out of me," Second Cashier said. "They were like, '*You were on something.*' No I wasn't. I was outside smoking a Black & Mild."

"In Galloway they actually have a paper—the whole thing devoted to the Jersey Devil," the first cashier said. "They sell it at the Pathmark. Basically it's all been regards to the Jersey Devil."

They each continued ringing up customers as they talked.

"Basically, what I know about it is that a person in the family—half-human body, half-animal body with wings—terrorized the Leeds family. Basically there was a curse—killed the children and everything else. But I used to threaten my kids to go to sleep at night. That everything? Have a good night."

"When did you see it?" I said.

"I think it was in tenth grade, and I was just standing on the porch smoking a Black & Mild, and I had my porch light on. And around here it's, like, completely dark or whatever, so the porch light doesn't really do anything. Looking up at the stars...

"Next thing you know I heard it flapped its wings one time—*whoomp*—and it like flew over me and I seen, like, a tail and it looked like bat's wings and everything like that—long *something* behind...

"My mom says it's because in school one day when I was really, really young, they tried teaching us about it. I don't remember that at all.

"Look, I'm getting chills just talking about it."

Another customer came in.

"Hello, how are you?"

"Good, thank you."

"I'm asking about the Jersey Devil," I said.

"Two seventy-nine," the second cashier said.

"He don't exist!" the customer said. "That woman's a liar! Ha ha!"

"See? And everyone has their own opinion on it. You know what I mean? Credit or debit? Oh, Wawa's.

"You have two twenty-one left on it."

"Really?"

"And, you know, my mom's one of them people that believe it don't exist—eight seventy-nine—and me? Things in the world does exist."

Another customer came in and asked for a pack of cigarettes from the second cashier.

"ID? I'm just making sure. Camel Crush?

"People don't explain it. When people see, you know what I mean, *things* they don't want to—it flew right in front of the tree, like, right across the street from my house. There's a tree. The whole tree shook and everything when it landed on the tree."

"But what is the Jersey Devil?" I said.

"It was born into a family," she said. "He was half-person, half-creature—nine seventy. Credit or debit?—and you know as a child he wasn't—have a good night—he wasn't accepted in his family or whatever, so that's when probably he ran off or something.

"They have something on The Travel Channel—have a good night—I know for a fact I saw it. Just look it up."

"Was your first thought that you'd seen the Jersey Devil?"

"No, my first thought was: I ain't gonna turn around and walk in the house. Literally I didn't turn around and walk in the house. Literally I backed up, grabbed the door. Because if I would have turned around, and it grabbed me from behind, I would have went crazy. Hello, how are you?"

"Good. Can I have a pack of Marlboros please?"

"Sure. Seven thirty-six. Thank you. Have a good one."

"And you didn't tell people?"

"My uncle, my aunt, my boyfriend and my daughter's god-dad was inside, and I didn't even want to walk in the house and tell them. I kept it quiet. Like, I was literally in shock. Until this day, I still don't even really like to talk about it.

"I just recently told my mom, and the reason why I didn't want to tell her is because of the *bull* crap. You know?

"But me? I believe. I know what I've seen and when it was—have a good day—and I think it was when I'd seen The Discovery Channel on it, is when I was like, 'Whoa! Is that possibly what you could have seen?' or whatever, you know? It just was crazy. You know what I mean? It really was crazy to me."

"Did your mother give you a hard time?"

"No, she didn't give me a hard time. She just said, 'Oh, it was from—you don't remember. School told you about it, and you came home.' And she said I was young at the time and I don't remember. And obviously you don't say something like that to kids. She says that they said a bunch of stuff in school.

"I know for a fact what I seen, and that wasn't no bird. She [her mother] put everything in her own mind. It wasn't a bird. It wasn't a bat. I seen its tail. I seen the claws. I seen its head. I seen the whole body structure. You know? I have good eyes, even at night. And I seen the whole body structure, and I believe that's what it was."

"Do you think it was, like, an animal, or did you think it was some kind of *supernatural*…?"

"Maybe. Um, [sigh]. Supernatural. It would have to be. I think. You know? Have a good night. You're welcome. I think it was supernatural you know."

FIFTEEN

Other conversations in chain-retail shops

The initial plan had been to spend all research hours not allocated to libraries or historical societies camped out in Wawa parking lots, conducting field interviews of this sort, but it became necessary to widen the ambit of my research to include the RadioShack at the Somers Point Shopping Center, the twenty-four-hour BAIT SHOP on Patcong Creek, the lineup of rolling-chair operators in front of the Tropicana casino on the boardwalk in Atlantic City, a hotdog cart in Chatsworth ("the Capital of the Pines"), any number of rest stops on the New Jersey Turnpike and Garden State Parkway, the New Jersey Transit atrium at Penn Station in New York City and the standing-room area ("Ashburn Alley") at Citizens Bank Park in Philadelphia during a Phillies game.

Of these encounters, the most haunting took place at the RadioShack, where the sales clerk, a young man of perhaps nineteen or twenty, began an informative talk on the Jersey Devil by stating, authoritatively, that "According to Weird New Jersey, New Jersey is actually one of the world's hot-spots for paranormal activity. *Apparently*. It's actually top on the list for residential places that would be haunted, or have some kind of supernatural relativity to them. *Allegedly*. I mean, *again*, this is all not based on anything. It's *hearsay*."

"But what is the Jersey Devil?" I said.

"Obviously, like every other myth, you have different versions," he said. "This particular myth—this is the part I wanted to get to—was that the house was apparently cursed, the one that he was locked in or wherever. And the curse was, if you were to take a picture of the house, the house would burn down. And the actual house burned down to its foundation. That actually happened. Someone did take a picture of it, and, coincidentally enough, it burned down—*according to myth*."

He supported a theory that held that the Jersey Devil had been invented by local business interests as a way to spur immigration to the region to supply labor for local industry.

"They were trying to promote ways for people to come in to New Jersey," he said, "to labor and to work with the economy, things like that. It may have just been a gimmick. I have no idea. It may have just been propaganda to propel that.

"But, like I said, Weird New Jersey is a really good source if you want a good, offhand source of accounts or sightings, whatever it may be. But historical references—you're really not going to get much more than what's already on record. As it is,

I have no idea. That's my best thing."

"So, its mother was a human being?" I said.

"Yes."

"It's got brothers and sisters?"

"Yes. Many of them."

"So, people are related to it?"

"Um, apparently. *Allegedly*."

"Did you ever meet anyone who's related to the Jersey Devil?"

"Allegedly as well yes. I've met maybe—about—several people who believe they are."

"When I was a kid, my grandmother told me I was related to it."

"Oh, so you're trying to learn more about your family. Good for you!

"Now in terms of names and things like that, does he have a name? I have no idea. Does he have a background besides the myth? I have no idea. I don't know if he was an actual gentleman and just disturbed or if he actually existed at all. I have no idea."

Later he said, "There's a reason why we were the Garden State. We were known for our garden-variety vegetables."

But in a way it was all merely training.

That first meeting with Harry Leeds had been a disaster. No seasoned journalist would have let the man out of the room without securing a taped confession. Instead, I'd just sat there next to my grandmother like I'd been happy slapped.

Ambushing strangers in Wawa parking lots seemed like one way to prepare for the rematch. That way, the next time I met Harry, I would not fail so spectacularly. I'd go up to him like Inigo Montoya and ask him what he had meant by all this nonsense. Why did he tell people that we all believed in the Jersey Devil? And why did he say he was related to the monster? And just how did he and them *Oceanville Leedses* think they fit in there, in BeBop's family tree, exactly? And why had he winked at me like that at the Galloway Municipal Complex? I would demand that Harry give a proper accounting of himself.

SIXTEEN

W.F. Mayers goes into the Pines

In the fall of 1858, a young reporter from New York City traveled by train across the state of New Jersey about fifty miles to Bordentown on the Delaware River. When he got there he transferred to a stage coach and traveled another twelve miles to the village of New Egypt on the frontier of the Pine Barrens, making piquant observations on the conditions of the roads ("oh! the horrors") and on the citizens he saw as he passed. A pair of "clodhoppers" leaned against a fence. A "curious old-world mortal" drove the coach. New Jersey itself, he said, was New York's "petulant little whiskey-drinking sister State."[46] In these and in other respects he was an innovator in his field.

David Haberly, a scholar of Brazilian literature at the University of Virginia, has identified the writer as William S. Frederick Mayers, aged about twenty-seven. Mayers was the son of a colonial chaplain, born in Tasmania, Haberly says. He had lived in France and probably Spain but he had moved to New York not long before he made his voyage into deepest, darkest New Jersey, an account of which appeared the following spring in a new magazine called *The Atlantic*, which had been founded a year earlier by some of America's leading literary lights—Ralph Waldo Emerson, Harriet Beecher Stowe, Henry Wadsworth Longfellow, John Greenleaf Whittier, Oliver Wendell Holmes.[47] Mayers' article, titled "In the Pines," contains the earliest known written reference to what would become known as the Jersey Devil.

Mayers story wasn't really about the Jersey Devil, of course. It was about the Pine Barrens and about their delightful residents, the famous Pineys (or "Pine Rats" to use Mayers' delightful term for them). And the monster he mentions wasn't the *Jersey* Devil either. Mayers says the locals called the creature

---

[46] Mayers, "In the Pines," The Atlantic (May, 1859)

[47] Haberly, *Facundo in the United States: An Unknown Reading* (on the internet)

"Leeds's Devil." But even in this respect Mayers was a kind of an innovator. From Henry Charlton Beck to Cornelius Weygandt to John McPhee, a literary history of the Jersey Devil is a history of writing about the Pine Barrens. Mayers was the first Jersey Devil writer who was really writing about something else.

In New Egypt, Mayers transferred to a horse-drawn buggy, which carried him to the Hanover Iron Works, a disorderly collection of buildings surrounded by forest. There he met a friend (identified only as "Mr. B") and together they continued on to a spot called Cranberry Lodge—a clearing in the woods that contained a "queer little cabin," two unusually large pine trees and no neighbors for four miles. From two Pine Rats, on the outskirts of Cranberry Lodge, Mayers first heard tell of Leeds's Devil.

At Mayers' request, Mr. B had led him on a tour of the surrounding countryside, and while wandering among the cranberry bogs, they came upon a Piney campsite, inhabited by Hannah Butler (the "Queen of the Pine Rats") and another unnamed male Piney. A "splenetic terrier" was also in attendance.

The Pineys were, in Mayers' description, filthy. The male Piney—wearing a "ragged jacket" and "what had once been a pair of trousers"—was using a piece of his own clothing to patch up his tent. Butler, a hobbling old "crone," was eating a tomato. When Mayers met them, they were screaming epithets at one another in a spray of partially eaten vegetable matter, hurling accusations of cranberry theft and providing other helpful social-class markers for the benefit of readers who may have failed to get the point—that these were not members of the countryside aristocracy.

During a gap in the screaming, the Male Piney made a seemingly innocent comment about the weather. A storm appeared to be *a'brewin*, he said.

"Ay, is there!" Butler said, "and a storm like the one when I seed Leeds's devil."

"Hush!" Male Piney said. "What's the good o' namin' him, and allus talkin' about him, when yer don't never know as he ar'n't byside ye?"

"I'll devil yer!" Butler said. "Finish mendin' up yer cover, yer mean cranberry-thief!"

And so on.

When Mayers got back to the lodge he asked Mr. B for the story of Leeds's Devil ("what fiend may he be, if you please?") and was obliged with a version of the story that differs only in the degree of detail with the standard version as reported by McCloy and Miller.

In 1735, in the "township of Burlington," B said, there had lived a woman known only as Mother Leeds, who was "shrewdly suspected of a little amateur witchcraft." One night as a thunderstorm blew outside, she gave birth to a child "whose father could have been no other than the Prince of Darkness."

The Leeds child had been born normal, but it quickly transformed into a monster with a horse's head, bat wings and a serpent's tail. It then assaulted its mother ("scratched and bepommelled" her) and flew out the window into the neighboring village, where it "played the mischief generally" for many days until a holy man succeeded in "repeating the enchantment of Prospero" and so exorcised the beast from the forest, but only for one century.

"Little children he devoured, maidens he abused, young men he mauled and battered," B said. "At length, however, Leeds's devil was laid,—but only for one hundred years."

As 1835 approached, the "denizens of Burlington and the Pines" had grown nervous about the Leeds Devil's return, B said, but so far only Hannah Butler claimed to have had "a personal interview with the fiend" and she was probably drunk (on Liquid Jersey Lightning).

Still, the monster could sometimes be heard howling and screaming and running about in the woods, and the Pine Rats—and many other New Jerseyans (though of a "higher order of intelligence")—would decline to wander about in the forest at night "unless secure in the strength of numbers."

It's hard to say how seriously we're meant to take Mayers as a reporter. The people he depicts are absurd people. The claims he makes about them are absurd claims. His Hannah Butler appears to be a thousand years old. Her pantsless companion is a threat to Western civilization. They trade insults in volleys of improbable dialogue. But Mayers' account of the Leeds Devil legend—whether due to the influence of his own writing or to its fidelity to a story that already had its own independent life—corresponds remarkably with what one still finds in discussions of the Jersey Devil today, at least in the *written* versions of the story.

Mayers seems to have been drawn to the Pine Barrens by the region's central contradiction: How had this wilderness survived in such proximity to the major urban centers of New York and Philadelphia? The Pine Barrens of the early nineteenth century had been home to active iron and glassmaking industries, with towns like Batsto and Hanover Furnace, which had homes, general stores, mansions and fully functional ironworks and glassworks, but by the middle of the century, a cheaper and more efficient source of iron had been found in Pennsylvania, and the Pine Barrens towns were being rapidly abandoned.

When Mayers toured the Hanover Iron Works in the fall of 1858, they had been shut down for three years. Instead of a lively, backwoods settlement, he saw empty mills, abandoned cottages and a population returning to subsistence lifestyles in the forest. The Leeds Devil story, as he tells it, is symptomatic of statewide social decay. His Pine Rats are a kind of agricultural pest. They are semi-feral, with "matted hair" and "wild, uncivilized eyes" behind which "animal cunning" lurks. They are the "degraded" descendants of Tories who fled into the Pines in the aftermath of the Revolution, and unlike their plucky, Yankee counterparts they are incapable of honest labor and have survived instead through organized theft.

"Completely besotted and brutish in their ignorance, they are incapable of obtaining an honest living, and have supported themselves, from a time which may be called immemorial, by practicing petty larceny on an organized plan," Mayers said. The Pine Rat stole wood, stole game, stole cranberries, stole anything "in fact that his hand can be laid upon." And if the neighboring farmers tried to defend their property, Pine Rats would set fire to the forest and destroy acres of valuable woodland out of spite.

Mayers said the Pine Rat was effectively a different species. They needed their own Louis Agassiz or Jeffries Wyman (natural philosophers, polygenists) to classify them according to the latest zoological principles, since they were not strictly human.

As with any other type of agricultural pest, the extermination of the Pine Rat was both natural and desirable. The Pine Barrens themselves, otherwise so ripe for cultivation, had been halted in their development by this race of immoral, drunken, barely articulate beings, who pillaged the natural resources, refused to work, stole from their more vigorous neighbors and threatened to set the whole thing on fire if their way of life was challenged.

Mayers did not himself believe in the Leeds Devil, I think it's safe to say. Nor did the audience he imagined he was writing for at The Atlantic. The true believers in this scenario were Pine Rats (and those other, unnamed New Jerseyans who, though of a "higher order of intelligence," refused to go into the woods at night). And in this respect too Mayers was a kind of innovator. As a kid growing up in South Jersey, I didn't believe in the Jersey Devil. But then, I didn't have to. I believed in Pineys, and they believed in it for me.

But the Pine Rat was on his way to extinction, Mayers said. "We shall not suffer his company much longer in this world, poor neglected, pitiable, darkened soul that he is." Cultivation, civilization and progress were coming. The railroad was piercing the Pines. Soon we would have farms and "happy homesteads" and "orchards heavy with the promise of cider, and wheat golden as home," instead of "silent aisles and avenues of mournful pine-trees, sheltering forlorn miscreations as our poor cranberry stealing friends.

"Civilization, like a stern, prosaic policeman," would have "no idlers in the path," he said. The Pine Rat would be "driven from point to point, from one means of subsistence to another," and soon, he would "have to make the bitter choice between regulated labor and starvation clean off from the face of the earth.

"There is no room for the gypsy in all our wide America!" he said. "The Rat must follow the Indian,—must fade like breath from a window-pane in winter!"

It didn't surprise me that Mayers envisioned the end of Pineydom. It surprised me that he was so rhapsodic about it.

Mayers would ultimately write three pieces for The Atlantic, including a seminal review of Domingo Sarmiento's *Facundo*— in which he further developed his ideas on civilization and barbarism—and a short biography of the Venezuelan caudillo José Antonio Páez.[48] Haberly, the Brazil scholar, identifies "Mr. B" as Nathaniel Holmes Bishop, a young adventurer, who hiked across the Andes as a teenager, and went on to make a "considerable fortune" (Haberly's words) in the cranberry business in New Jersey.

Even before his Pine Barrens piece appeared in print, Mayers left America, sailing in February 1859 for Asia under contract with the British Foreign Office as a Chinese interpreter. He would rise through the ranks of the diplomatic service and eventually become a secretary in its Beijing delegation. Haberly calls him "one of the most distinguished sinologists of his time." He died of typhoid in Shanghai in 1878.

Mayers' "In the Pines" did not usher in the great flood tide of Jersey Devil stories that established the tale as a permanent feature of the written culture of the region. That would come fifty years later. Maybe the media environment was not sufficiently developed to accommodate such a frenzy. Maybe more stories *were* written but didn't survive or haven't been discovered yet, but more likely, I think, the story receded into the background, into folklore. But when it did break out into the open again, it seemed to do so in paths that were first established by Mayers.

Mayers was incorrect of course in his prediction about the end of the Pine Barrens. As John McPhee has noted, the trend that Mayers anticipated was in fact the reverse of the one that took place, and the woods gradually lost population from their

---

[48] Haberly, Facundo

peak in the early nineteenth century, returning more or less to their "pre-Colonial desolation" and becoming a "separate and distinct world" (McPhee's words).[49] But Mayers was more discerning as a prophet of natural history. The Pineys *would* get their own Agassiz and Wyman—their own natural philosophers—who would measure, collect and finally label them as a kind of separate species. But that would take some time too.

SEVENTEEN

Daniel Leeds is 'Satan's harbinger'

Following the defeat of the Keithians in the fall of 1692, Daniel Leeds and his allies had fallen, in the historian Jon Butler's words, into "desperate acts" of their own.[50] Keith would stop orthodox Quakers in the streets and subject them to elaborate harangues. Keithians would run into Quaker meeting houses, harass the congregations, and then run out. In a letter signed by Jennings, Cooke, Lloyd and John Delavall, and submitted to the Pennsylvania governor's council around this time, the Public Friends called Keith, "crazy, turbulent, a decryer of magistracie, and a notorious evil instrument in church and state."[51]

In the historian Gary Nash's account, the climax of this campaign came in early 1693, when a group of Keithians infiltrated the largest meeting house in Philadelphia the night before services and built their own gallery. The next day when worshipers arrived, they found themselves caught between two groups of angry Quakers. During the ensuing melee, carpentry tools were produced as each group fought to tear down the other's gallery. "Posts, railings, stairs, seats—all went down before the angry blows of the two opposed camps," Nash

---

[49] McPhee, *The Pine Barrens* (1968)

[50] Butler, Gospel Order

[51] Edward Cody, "The Price of Perfection: The Irony of George Keith" in *Pennsylvania History* (Jan. 1972); cites the Minutes of the Provincial Council.

writes.[52]

But, as the historian Butler says, this episode "signaled defeat, not victory" for the Keithians. Keith would continue to tour the region and hold separate meetings, but his following steadily "dwindled" (Butler's word). In 1694, the London Second Day Morning Meeting reprimanded Keith. The next year the London Yearly Meeting would disown him entirely. But the Quaker leadership in London also criticized Jennings, Lloyd and the rest of the Philadelphia Public Friends for their aggressive pursuit of the Keithians in the courts, and they ordered Jennings and company to refrain from further attacks.[53]

For Daniel Leeds the aftermath of 1692 might have felt like a weird kind of liberation. By 1693, Bradford had accepted an offer from the New York Council to become that colony's official printer, and he had set up a new printing operation in Manhattan. His first publication, New-England's Spirit of Persecution, would be an account of the libel trials. Daniel would soon move his family across West Jersey to Leeds Point on the coast. Whether this new homestead signified exile or refuge hardly mattered at all. Leeds was now beyond the reach of the Public Friends, under whose censorship he'd been operating his entire career. He was now free, more or less, to write what he wanted, and Bradford was free to publish him from the safety of New York.[54] And they still had the almanac—one of the most popular publications in the colonies—to hit their Quaker enemies over the head with once a year.

Leeds' first pamphlet in this new phase of the collaboration with Bradford was *The Innocent Vindicated* (1695), which began with a quotation from Proverbs Chapter Ten that may have been a reference to the libel trials: "He that uttereth a slander is a fool." In it Leeds dealt with familiar characters—Boss, Keith, Jennings—and gave an account of his own confrontation over the Chesterfield Certificates at the Burlington Meeting in 1694. Leeds also said that his fellow Keithian Peter Boss had been

---

[52] Nash, Quakers and Politics

[53] Butler, Gospel Order

[54] Note also the expiration of the Licensing Order, which had established tight control over printing, in 1694-95

the victim of an attempted smear campaign perpetrated by Jennings. Leeds said Jennings was making enquiries about Boss and his friends, both in America and in England, to uncover any unsavory connections that could be used against the Keithians.

Leeds' next work was *News of a Trumpet Sounding in the Wilderness* (1697). This was Daniel's statement of faith, explaining his break with the Quakers. Rereading it in light of his decision to leave Burlington, the title seemed to have new resonance. The libel trials, after all, had been explicitly about *silencing* the Keithians. During one of his speeches at the trial, Keith himself had said, "when a man is wronged, and can have no other Remedy, printing is his last." Leeds claimed that Jennings had threatened the group at one point, saying, "if I draw forth my hand against you, I WILL Not pull it in again till I have Quieted you ALL."[55]

But in this task at least they had failed completely. The Public Friends may have won the struggles for control of the Quaker Meeting system in 1692, but the Keithians were now freer to criticize the Quaker leadership than they'd ever been. In their choice of title, Leeds and Bradford seemed to be making a statement. Here I am, blowing away on my trumpet in the wilderness of Leeds Point, Leeds seemed to be saying, and there's nothing you can do to stop me.

After 1695, if the Philadelphia Quaker establishment wanted to silence Leeds and Bradford, it would have to use means other than property seizures, fines and arbitrary incarceration. Eventually a Quaker response did come together, and when it did, it took an instructive form.

In 1700 a Quaker named Caleb Pusey, a Public Friend who had for years been involved in the oversight of Quaker publications, wrote a reply to News of a Trumpet in which he set forth Daniel Leeds' "Crooked Ways in the Wildernesse" to the view of the "Impartial and Judicious."

Pusey's work was published in Philadelphia by Reynier Jansen. It numbered seventy-three densely reasoned, pedantic

---

55 Leeds, News of a Strumpet (1701); this is reported as "quelled" in New-England's Spirit of Persecution.

pages in which he defended Quakers whom, he said, had been "abused" by Daniel Leeds and cited instances in which that wicked man ("our present Adversary") had used false citations from Quaker books and put wrong meanings onto Quaker words.

It was an obscure document, seemingly ignored by historians, but for someone interested in the Leeds family and how the idea of a Leeds Devil might have grafted itself on to the family history, it had an altogether more stimulating aspect.

Daniel Leeds had settled Leeds Point. His descendants still lived in the town. Local high school kids still made nocturnal pilgrimages to the site of his plantation looking for the former Leeds Devil. And now, here I was reading a pamphlet about the man, written by a contemporary, and it was titled *Satan's Harbinger*.

Maybe not the devil himself but at least a close associate.

EIGHTEEN

The spiritual and carnal whoredoms of Quakers

I read *about* Satan's Harbinger way before I ever saw the document itself. I remember sitting in the basement of the Sterling Memorial Library at Yale University in New Haven, Connecticut, in the spring of 1999. It was a big, bright room full of cabinets holding rolls and rolls of micro-fiche, megabytes of arcane texts—pamphlets and newspapers and magazines—most of which would never be read by anyone. I had one of the rolls in the machine and was scanning one of Daniel's pamphlets at random—*A Challenge to Caleb Pusey, and a Check to his Lyes & Forgeries*—and the first paragraph began:

"It is three years since I published a Book, called News of a Trumpet, &c, which has vexed and gall'd the Quakers...and some Consultations there has been among 'em, as I am told, to bring forth an Answer, which accordingly I have long expected & at last have met with a right Scarrilous Pamphlet, signed by one Caleb Pusey, Satan's Harbinger, by Title, wherein he pretends to an answer (here and there a bit of) my said Book."

I remember thinking I'd found it—a member of the Leeds family, living in the place he was supposed to be living, around the time he was supposed to be living there, and one of his peers was describing him in print, in language that was strongly suggestive of the demonic. I never expected it to be so easy. I think I feel a little differently now.

Sterling Library didn't have a copy of Pusey's pamphlet. At the time, the only copy of Satan's Harbinger I could find was held at a university library somewhere in Australia. For a modest fee (ten dollars + shipping and handling) they would send photocopies, but through some combination of financial illiquidity and native suspicion of the postal services, I was unable to see this as a viable research possibility. The only copy of Satan's Harbinger might as well have been located six inches beneath the lunar surface. I never read it until it became available over the internet.

In retrospect, it seems characteristic of Daniel Leeds that one should learn about all the terrible stuff that people said about him through the medium of his own writing. The public relations principle that you shouldn't spill ink rehashing the arguments of the enemy was lost on him. He seemed to have no problem republishing the criticisms leveled by other, often less well-known, writers. In fact he did so with real gusto.

If Satan's Harbinger was the great causative event, the source of the Leeds Devil whose echoes could be heard, as folklore, three centuries later, I got no sense of this potential from Daniel Leeds himself. Daniel's reaction to Pusey, though at times angry, was measured and reasonable. Pusey had misrepresented his arguments, Leeds said. The man's pamphlet had been needlessly personal. It was full of "Lyes" too of course but this charge seemed almost pro forma. If there was anything epic or earth-shattering in the exchange, I missed it.

Likewise, when I finally found a copy and read it, Satan's Harbinger was not the wellspring of salacious mudslinging that I'd hoped for. Despite the sexy title, it read like dull propaganda, full of cross-references and citations and arcane accusations that seemed to have little relevance to matters of any import three hundred years later. On page eighty-eight, Pusey publisheth a letter. On page ninety, he produceth a quotation.

And so on.

Pusey's central claim was that Daniel Leeds "in a very palpable manner" and "to his own shame" had "ventured to abuse" Quakers at a very shameful rate. The actual villain in the wider story, it seemed, was still Keith, whom Leeds merely *announced*. There had been lots of name-calling though, apparently, and much of it was helpfully reproduced by Pusey. Pusey had called Keith an atheist. Pusey had called Leeds a "disingenuous, unfair, envious and conceited man." Leeds had called the Quakers "Muggletonians." Pusey had said it was Leeds who was the real Muggletonian. And so on.

The central point of contention was whether William Penn had once described Jesus Christ as a "finite" and "impotent creature," as Leeds claimed Penn had done. Pusey said this was nonsense. Penn had done no such thing, and he demanded that Leeds issue a retraction. Since Penn had made these remarks in print, settling the question would seem to have been a simple matter of consulting the nearest copy of whatever relevant document, and for what it's worth, a quick search of Penn's *The Sandy Foundation* (1668) turns up the following observation, "That the Finite and Impotent Creature, is more capable of extending Mercy and Forgiveness, than the Infinite and Omnipotent Creator," in which Penn seems to have been referring to Jesus Christ. But apparently it was all more complex than that.

Leeds, for his part, said he was trying not to be too judgy, merely stating facts. He couldn't see why Pusey was so incensed on this point of Jesus' finitude. "I know Persons of several Societies of Christians (as well as W.P.) hold Christ, as Man, to be Finite and Impotent, but as God, Infinite and Omnipotent," Leeds said. Pusey called this claim a "horrid Abuse" put upon Penn. The whole thing has echoes of Keith's fight with William Stockdale from nearly a decade earlier.

By 1701, Keith himself had left England and returned to the American colonies. He was now, of all things, an Anglican minister, "tho' of the meanest Class" (Pusey's words).[56] He

---

[56] Pusey, *Proteus Ecclesiasticus* (1703)

had resumed his campaign against the Quakers, traveling from colony to colony, interrupting Quaker meetings, conducting unauthorized preaching expeditions and generally making a nuisance of himself.

As Pusey put it, it was "no Secret in the parts of America, between Piscataway and Philadelphia, where he hath travelled in his work of Envy, what accusations (tho' false) he hath openly brought against the Magistrates of Pennsylvania."[57] By all appearances, Keith had simply picked up his fight against the Quakers in a different costume.

Keith interrupted Quaker meetings in Rhode Island, New York and Pennsylvania. Though he did not go himself, he sent an associate ("a rash precipitant person" who by "his garb looked like a Minister of the Church of England") to the Yearly Meeting in Shrewsbury to read "certain abusive manuscripts" to its members.[58] He carried letters of recommendation with him on his travels. One letter, which appeared to be from an Anglican bishop, stated that Keith was a designated instrument intended to bring souls to God and therefore should be treated kindly. At a Quaker meeting in Rhode Island, Keith arrived with two confederates who identified themselves as ministers of the Church of England. After one of the local Quakers had stood up and given his testimony ("to the Comfort and Edification of the Meeting in General"), Keith rose and offered a kind of rebuttal, saying that the man had spoken, "many good Truths, but mixed with Error."

This was not how the Quakers did things.

"Reply was made, that we desired to enjoy our Meetings peaceably (not being yet ended); and if he [Keith] or they had any thing to offer AFTERWARDS the House should be left to him." But, in Pusey's account, Keith "still pressed for audience, and being in a Turbulent frame, called to the Governour in a Commanding way to ORDER that he might be heard; and that the AUDITORY might BE COMPELLED TO STAY and HEAR HIM; or else HE WOULD COMPLAIN to the QUEEN of him."[59]

[57] Pusey, Proteus Ecclesiasticus

[58] Pusey, Proteus Ecclesiasticus

[59] Pusey, Proteus Ecclesiasticus

The historian Jon Butler says there is in fact "considerable evidence" that Keith's tour of the colonies was part of an orchestrated plan conceived by Keith with Thomas Bray, founder of the Anglican missionary group the Society for the Propagation of the Gospel in Foreign Parts, to deliberately sow discord among the American Quakers and send them running for the comparative peace of the Church of England.

Meanwhile, Leeds kept up his pamphleteering. In 1701, he published *News of a Strumpet*, probably the most incendiary of his anti-Quaker tracts. A more complete title of this work would be *News of a Strumpet Co-habiting in the Wilderness or, a Brief Abstract of the Spiritual and Carnal Whoredoms and Adulteries of the Quakers in America*—but even that wouldn't be the full title, which stretched on to cover most of the first page. It was not the work of a defeated man.

In the preface to the pamphlet, Leeds said he did not put his name on the document, signing instead with only his initials ("as the Quakers use to do") since his reputation in the region was so poor that he didn't want readers to know he was the author and therefore be prejudiced against it. "Thereby if you know me not, you may read before you Judge," he said.

Having seen the outlandish title beside Leeds' name in bibliographical dictionaries long before I ever found and read a copy, I expected Strumpet to be the work of a madman, the piece of evidence that would convince me finally of Daniel's insanity. But here too he seemed strangely measured and reasonable even, given that it was essentially a laundry list of alleged sexual crimes by Quaker ministers.

Leeds said he wrote Strumpet in direct response to a claim made by Pusey in Satan's Harbinger—specifically the statement, on page forty-seven, that Pusey knew of no Quaker preachers who had been "unlawfully concerned with women," as Leeds had alleged. Pusey said if Leeds knew of any such preachers, "He should either have let us know who they were, or else have been silent about it." Leeds chose to let them know.

News of a Strumpet presents Leeds' list of twenty Quaker fornicators as "unclean birds," which he removes one by one from their cage for examination. There is Thomas Thurston, who "betrayed an eminent person's wife, in Maryland, to the sin of Adultery, by pretending he had a motion from the spirit to get her with Child." There is John Moon who "conferred honor on his Maid Servant at Philadelphia by sporting with her, till he caused her Belly to swell." Here is Robert Ewer, who was "taken on bed with his Neighbor's Wife, with her Coats up &c." Here is Jacob S., who, while his wife was in childbed, was found, "tampering with his Neighbours wife in the woods." Christopher Holder, an "effeminate loving Preacher to the Women in Rhode Island" was found "lying with another man's wife in a field of Corn." And so on.

Strumpet contained some straight political criticism as well, accusing the Quakers of cronyism for instance—for choosing "one another for Justices" and for enjoining followers to choose Quakers for the colonial assembly (for "crowding Offices upon one another") and for presiding over a tax system that unfairly benefited their coreligionists—and accusing them of hypocrisy. The Quakers sold strong drink to the Indians while enforcing fines for selling strong drink to the Indians, Leeds said. Summarizing political conditions in the colony, he said the "Privileges of West Jersey that the Quakers have so long stood up for and boasted of, is for them to lord it over their neighbors, and command their Purses."

But mostly it was salacious gossip. William Yardley, an "old Preacher" (and distasteful to women), had "offered to lay with his maidservant" and she refused, "whereupon he renewed his assaults on her." John Gilbert was accused of lying with both "a white woman and a Negroe woman." William Bile proposed retrograde legislation against widows. Henry Jennings "had several Bastards before he was discovered, he not being suspected, by reason of his being so demure a Quaker, and his carriage so Saint-like." And so on.

The worst offender—the "most aspiring bird in the CAGE"—was Samuel Jennings. Though Jennings was not accused of any sexual impropriety, he had displayed "intolerable Pride" and talked of himself as if "he were the Almighty."

Given Jennings' anger at the accusations made by Peter Boss in a single private letter, and the lengths to which he and the Public Friends had gone to prosecute the Keithians for slighting speech, it's difficult to imagine Jennings' reaction to this far more comprehensive, far more public, attack. And it's tough not to see Strumpet as a continuation of the controversy of a decade earlier—as an act of retribution against the Public Friends for their judicial excesses in 1692, as Daniel at last getting Jennings back for throwing his associates in jail and blowing up his life in Burlington.

But though Leeds' motives might have been personal, his writing was part of a wider campaign that had broad political consequences. When the proprietary Quaker colony of West Jersey finally *surrendered* to the crown (William Penn's word), there was no single reason. Anti-Quaker factions from St. Mary's Church in Burlington (where Leeds and other ex-Keithians were charter members) had been urging colonists not to pay taxes, part of an effort to undermine and sabotage the colonial government. When a mob of anti-Quakers broke into the jail in Burlington and released several "fomenters of discord" it was just one of a series of "petty revolts" including "court interruptions, jail rescues" and "cracked heads, but not deaths" (the historian Kemmerer's words) that were occurring across East and West Jersey at the time. The old dispute between the Nicolls patentees and the proprietors added to the discord—or maybe it was the main cause of the discord. Or maybe the Crown had simply been determined all along to seize the colonies and merely used the infighting as a pretense.

But in Quaker West Jersey and Pennsylvania, it's hard not to imagine Daniel Leeds wasn't held at least partially responsible for the end of the Quaker proprietary colony. He had become a public face—perhaps *the* public face—of a movement that, for more than a decade, had been responsible for many acts of mischief and outright sedition that had been designed precisely to bring about this capitulation.

NINETEEN

Daniel and the Cornbury clique

Whatever the causes, on April 15, 1702, the proprietary government of West New Jersey, along with the governments of East New Jersey and New York, were surrendered to the English Crown. William Penn decried this act as having been "knavishly contrived to betray the people."[60]

Not only were the Quakers relieved of their proprietary colony, the Crown installed, as governor of the combined colonies, Edward Hyde, Third Earl of Clarendon, aka Lord Cornbury, widely regarded as the most corrupt and venal official in the whole long history of the British Empire.

Cornbury was widely known to have both solicited and accepted bribes. He plundered the public treasury and mismanaged public affairs. And in addition to these more conventional forms of malfeasance, he was a transvestite, known to walk upon the ramparts of the governor's quarters each evening dressed in drag. It was a widely known fact that Cornbury dressed in women's clothing each day and that he had once opened a session of the assembly wearing earrings and an elegant gown, the better to evoke the presence of her majesty the queen, whom it was his solemn duty to represent.

Until recently, a painting hung in the New York Historical Society on Central Park West depicting a strikingly unattractive person in a powder-blue ball gown, a spray of jewels in her hair and a five o'clock shadow thrown across her jowly cheeks, and this painting was said to show Cornbury as he might have looked on one of his sprees. The historian George Bancroft, writing in the 1830s, said Cornbury represented the worst tendencies of the English aristocracy, "arrogance, joined to intellectual imbecility."[61] In one popular story, the governor

---

[60] Quoted in Kemmerer, Path to Freedom

[61] Bancroft, *History of the United States of America from the Discovery of the Continent*, vol. ii (1837)

regaled guests at a state dinner with a "flowery panegyric" on the subject of his wife's ears, which he felt to be of surpassing shapeliness, and at an opportune moment during the meal he invited the men present to line up and take turns examining the ears up close.[62] The historian Patricia Bonomi—who does not share this conventional view and has led an effort to revise Cornbury's historical legacy—calls him "notorious in the historical literature as a moral profligate, sunk in corruption, and perhaps the worst governor Britain ever imposed on an American colony."[63]

Naturally, Daniel Leeds' career flourished under the Cornbury administration. In August 1702, four months after the surrender, Leeds was appointed to serve on the colonial council. Two years later, he was appointed to the colonial assembly. He seemed to be spending more time west of the Pines in the neighborhood of Burlington at this time, while Keith and other Anglicans established St. Mary's Church, an institution that one historian (Kemmerer) has referred to as a colonial Tammany Hall. According to the *Burlington County Court Book*, a comprehensive and convincing record of jurisprudence in the colony, Leeds' appointments, and the promotion of Thomas Revell, were in reward for good works in defeating the Quakers and installing Cornbury.[64]

In Kemmerer's not-at-all-controversial account of the Cornbury regime, the governor ascended to power as various factions were engaged in a bidding war for his services. Cornbury—unhappy about the size of his salary, the duration of his contract and his lack of influence over land distribution, which he'd hoped to parlay into his fortune—became a participant in something called the Blind Tax., a scheme conceived by two enterprising political functionaries, Richard Saltar and John Bowne, who traveled the countryside soliciting moneys

---

[62] Ormonde De Kay, "His Most Detestable High Mightiness," in *American Heritage* (1976); The often repeated words "flowery panegyric" appear to be De Kay's.

[63] Patricia Bonomi, *The Lord Cornbury Scandal: The Politics of Reputation in British America* (1998)

[64] *The Burlington Court Book of West New Jersey: 1680 – 1709*, George Miller and H. Clay Reed eds. (1944)

for the redress of grievances. The tax was called *blind* because the taxpayers were not told what it would be used for or even whose pockets it would eventually end up in.[65]

Depending on whom you believe, Saltar and Bowne extorted either eight hundred pounds or fifteen hundred pounds from the good people of New Jersey in this way. When the money was delivered to Cornbury, he would not deign to touch it but instead caused it to be left in the hands of an associate. In this version of events, the money effected a striking change in Cornbury's attitude between the first and second sessions of the colonial assembly, as a result of which, in East Jersey, he favored the Nicolls patentees in their struggles against the proprietors. In West Jersey, he favored the Anglicans (including the ex-Keithians) over the Quakers. As Kemmerer puts it, "In exchange for the help of the anti-proprietary party, Cornbury was expected to protect the people of the Nicolls patents from the proprietors, and to aid the Anglicans in their proceedings against the Quakers."

Cornbury arrived in Burlington and immediately appointed a high sheriff, a coroner and a clerk, all of them Anglicans. Quakers were either barred or strongly discouraged from serving on juries on the pretense (an old Quaker-baiting trick) that they refused to swear oaths. As the Burlington Court Book describes it, Cornbury's arrival marked "not only the end of the Quakers' judicial supremacy in Burlington but also their complete withdrawal from the court."[66]

According to the historian Edward Cody, not long after Cornbury's arrival in the colonies, the governor hosted a dinner in New York attended by George Keith and John Talbot. Talbot, a member of the Society for the Propagation of the Gospel, would serve as the first rector of St. Mary's Church in Burlington. Among the subjects discussed was the Anglicans' treatment (their perceived mistreatment) at the hands of Quakers in Flushing, where Keith and Talbot, as usual, had tried to interrupt a Quaker meeting but the Quakers had resisted. Cornbury's response was to supply Keith with a letter

---

[65] Kemmerer, Path to Freedom
[66] Burlington Court Book of West New Jersey

authorizing him to speak without interruption at any Quaker meeting, in effect giving Keith official government support in his work of Traveling Envy and Sabotage.[67]

The real, documentable funny business involving Daniel Leeds began in the fall of 1704, when an election was held to determine control of the colonial assembly in New Jersey. When the votes were counted, it appeared that the Quakers and their allies would hold a majority of two seats over their Anglican and anti-proprietary rivals. But here Daniel Leeds and Thomas Revell intervened, objecting that three of the West Jersey Quakers—Thomas Lambert, Thomas Gardiner and Joshua Wright—who'd won seats in the election were ineligible because they didn't own the one thousand acres of land required to serve. On the basis of this "bare suggestion" (Samuel Jennings' words) Cornbury promptly refused to affirm their seats and moved on.[68]

The next day, Lambert, Gardiner and Wright returned with copies of surveys proving that they did own the required land, but again Cornbury, outrageously, refused to affirm them. Daniel Leeds meanwhile had written a letter to the assembly saying that it was difficult to tell if the Quakers met the land requirement and that "further enquiry" was necessary. He requested fourteen days to study the matter.[69] Jennings would later call this move a "trick."[70]

On December 7, the assembly and Cornbury met and the Quakers again requested a hearing. Lambert, Gardiner and Wright again showed that they met the land requirement, and the assembly asked Cornbury to allow the Quakers to qualify themselves and take up their seats, but before this could be done, Cornbury abruptly closed the session. It would not meet again for one year, during which time the Anglican and anti-proprietary groups would maintain control over the legislative body.

---

[67] Cody, Price of Perfection

[68] Tanner, Province of New Jersey, citing the assembly journal

[69] A copy of this letter is in Samuel Smith's *History of Nova Caesarea* (1765)

[70] Jennings supposedly said this in his remonstrance, a copy of which is given in Smith's History of Nova Caesarea

In this way, the "Cornbury clique" (as later historians would call them) executed a bold and (at least temporarily) successful power grab. This group included Attorney General Alexander Griffiths, Hugh Huddy, and Richard Townley as well as Leeds and Revell. "The entire Ring," the historian Kemmerer says, "belonged to St. Mary's Church in Burlington, where hatred of Quakers was the rallying cry." The group seems (to me anyway) to have succeeded Keith in a decades-long fight with the West Jersey Quaker establishment

During the twelve months that Cornbury's allies, enabled by Leeds' fraud, illegitimately held control of the assembly, three relevant laws were passed: a land tax on proprietors, a militia act requiring all males aged sixteen-to-sixty to muster four times per year, and a highway act that was used for general mischief purposes. Under the new militia law, anyone who failed to muster—pacifist Quakers for instance—was subject to quarterly fines. Under the highway act, government officials could seize or divide private property on the pretence that it was needed for the building of roads, a power they used disproportionately to seize and divide the property of their political enemies. Lewis Morris, a future governor of New Jersey, would say that these "layers out of the Highway" were "the most inveterate party men" who "pull'd down their enemies inclosures," and "laid ways through their orchards, gardens and improvements."

Morris described one incident where the Cornbury gang targeted a political enemy (a "gentleman at whom they had extraordinary pique") by using the highway act to seize his property and build a bridge over a mill pond, requiring the man to pull down his dam and his mill, even though he offered to build a bridge over the same stream, at his own expense, in a more convenient location (Morris failed to disclose that he was the gentleman whose mill, dam and bridge were targeted in this way).

It couldn't last.

In December 1705, when the assembly reconvened, the question of the three West Jersey Quakers was again taken up. This time the assembly acted with more determination. The West Jersey Society had written to the home government in

England requesting help in the matter, and the committee of the Lords Trade, who oversaw colonial affairs, had instructed Cornbury to not interfere in the business of the assembly. Though he resisted, Cornbury agreed to hear discussion on the matter of Gardiner, Lambert and Wright. There had been a shift, maybe, in the balance of power.

After a brief interview with the men, Cornbury dismissed the Quakers, saying he would summon them again if he needed them.[71] But the assembly had resolved not to let the matter continue and refused to proceed with new business until the Quakers were sworn in and the legislature was restored to its full membership. This action, in the historian Tanner's account, was decisive in meeting the "arbitrary" conduct of Cornbury. Lambert, Gardiner and Wright took their seats and the Quakers and their allies resumed control of the assembly.

In Tanner's reading, Cornbury's bad behavior turned political will against him and helped give control of the assembly to his enemies, to the extent that the Quakers opened the next session of the house with a sarcastic statement of thanks to the governor for putting them in power. Before long the highway and militia acts were repealed.

In a speech, sometimes known as the *Great Remonstrance*, Samuel Jennings, who had been made assembly speaker under the new Quaker majority, described the state of affairs in the colonies under Cornbury. The Quakers had suffered tremendously since the surrender, Jennings said. They were barred from service on juries and harassed repeatedly under the militia act. Cornbury was avaricious and depraved in his nature. He trampled and invaded the rights of the proprietors. His administration was shot-through with corruption and tyranny.[72]

In some accounts, Jennings was merely coauthor of this remonstrance. In others he delivered it personally before the assembly with Cornbury in attendance. In Bancroft's account, Cornbury croaked "Stop!" in his ineffectual way as Jennings carried on "meekly and distinctly" with his litany of accusations and grievances.[73]

---

[71] Tanner, Province of New Jersey

[72] From the account of the remonstrance in Smith's Nova Caesarea

[73] Bancroft, History of the United States

Robert Quarry, a crown official, would later describe the denunciation of Cornbury by Jennings and Lewis Morris as "false malicious unjust and most barbarously rude." Jennings and Morris, in Quarry's words, had "shewed their resentments by scandalous...libels, and all that malice with *the help of Hell* could invent."[74] But their speech nonetheless had its intended effect.

The next year Cornbury would be recalled to England. With his patron gone, Daniel too would soon be out of power. In a letter to the Lords Trade in London Trade, William Penn himself recommended that Leeds and Thomas Revell be left out of the colonial government, since this would "tend most to the public quiet and Satisfaction of the people of those parts, which I take to be of moment at this time, on divers accounts. One Keeble that is to be with ye Lords, knows them both, pray ask him & favour his proposal of a Noble Staple, Potash, to encrease our Returns."[75]

Undone in the same sentence as a potash deal.

With Cornbury gone, the West Jersey Society and other aggrieved parties made moves against members of the governor's old administration, but the home government would act only against Leeds and Revell (in Tanner's account) due to their "indefensible conduct in abetting Cornbury in keeping the three West Jersey members out of the second assembly."[76]

The Cornbury clique enjoyed a brief reprieve during the governorship of Richard Ingoldesby (1709-1710) but under Governor Robert Hunter, moves again were made. In February 1713, Thomas Byerly, a member of the colonial council, filed a complaint against Leeds, alleging that he had falsified surveys. According to an entry in the New Jersey Archives, Daniel was called before the Burlington Council on February 23, 1713 and ordered to bring copies of the surveys. Two witnesses—John Gosling and Nathaniel Crips—testified that Leeds had in fact altered the documents.

---

[74] Quoted in Bonomi, *The Lord Cornbury Scandal*

[75] *Documents Relating to the Colonial, Revolutionary and Post-Revolutionary History of the State of New Jersey, vol. iii*, ed. William Whitehead (1881)

[76] Tanner, Province of New Jersey

The next day the court reconvened and more witnesses were called but Leeds refused to turn over his books on the advice of friends. After that, it seems like he stopped cooperating altogether, claiming illness.

An entry in the New Jersey archives dated March 17, 1713 states Leeds was plainly guilty of "many frauds" and "Malversations" during his tenure as surveyor general and says he was banned from further office. The only reason criminal proceedings weren't initiated against Leeds was that the attorney general, Alexander Griffiths, was a Cornbury holdover and he refused to cooperate.

It took some time, but Governor Hunter eventually had Griffiths removed and the push against Leeds continued. Officially Griffiths was suspended for "sundry misdemeanors, neglects and contempts of duty" but in reality (in Tanner's account) it was for failing to prosecute Leeds.

Under a new attorney general, Thomas Gordon, the trial of Daniel Leeds finally took place in 1716. Whether it was a retrial of the 1713 case or an entirely new set of accusations, I couldn't really tell. Despite no shortage of charges or witnesses willing to level accusations, the records of the Supreme Court in Burlington merely say that Daniel was acquitted. But his career was over. He would never hold public office again. He died in 1720.

Somebody was probably mad at the Leeds family and made it up.
The words happened to belong to Donn Shearer, but I heard them often enough in my wanderings to know the sentiment was shared by many others. The idea that anger or some kind of grudge could be at the root of the Jersey Devil story was so pervasive that it seemed less an explanation of a historical phenomena that had taken place sometime in the past than an ongoing application of the principle—conflict, anger and the satanic went together in the popular imagination. People *still* associated controversy with evil and with the devil. It was its own kind of evidence for the proposition that maybe they had done the same thing three hundred years ago too.

But such speculation wasn't strictly necessary. Again, Leeds' peers at the time had been using language that compared him to, if not *the* devil, then at least *a* devil.

In the middle of Cornbury's tenure, when Leeds was at the height of his political and pamphleteering offensiveness and when the Quakers had been seemingly powerless to stop him, a Quaker almanac-maker named Jacob Taylor had, in the introduction to his own almanac, called Daniel Leeds *Rhadamanthus*, Virgil's king of the underworld, invoking the heathen gods and at least one interpretation of the devil.

With his characteristic diplomacy, Leeds had responded by going on the offensive. Taylor "Cannot for his Conscience use Heathenish words in his Almanack," Leeds said, "no, not so much as the Names of the Months, yet he can for all his Conscience use this heathenish word, and more, elsewhere to put out his venom against me.

"Well, but if I am Judge of Hell, let him take heed hereafter of abusing me, as he has done, lest when he comes there to be judged, I should Sentence him to be tormented according to his Deserts."[77]

TWENTY

Weather events, and I fail to ask an important question

I sat in the kitchen at my Aunt Maureen's house in Northfield with BeBop, a big bay window opening onto the neighbors' yard, the last flakes of a dying snowstorm floating quietly down behind her. Aunt Maureen was a lady of great modesty and rectitude, and the neighbors' yard was filled with bright plastic toys. There was a big trampoline that the kids seemed to want to get as close to her kitchen window as possible. But on this day the snowstorm had buried the bright plastic toys, and all was quiet in the offending yard.

We sat in the kitchen, the diffuse afternoon light coming through the window. I had an old postcard with me for some reason, a Currier & Ives print depicting a train stuck in a snow

---

[77] Leeds, *The American Almanack for the Year of Christian Account 1706* (1705); I was unable to find Taylor's actual statement.

bank on a mountainside.

"Snow-Bound."

"That's a poem," BeBop said. "John Greenleaf Whittier."

I remember being kind of surprised she knew that.

In the image on the postcard, a group of men had emerged from the train with shovels. They were clearing the snow from the tracks. The train's headlight shone down on them and into the remains of the avalanche that had stopped the train. In the background a few Rockefeller Center Christmas trees loomed. Light shone from the train windows, and it looked like this little piece of civilization, warm and secure and benighted in the snow on the hillside.

Later I went back and read Greenleaf Whittier's poem, which began with an epigraph and a dedication. The epigraph was from *The Occult Philosophy* of Heinrich Cornelius, an early sixteenth-century magician and astrologer, and the lines excerpted from his book had to do with spirits. Apparently there were two types, light and dark, and they drew their energy from the kind of light that surrounded them. The spirits of darkness were stronger at night (unsurprising), but the good spirits could be "augmented" not only by the divine light of the sun but also by the ordinary wood fires of a common domestic hearth. "To the memory of the household it describes," the poet dedicated his work.

Incidentally, Whittier was a Quaker.

This was the first time that I'd gone to talk to BeBop about the family folklore. I had an actual tape recorder that I brought with me, current whereabouts unknown. The only surviving artifact of this conversation is a transcript of two paragraphs in which BeBop gave me her version of the Jersey Devil creation myth. In every respect it's the orthodox version of the story as it appears in McCloy and Miller's book, except that in BeBop's version, the Jersey Devil is the thirteenth child of Deborah Leeds—the archetypal Mother Leeds is converted into a particular woman with a real history, a first name and a husband and descendants who still lived in ranch houses in suburbs across South Jersey.

I had tried to interview my grandmother. Something still

feels faintly obscene about this—not that BeBop was anything but supportive of this project. She loved talking about Leeds Point and about her childhood in that place. She wanted someone to write a history of the family and I was one of the few people available.

As fact-finding missions, though, these conversations were failures. I had no idea how to interview anyone—how to capture fragments of a life and catalogue them for arrangement someday in some meaningful order—certainly not my own grandmother's life. But as social events they were more successful. I know I enjoyed my grandmother's company because I came to enjoy things that she enjoyed. Seafood for instance—clam chowder and scallops mostly. And the Philadelphia Phillies. These things had never been too popular before in my house, but they were sort of reintroduced, into my life anyway, through the vector of my grandmother.

A lot of old Leeds Point people didn't seem to like seafood, having eaten so much of it growing up, but BeBop had made her peace with fish. She told me she'd cooked eels for her own children. Her own grandmother pickled eels to store in the basement for winter. They were an excellent food for little kids, she said: no bones.

"Did you ever see an eel in the frying pan?"

"No."

"Well, they squirm all over," she said, and she laughed.

Somehow I couldn't picture Aunt Maureen or Aunt Cass eating an eel, but BeBop said they did.

I would ask questions but they were never quite the right questions. BeBop would answer patiently, but the whole enterprise had been handicapped by my misimpressions. Her memory was excellent, but then there was not a great deal to report. Leeds Point was not the cultural epicenter of South Jersey in 2002, and it had not been the cultural epicenter of South Jersey in 1922 either. It was a quiet peninsula sticking out into the salt marshes on the outskirts of Atlantic City, and nothing much had happened.

Some details I did manage to collect. There had been a pear farm across the street. She went to a one-room schoolhouse. One of her classmates, Milt Hynser, called her "String

Bean." There was a bottomless spring in the woods at the end of the road. Their mother forbade them from walking in the meadows, which was what they called the salt marshes. BeBop didn't enjoy being called "String Bean." Aunt Dottie had been compelled to take piano lessons. BeBop was kind of a tomboy and was happy to have avoided them.[78]

They had been embarrassed by their father's bootlegging, and the children made fun of them at school. Their grandfather, Charles, had gone to sea as a teenager and would sometimes tell the children stories, but BeBop couldn't really remember these stories. In the winter, when he wasn't fishing, he would cut firewood for one of the neighbors who had money.

She knew how to stun a chicken—in preparation for beheading it—by swinging the bird around by its feet. Her brother Bobby dreamed of walking across the marshes to Atlantic City and would get in trouble when he went out onto the mud and came home with the evidence all over his socks. When I asked her how the family had left Leeds Point or what she did afterward, she seemed to either not remember or to not want to talk about it.

Where I feel my failure most acutely is in the sound of her voice, which I want to communicate but am utterly unable to reproduce. There was something old-fashioned in it, in its nasal qualities. And in the sound of her laughter, which was continuous. She pronounced the name Deborah De-BOR-ah, accent on syllable two. And she referred to her own mother as *Mother*, as in, "Mother was a gourmet cook." Looking back I think these two details might be the strongest evidence— maybe the only evidence—that Deborah Leeds and Mother Leeds had been part of the oral tradition, the informal, family tradition, dating back to the time before BeBop, before the sources ran out.

She and Aunt Dottie were accomplished talkers, storytellers, but neither was really the type to impose a grand, over-arching narrative on her life. To listen to them, the family history was mostly made up of weather events. There was the

---

[78] The internet has no record of a "Milt Hynser," but that's what BeBop said.

nor'easter in 1962 when BeBop and the family were living on the top floor of an apartment building on Vermont Avenue in Atlantic City. The island was submerged ("the ocean met the bay") during successive tide cycles, and people's furniture floated down the streets. The hutch, which would later hold various decorative plates and fancy silverware and Hummel figurines in my childhood living room, "danced" (my mom's word) back and forth across the apartment as the wind blew and the building swayed.

"They always say that's a good, sturdy house that sways like that in the wind," BeBop said.

At a point during the storm, the family fled the top-floor for the comparative safety of the basement apartment where my Aunt Cass and Uncle Bud lived. That they believed themselves safer in a basement, despite the flooding, is a fact my mom submits as evidence that they could not have been too comfortable swaying back and forth at the top of Vermont Avenue.

A famous blizzard hit years later, after most of the family had moved offshore. Communication was cut off between the island and the mainland. Haddon Hall was turned into a temporary barracks for workers who couldn't get home. My Uncle Maurice walked first to my Uncle Craig's house in Northfield, then to the Rugby Inn to buy beer in the heart of the storm.

In the big storms it seemed, the white noise of daily life stopped for a moment. You could hear things that were ordinarily inaudible—little blocks of time pulled out of their surrounding matrix of unremarkable time and set aside for later observation.

There was one question I wanted to ask BeBop but never got a good answer. It had to do with Deborah Leeds. BeBop said she'd first heard of the Leeds Devil from Charles, her grandfather, and that all the Leedses in Leeds Point were related to the Jersey Devil. But what about the name Deborah? Did Charles tell her that part of the story too?

By the time I started talking to BeBop, Deborah's name and many parts of her story had already appeared in print. Cynthia Lamb had written her book. A few family trees had been assembled that identified Deborah and traced the Leeds' ancestry through her and Japhet to Daniel and Thomas Leeds.

I'd wanted to know if BeBop learned Deborah's name by talking to people, to her family members, of if she'd read about it as an adult, but it wasn't until later that this seemed like an important question, and although I asked her a number of times, I was never really sure she understood what I meant.

TWENTY-ONE

Uncle James shoots the sheriff of Henderson in the ass

I took the casino bus down one weekday in early September. Beside me sat a man from Henderson, North Carolina. He'd started out a few rows back, but after a short argument with his traveling companion, he plopped down next to me and fell deeply, instantly, asleep with a styrofoam coffee cup (mostly empty) in his hand. He woke up for one moment during the driver's usual welcome-aboard speech.

"Hello. My name is [inaudible] and I'll be driving your coach today."

"Then get us the fuck out of here," my new best friend said, and instantly he fell back asleep again.

An hour later, somewhere in the Pine Barrens, he woke up again. A solitary droplet of coffee that had been hanging from the lip of his cup for some time had fallen at last onto his jeans. He looked down wistfully at the spot and began to speak.

He was sixty-eight years old, he said (I'd had to guess for a while), but people usually thought he looked sixteen years younger (I did not). He had one remaining tooth in his head. He weighed one hundred and thirty pounds (I was not required to guess) and he "probably had more Indian blood in him than Black blood—three-fourths Cherokee." And his Uncle James had once shot the sheriff of Henderson, North Carolina, in the ass.

During the years of his marriage, his weight had been up to one-forty, but it had slowly dropped back down again over the years since his separation, and he fit easily into the standard Greyhound seats. He was unsympathetic toward people who found bus travel inconvenient.

His Uncle James, whom he took after, had owned a very fast car that he used to drive through the town of Henderson at high speeds. But the sheriff of Henderson also had a fast car and he would chase Uncle James and usually catch him, though usually not until they'd reached the outskirts of town.

My fellow passenger said that when he grew up and got a car of his own, he too liked to speed through Henderson and would be chased by the same sheriff, but he respected the sheriff, in part because of what had happened to Uncle James.

Back in the late Sixties or early Seventies there had been a manhunt for an escaped convict, which had led county authorities onto Uncle James' property. When Uncle James heard noises outside, he emerged from his house with a shotgun and called out three times, "Who's there?" When no one answered he fired the warning shot that accidentally struck the sheriff of Henderson in the ass.

The case went to court, but at the trial the sheriff spoke up in defense of Uncle James, saying it wasn't his fault since he'd shouted three times and no one had responded.

"This was a big deal," the man said. "A white sheriff, standing up in a court in North Carolina in the Sixties, and saying, 'Don't throw the black guy in jail who shot me in the ass.'"

He plays blackjack and three-card poker, he said. He used to go to Vegas a lot—more customer-friendly than Atlantic City, Vegas. And the food is better. He said he lost three hundred dollars in Atlantic City recently.

"No, I didn't *lose* three hundred dollars," he corrected himself. "I *invested* three hundred dollars." But when he asked for some "comps" for him and his friends, he was refused.

"In Vegas they would have done it."

We crossed the Mullica and the marshes opened up. My seatmate said he could tell things about the wind by looking at the clouds. I looked up at the clouds but couldn't tell anything.

A few weeks earlier, in August, there had appeared in The Cape May County Herald a photograph of Donn Shearer attacking Joe Fulginiti with a sword. "Pirates Invade Lighthouse," the headline said. Apparently it was National Lighthouse Day and the simulated attack was part of celebrations honoring the Cape May Lighthouse, which was turning one hundred years old. Joe, identified as "Gray Beard," was wearing a white sash around his waist and appeared to be wilting under a determined assault from Donn.

"There was swordplay and a couple of scalawags were recruiting youngsters for a life at sea," the story said.[79]

The end of summer is a melancholy time in a beach town, even one like Atlantic City, which was taken over by twenty-four-hour party people decades ago. The school year begins and the Pennsylvanians close up their big beach houses for the winter. They can be seen all over in places like Longport and Margate, loading up their SUVs with their kids' big plastic toys.

The man from Henderson gave me a fist-bump when he exited the bus.

In the casino, I got two or three dollars back with my bonus credits. I looked up at the names across the slot machines as I played:

- Alien Egg
- Wild Dolphin
- Enchanted Unicorn
- Get Nuts
- Shrimp Mania

---

[79] *Cape May County Herald*, August 7, 2010

TWENTY-TWO

A visit to the Booseum

The history of Atlantic City is in two bedrooms on the second floor of a modest residential house in a quiet neighborhood in Margate, New Jersey. The house is owned by Allen "Boo" Pergament, a retired employee of the South Jersey Gas Company, amateur historian and volunteer at the Atlantic County Historical Society. One of the bedrooms used to belong to his daughter.

The town of Margate, south of Atlantic City on Absecon Island, is one of the fancier beach towns along the South Jersey coast, famous for its giant elephant statue ("Lucy"), which lives on the beach block between Decatur and Washington Avenues. But back toward the bay, where Boo lives, things are quieter. There are no Brazilian bikinis or outlandish statuary. Boo's house wouldn't be out of place if you dropped it down in my neighborhood in Egg Harbor Township.

When I was a kid, Boo had been a famous basketball coach in the region, though maybe "tutor" is the better word. He ran a regular basketball clinic out of the gym at Holy Spirit High School in Absecon, where I spent a lot of time as a kid (my dad was an assistant football coach there). I never went to Boo's clinics, but some of my friends did, and they developed these astonishing, high-arcing jump shots that they launched almost vertically into the air. It looked unorthodox, but it must have been effective. Three of them, just from among my friends, went on to play basketball in college.

Boo also organized the prestigious Seagull Classic basketball tournament at Holy Spirit with Father Ed Lyons, a teacher at the school. This was also a big deal locally and attracted powerhouse teams from around the country, among them Atlantic City High School itself. In 1987 during a game between Atlantic High and Mater Dei High School of California, a fight broke out in the stands. One person was shot and three others stabbed as the fight spilled onto the court and into the hallways of the school, and a few years later the tournament was discontinued.

Boo had been a basketball fanatic for years. In addition to the clinics and tournaments, he used to go to games every night of the week, sometimes multiple games, he said, and then a few years ago, quite abruptly, over the course of a few weeks, he had given up basketball and thrown himself with comparable enthusiasm into historical preservation work, assembling gradually the large collection of photographs and artifacts from Atlantic City history that now took up most of the second floor of his house.

Like Heritage Day and the Knights of Lucerne, Boo seemed to be a vector. If South Jersey did possess a heritage, Boo was one of the ways it was being preserved. Since I'd never met the man, I resolved to talk to him and see his collection.

I took the NJ Transit bus up Ventnor Avenue and walked a few blocks back to the house where Boo lived. From the outside, the place was unremarkable. A little stained-glass ghost decoration was suction-cupped to a window, but otherwise there was no indication of the Booseum within.

I probably hadn't seen Boo in sixteen years, but he seemed exactly the same. He gave me a folder of documents that he'd photocopied and led me upstairs to the collection.

"You are now in the midst of the Booseum," he said.

The door to the room that housed most of it still had his daughter's name on it. Inside, were glass display cases full of relics, binders full of postcards, binders full of photographs, shelves and shelves of old books, crates of photographs that Boo'd had enlarged and set in plastic sleeves. He said he'd bought the display cases from a trophy shop (I think) that was going out of business and gave him a great deal.

There were a great many arcane objects that Boo had collected over the years. Among the prize artifacts was the Morris Guards uniform of Joe Hackney, "Probably the greatest athlete in Atlantic City's history," Boo said. There was a cowboy outfit that had once belonged to Ben Cotey, owner of a club called The Dude Ranch that used to be on Connecticut Avenue and the boardwalk.

He produced an old bathing suit from somewhere, ("this

old bathing suit") shaking his head as he did so, and then a pair of roller skates. "Got these skates that have nothing to do with Atlantic City. They're kind of symbolic."

Boo's particular forte was old photographs, and this part of the collection was enormous. Boo said the plan was to organize the photographs geographically according to the Atlantic City street grid. Photos would be arranged according to the scenes they depicted, and then by date taken.

When I told him I'd lived on Sovereign Avenue as a kid, he produced a photo of Nicholson's Bar, which used to be on the corner of Sovereign and Atlantic Avenues. It was a "famous" bar, Boo said.

He showed me a picture of Caldwell's liquor store which was also nearby ("that was also well known") and a photo of a house in the neighborhood where a famous doctor once lived.

Then he removed an old book from a shelf and passed it to me.

"Just hold that in your hand," he said. "*Carefully.*"

Some time elapsed.

"Ever hear of Jonathan Pitney?"

Pitney is a founding father of Atlantic City.

"Sure," I said.

"Ok. This is one of his books."

I held the book.

"I have three of his books," Boo said. "They're just from his library. And I always feel the same when I touch this. I feel like I'm transported back into time."

Boo took the book back and put it on the shelf.

"Was that a bible?" I said.

"The book is insignificant," Boo said, and he continued on with his tour.

A moment later he picked up the book again and looked at it. "It's...*Testament and Psalms*," he said. "I knew it wasn't a bible."

Boo had bricks from old apartment houses. He had plaques from off the old hotels, long since torn down—artifacts from a version of the city that was no longer available in the real world. There were pieces of the Traymore, the Hotel St. Charles, the Marlboro-Blenheim—old hotels, all gone now. There was a brick from the old Atlantic City High School, which the city had torn down not long after it named the surrounding neighborhood a historic district.

"That's the post office that just came down," Boo said, showing me one brick. "This is the Senator Hotel. Lighthouse from 1857. That piece of tile is the Vermont Apartments. This piece of tile, the Vanderbilt Apartments. South Jersey Gas Company, where I worked."

"How did you get them?" I said.

"Walked up and ripped it off," he said. "Bare hands."

Boo had a deed for piece of land that was once owned by the Leeds family—"prime property" he said. "It goes right through Brighton Park, right through where the Claridge Hotel was, over to where the Traymore was. I have the original deed to that—pretty neat piece."

In the folder he gave me were photocopies of pages from books that Boo thought might be helpful. There were excerpts from William McMahon's *Historical Town of Smithville*, and from McMahon's *Historical Towns of Smithville, Vol. II*, and also from McMahon's *Tales of the Historic Smithville Inn – in the Towne of Smithville* and also from *South Jersey Towns: History and Legend* (with a chapter on the Towne of Smithville) also by McMahon, I think.

"This particular guy," Boo said, "Bill McMahon—he wrote the same stuff ten times over."

Boo had copied a few pages from A.L. English's 1884 *History of Atlantic City*, dealing with the "Leeds' possession of the island." According to English, Jeremiah Leeds (a grandson of Japhet and Deborah) bought pieces of Absecon Island from its various owners—James Steelman, Reuben Clark, the Conover family (John, Enoch, James and Joseph)—in the late eighteenth century. It could be "reasonably inferred," English said, that Jeremiah's "continuous occupation" of the island had begun by about 1795, and that he and his family had been "fixtures" on the beach by 1800.[80]

Jeremiah raised livestock, corn and rye on the island, English said. Grain was so abundant that coastal fishermen

---

[80] A.L. English, *History of Atlantic City, New Jersey* (1884)

("shallopmen") who landed there to buy supplies would say that they were "going down to Egypt to buy corn." For many years, Leeds was the island's only occupant. "He first erected a home near where the Island House now stands, but later moved it to the foot of Massachusetts Avenue, on the margin of a road that for many years was the main highway from the inlet to Hill's Creek. Here he cleared a farm, which afterwards became known as 'Leeds Plantation,'" English said.

When Jeremiah died intestate in 1838, the Orphans Court of Atlantic County appointed a Japhet Leeds (a descendant, not Deborah's husband) and John Clemente to divide the property among his heirs, and in 1852 it was Jeremiah Leeds' children who sold their stakes to Jonathan Pitney and Enoch Doughty—two representatives of the Camden and Atlantic Land Company—in what would be the first act in the story that resulted in the creation of Atlantic City. The Camden and Atlantic Railroad (the second act) got its charter the same year.

Jeremiah's son Chalkley, who was alive when English wrote his book and who was interviewed by the young reporter, told English that his father had first settled Absecon Island in 1783. Chalkley's earliest memories were of the homestead on Baltic and Massachusetts Avenues. There was a salt works at the time, Chalkley said. Most of the visitors before the railroad were sportsmen who came to hunt (to "gun" in Chalkley's word) and to fish. To accommodate them, a "fish house" had been built near Clam Creek in the Inlet.

The reminiscences of early visitors to Absecon Island were unanimous on the generally repellent character of the island, its many unpleasant qualities, its hostility to settlement, the gray depression evoked by its combination of sand, sea and sky, the harshness of the wind and the abundant, aggressive and vampiric insect life. Samuel Richards, whose family provided most of the money needed to build the railroad, said of his first impression, "It was the most horrible place to make the termination of a railroad I had ever seen."[81]

After the town's incorporation, the residents were still

[81] Quoted in Sarah Ewing and Robert McMullin, *Along Absecon Creek* (1965)

mostly Leedses. Robert Leeds was Atlantic City's first post-master. Chalkley was the first mayor. On May 1, 1854, he was elected in an informal ceremony. "Eighteen votes were cast in a cigar-box, secured with yellow tape," Alfred Heston, the historian, who claimed to have been a witness, wrote.[82] Chalkley's first act as chief executive was to award a liquor license. Within a year he would be out of office.

At a dinner in 1889, a man named Peter Boice stood up and gave an account of his reminiscences of Jeremiah Leeds, whose grain he'd helped harvest when he was a young man. Boice said that, at the time Leeds settled it, the "greater portion of the island was sand hills, duck ponds, swamps, brier thicks." Wildfowl were so plentiful they could be killed with clubs. Heron could be hooked around the neck with long poles. It was not surprising that the island was a destination for hunters, Boice said, but Leeds survived mostly by raising cattle and grain. "Though he lived a lonely life he generally had an abundance."

At the time of his death, Jeremiah owned more than 1,068 acres on the island and another two hundred and fifty-one on the mainland. He had a much younger wife, Millicent, who outlived him by many years and who, after his death, opened Aunt Millie's Boardinghouse, which was either Atlantic City's first boardinghouse or its first whorehouse, depending on whom you ask.

Jeremiah died at age eighty-four from "a cancer on his lower lip, which had worried him for the last forty years of his life."[83] He had never much cared for the men who came to the beach to shoot his birds.

According to the historian John Hall, toward the end of his life, Jeremiah liked to tell a story from his childhood.[84] At the time of the Revolution, two British ships had entered Great Bay ("in full view from Leeds Point") and a party of marines landed on shore to forage for supplies. The soldiers ordered John Leeds (Deborah and Japhet's son) to round up his cattle

[82] Heston, *Abesgami: Annals of Eyren Haven and Atlantic City, 1609 to 1904* (1904); Heston says he was present at this event.

[83] John Hall, *The Daily Union History of Atlantic City, New Jersey* (1899)

[84] Hall, The Daily Union History

and then selected two of the fattest cows, confiscating them without paying the family. But the cows, Jeremiah said, had belonged to him and his to brother, and they had been worth between six and eight dollars apiece.

"This event had its effect in making a soldier of the Quaker boy in the war of the Revolution which soon followed," Hall wrote.

Today in Atlantic City, on the corner of Michigan and Atlantic Avenues, half a block from the current site of the Atlantic City bus terminal, are a Ralph Lauren Outlet store, an Under Armour Factory House, a Nautica Outlet store and a Banana Republic outlet. On the north side of Atlantic Avenue, facing south, there's a waymark noting the location of the house of Jeremiah Leeds, who, it says, came from Leeds Point with his ten children in 1785 and built the first permanent structure on the island from cedar logs.

"That land is now occupied by the terminus of the Atlantic City Expressway and the recently improved gateway corridor to the resort."

TWENTY-THREE

Boo's jump shot, and other Atlantic City icons

Boo said he had little interest in the Jersey Devil and that, before I asked him, he'd never really investigated the story.

"If I had time to do that, I could have found other things in Atlantic City that I'd prefer to know," he said.

When I asked him where he thought the story might have come from, he said, "There's things like that that find their niche. I'm not one that can tell you even *how* it happens. I can only tell you *that* it happens—that something becomes, for lack of a better word, so romantic that it's neat. People enjoy hearing about it. They love that type of stuff. There's other things like that that people become so enamored with that they enjoy that, and it grows up and it sticks with generation to generation. It prolongs itself, and there's not a simple answer to why or how or whatever. It's just something that sits easy with people, comfortably. And it sticks to an area. It's native to this area.

"Why does something like the diving horse become such a symbol? It's the biggest icon in Atlantic City's history, more so than the lighthouse or the rolling chair or Convention Hall or anything. There's no question in my mind about that. How can something like Lucy persevere all these years—one hundred and thirty years?

"If you were able to find out the truth it might simply be that she [Mother Leeds] said something that somebody took in a certain way, and then somebody else repeated it, and that's how. Just like a rumor starts or whatever.

"And then it goes down from generation to generation. It gets perpetuated, but it's based on absolutely nothing at all."

Boo said he was constantly fielding questions from around the state, from around the world even—from documentarians and journalists and writers and historians, amateur and professional, who needed information on Atlantic City. He had consulted for the HBO series *Boardwalk Empire*, which is set in Atlantic City during Prohibition. Someone from *New Jersey Lifestyle* magazine had just called looking for pictures for a story on the new hotel, The Chelsea. A crew of "ghost hunters" (Boo's words) interviewed him for a short film on the Atlantic City lighthouse, which someone (no idea who) says is haunted. A group of strangers in Florida recently called him to settle an argument they were having in a bar. "How the hell did they get my number?" he said. But he wasn't complaining. He felt very privileged to have the time and energy and good fortune to devote himself to these projects.

"You know what. I'm trying to do every hotel, guest house, hall, apartment in Atlantic City's history, every contestant in the Miss America Pageant. I have a pile of letters this high that I'm trying to categorize. These are all major projects that would stop anybody. And they aren't even the main things I'm busy with."

I asked him about the arc on a jump shot, and he seemed pleased.

"I'm glad to hear you say that, because some of my friends

mock me about that." He made me put my hand up to simulate a defender in basketball as he explained his rationale. An "upside-down U" gets "more shots off" and frustrates defenders and "it's clean," he said.

He hadn't coached basketball in fifteen years, but he sounded like he was giving a half-time speech.

"I believe it fervently," he said. "I can't get people to do it enough."

Later he said, "Somebody should capture every drawing of the Jersey Devil, every interpretation, and show them all together."

TWENTY-FOUR

Today's morons, yesterday's disowned Friends

Whatever *else* the Jersey Devil might be, it is first a story. It has setting, characters, a basic plot, even a kind of moral logic. Themes of poverty and sexual misadventure are consistent across its history.

The Jersey Devil is always an unwanted child. Henry Charlton Beck calls it, "New Jersey's most celebrated of all unwanted children." A woman, old and poor, puts a curse on her unborn. The proximate sin may be blasphemy, but the original sin is whatever moral failing caused her to conceive a child she didn't want and couldn't care for in the first place.

In the 1890s, Henry Herbert Goddard and Elizabeth Kite went into the Pines. Goddard was a psychologist and the Director of Research at the Training School for Backward and Feeble-Minded Children in Vineland, New Jersey. Kite was his capable assistant. In November 1897 a young girl, later made famous as *Deborah Kallikak*, came into their care. She was eight years old and had been born in an alms house. Her mother had been married twice. Neither of the men was Deborah's father and neither would agree to care for the girl.

After an unsuccessful stint in school, Deborah was admitted to the Training School in Vineland, where her doctors began making detailed observations on her physical characteristics, personal habits, intellectual aptitude and moral intelligence. She was of average size and weight, her admissions form noted, with "no peculiarity in form or size of head." She had a "staring expression" and was "excitable but not nervous." She was "not affectionate and quite noisy." She had a "jerking movement in walking." She could throw a ball but not catch one. Her grandmother had been classified "somewhat deficient." Her grandfather, a "periodical drunkard," had been classified "mentally deficient." Deborah herself was declared "possibly feeble-minded."[85]

A diary, kept over a decade of her custody, traces the progress of her education and the sad conclusions forced upon her caregivers. In 1900 it was noted that Deborah was disobedient, graceful, a "good captain" and "good in entertainment work." She could follow the commands halt, right-face, left-face and forward-march. By 1904 she could play "Old Black Joe" on the cornet. By 1908 she could write a fairly good story but had "little idea of the use of capitals." She was "bold toward strangers" yet "kind toward animals." She retained a good many interesting facts concerning nature work.

By Christmas 1909, she requested a pair of nice shoes and several varieties of colored ribbon, but her education in basic arithmetic and spelling were failing, and her teachers were giving up on her. In April 1910, she was given the Binet-Simon intelligence test and determined to have the mental aptitude of a nine-year-old. She could count and knew what a fork was and knew what a chair was but struggled at rhyming. She did not know money.

On the basis of the Binet-Simon test, and on their own steadfast observations, Goddard and Kite declared Deborah to be a "high-grade feeble-minded" person or "moron," the kind of wayward girl that fills up our reformatories and gets into "all sorts of trouble and difficulties, sexual and otherwise."

Despite their careful attentions, no progress had been made toward the development of Deborah's "higher intelli-

---

[85] Goddard and Kite's account, *The Kallikak Family: A Study in the Heredity of Feeble-Mindedness* (1912)

gence or general education." All her instincts and appetites led toward vice. If released from the institution, she would be easy prey for evil men and lead a life of viciousness and depravity. Deborah was a good-looking girl with many attractive qualities that had given her teachers hopes that, with enough hard work and guidance, she could one day lead a decent life. "Such hopes," Goddard and Kite wrote, were "delusions."

Following their experience with Deborah, and with large numbers of other feebleminded persons at the school, Goddard and Kite undertook a project of forensic genealogy to determine the origins of the hereditary taint that had condemned their young charge to a life of wickedness. For two years staff at the school devoted themselves to this project. Hundreds of families were interviewed, volumes of records were consulted, miles and miles were traveled as scientists sought to identify the source of Deborah's feeblemindedness.

In research of this kind, Goddard and Kite said, the feebleminded moron presented special problems. Unlike the lower orders of intelligence—the imbecile or the idiot for example—the moron could appear normal to the uninitiated, but with sufficient preparation and training, the signs became unmistakable. Owing to their greater sensitivity, women were considered best for this work.

Goddard and Kite learned to identify morons on sight, and they wandered the region seeking out the slack-jawed and dull-eyed, the poorly shod and helpless. Goddard worked for a time at Ellis Island, picking out morons from the crowds of immigrant passersby. They learned to identify feeblemindedness in people they had never met, dead persons mostly, a skill of immense value in reconstructing Deborah's scarred and degraded family tree. They could identify feeblemindedness in fictional persons. The subject of Jean-François Millet's painting *Man with a Hoe* was a "perfect picture of an imbecile," Goddard said.

The work was slow and difficult, with many unforeseen challenges. Drunkenness, for instance, was a challenge. If a man was a habitual drunkard it was difficult to tell if he was truly feebleminded or merely pissed as a lord. But of course habitual drunkenness was itself strongly suggestive of mental defect. Kite entered one house that contained nine mental defectives. Conditions inside were horrific, she said. The father, a large man, sat helplessly in one corner. From their hygiene, the expressions on their faces and the state of their clothing, it was clear to Kite that she was in the presence of feebleminded morons, people who would likely reproduce at twice the rate of the general population and so "clog the wheels of human progress" (Kite's words).

Goddard and Kite interviewed defective parents and defective children, and the defective parents of defective children, and at last the problem yielded to the perspicacity of their science. Their conclusion, published in 1912 as *The Kallikak Family: A Study in the Heredity of Feeble-Mindedness*, was that the problems of Deborah Kallikak, and of large numbers of other Pine Barrens residents, were traceable to the sins of a certain "Martin Kallikak" (not his real name) who had been a soldier in the colonial militia at the time of the American Revolution.

Martin had been stationed along the King's Highway during the war and there, during off-duty hours, when "the fires of patriotism burned lower than other fires within him," he had found means to *quench his own thirst* in the company of a young bar girl, a native of the region, whom he'd met at one of the many taverns along the highway, and in consequence of this union she bore him a son.

Martin's military service was cut short (arm wound, accidental), and he returned to the farm, where he married a Quaker girl from an English family in the front ranks of colonial society, and from this healthy union emerged a family of intelligent beings, including lawyers, ministers, merchants, pioneers, and many of the leading citizens of the province, men and women whose varied activities "have constantly tended to increase the preserving force of our commonwealth, lifting its energies to an ever broadening outlook" (Kite's words).[86]

But from that first squalid combination with the nameless tavern girl sprang a band of illegitimates, confirmed alcoholics, sexually immoral persons, epileptics and criminals who have

---

[86] Elizabeth Kite, *The Survey* (1912)

scandalized the region for generations, inciting comment among the neighboring townspeople who "retained a vivid impression of the strange doings and disorderly ways of these wild people of the woods."

"This is the ghastly story of the descendants of Martin Kallikak Sr., from the nameless feeble-minded girl," Kite wrote.

Goddard and Kite's The Kallikaks is probably the most important creative work ever produced about Pineys and the Pine Barrens. In a sense, the literary history of the region since about 1935 has been an extended attempt to live down the legacy of Goddard and Kite. The natural historian Stephen Jay Gould, who neatly disassembled its claims in his book *The Mismeasure of Man*, says that the Kallikak family "functioned as a primal myth of the eugenics movement" for decades after its publication. The historian John David Smith, in his account of the fiasco, says The Kallikaks was such a sensation that there was talk of a possible Broadway adaptation following its release.[87]

Goddard and Kite's research was positively reviewed in the scientific literature, where readers likened the discovery of the Kallikak family to an important archeological find.[88] Leila Zenderland, another historian, notes that the study was warmly received by the Nazis. Hitler himself may have owned a copy. While the agents of the Reich were burning other books, they busily printed a new edition of *Die Familie Kallikak* in 1933.[89]

As a result of the book's popularity, a certain image of the Pineys took shape in the popular imagination. In news coverage of the region, writers emphasized the threats posed by Pineys to the American way of life. "Bad Blood a Danger to American Democracy," blared the headline of one such story, which proceeded to describe the "dangers of defectives" in

---

[87] Smith, *Minds Made Feeble* (1985)
[88] *American Journal of Psychology*, c. 1913, quoted in Hugh Tullner, The Imaginary Birth and Slow Death of the Pineys (a student essay)
[89] Zenderland, *Measuring Minds: Henry Herbert Goddard and the Origins of American Intelligence Testing* (1998)

our "communities."[90] Of the discovery of the Kallikaks, one newspaper wrote, "There could hardly be a more thorough demonstration of the effect of the fouling of the blood descending through generations, and the result also of a clean heritage."

The feebleminded moron did not make up the most loathsome strata of society, Goddard and Kite said. The idiot and the imbecile were lower but less dangerous because too stupid to breed in sufficient numbers. By contrast the moron could appear charming and attractive (though utterly without moral intelligence) and herein lay an important tenet of Goddard and Kite's system of belief. Because of their low *moral* endowment, feebleminded morons exerted an enormous influence on society at large. They led non-morons into temptation. And because they could not control their sexual urges, they reproduced at alarming rates.

"The idiot is not our greatest problem," Goddard said. "He is indeed loathsome; he is somewhat difficult to take care of; nevertheless, he lives his life and is done. He does not continue the race with a line of children like himself, he never becomes a parent. It is the moron type that makes for us our great problem."[91]

Goddard and Kite's central claim was that the horrors of the Piney race were a result, not of opportunity or education, but of breeding. It had been a perfect test case. The two strains of the family had lived within the borders of the same state, often within miles of one another, for generations. Any differences of environment had been purely of their own making. The only variable had been the "tainted" blood introduced by the anonymous bar girl.

Goddard said the feebleminded were effectively a different species, a "vigorous animal organism of low intellect but strong physique—the wild man of today."[92] He coined the pseudonym Kallikak—from Greek works *kalos* and *kakos*, meaning *good* and *bad*—to reflect the divergent destinies of the family resulting from the two strains of blood.

[90] *Pullman Herald*, February 3, 1922
[91] Goddard and Kite, The Kallikak Family
[92] Goddard, *Feeble-mindedness: Its Causes and Consequences* (1914)

For Goddard and Kite, the morons of the Pine Barrens made up part of a "feeble-minded menace" that numbered between three hundred thousand and four hundred thousand persons and posed a threat to democracy. It had been a "singular coincidence," Kite wrote, that the Kallikak half-brothers should have been born around the time of the American Revolution, each in his way a "direct outcome" of the forces that made possible the establishment of the republic. *All men created equal* had been a basic principle of that republic, but as she herself had helped demonstrate, all men were not created equal, Kite said. They were born with different aptitudes, moral and otherwise. A new social contract was needed to make the dreams of the founders more nearly true.

Goddard and Kite were influential within the wider eugenics movements taking shape in the U.S. and around the world. By 1911, in his own account, Goddard had administered the Binet-Simon intelligence test to about two thousand children, some of them as old as age fifty. He would go on to become part of a team of army scientists commissioned to design tests to sort men according to their aptitude for military service. He translated Alfred Binet's books into English and is credited with introducing the term "moron" into English. The Training School was recognized as one of the first institutions for the study of "mental deficiency" in the U.S.

Among the results of their work were proposals to segregate or sterilize Pineys to curb the rampant reproduction of the unfit. A sterilization law that would have applied to morons passed in the New Jersey legislature in 1911 but was declared unconstitutional two years later. Another proposal in 1914 was rejected. Governor James Fielder, after a tour of the Pines in 1913 had said, "The state must segregate them, that is certain. I think it may be necessary to sterilize some of them."[93]

Goddard for his part was in favor of segregating the Pineys in colonies to prevent sexual contact with persons of normal intellect and moral standing. Marriage prohibitions would be

[93] Quoted in Robert Mason's *Contested Lands: Conflict and Compromise in New Jersey's Pine Barrens* (1912). Mason says the quote originally appeared in *The New York Sun* for June 29, 1913

useless in the face of this menace. The moron had no more respect for marriage than he did for any other social institution. Castration was one possible solution but, alas, it was probably not politically feasible owing to an unfortunate and wholly superstitious resistance to this humane practice on the part of otherwise healthy males. But somehow morons must be kept away from normal folk, Goddard said. They must be kept from reproducing, whether through sterilization or colonization. Above all, he wisely counseled, we must *keep them happy*.

In Goddard and Kite's story, Martin Kallikak's bastard child had retained his father's ancient family name, but he also retained the tainted blood of his mother. In early life, the child had shown some promise, but eventually the "degenerate tendency" asserted itself. He built a hut and started a family. County land records showed the gradual expansion of his holdings as he added a half acre here, a third of an acre there, but otherwise "no gleam of ambition" had illuminated the dark path of his life.

It had been a large family, the scientists said. The unnamed Mother Kallikak had given birth to twelve children before she succumbed to the inevitable. "Overworked" and "scantily clad," she died giving birth to a thirteenth child.

For a while, I thought the Kallikak family might have actually *been* the historical Leeds family (apparently, they were not).[94] But this hardly seemed to add or subtract to the situation. The Leeds Devil wasn't just associated with Pineys. The Leeds Devil *was* a Piney. Born on the periphery of the woods to Piney parents, and presently living in the Pine Barrens themselves, the Leeds Devil was a product of the same moral logic that underlay the Piney creation myth.

Mother Leeds was an archetype of the Piney situation. Mired in poverty, unable to care for her children and yet unable to stop producing them, she was symptomatic of the ram-

---

[94] See J. David Smith and Michael Wehmeyer, "Who Was Deborah Kallikak?" in *Intellectual and Developmental Disabilities* (2012)

pant reproduction of the unfit. And at the root, this thinking held, there must be some original sin. In Deborah Kallikak's case, this had been her ancestor's sexual dalliance with a member of the wrong social class. In Mother Leeds' case, it was the black magic (inspired by poverty and immorality) that she put on her own unborn. But in both cases, the result was a kind of separate species, a vigorous animal organism of strong physique but low intellect, a kind of wild-man of today. The result was Pineys.

Goddard and Kite, incidentally, were Quakers. The high levels of feeblemindedness they found in the Pine Barrens were strongly suggestive of some original transgression on the part of the region's settlers. Kite said that the Piney problem was a direct consequence of the region's Quaker history. The Society's method for dealing with repeat sinners, she said, was to expel them from their ranks. In this way they had "unconsciously" thrown "upon society at large the responsibility of caring for what they themselves had failed to control."

By a neat trick of hereditary morality, the sinfulness of the children was seen was seen to indicate original sin on the part of the ancestors. But while the sins of the Keithians had been their "unbounded ambition" (Sam Jennings' words), the sins of the Pineys apparently had to do with whatever relative absence of ambition caused them to remain in the same region even as their economies, local industries and fellow townspeople abandoned them.

But for Goddard and Kite, immorality was immorality. Sin, whether of the Keithian or the Pine-Rat type, manifested across generations, and some sinister hereditary taint would have connected the destinies of Daniel Leeds and Deborah Kallikak. As Kite put it, "Today's morons" were yesterday's "colonial outcasts" or "disowned" Friends.

TWENTY-FIVE

'Lenin tried something different'

Bus back to New York in what must be December. A young man two rows behind me is declaiming exquisite nonsense at high volume to his long-suffering "papa" who sits beside him saying nothing—he just sighs audibly every few minutes.

"I stole two cookies for you, papa!" the young man says, "from Starbucks!

"I was the thousandth customer!"

They had lost a bit of money, these two, in the last few hours. At the casinos. They had been going to get massages, but now there was no way. Mama would be displeased. If they hadn't lost so much money at the casinos, they would certainly not be traveling by bus. They would be traveling by Lincoln Town Car. They'd have gotten massages and taken a Town Car. As a fellow passenger, it's a little hard not to take this kind of talk personally.

One of the Starbucks employees had been staring right at him as he stole that cookie, but the employee hadn't done anything.

They are smokers. At least the son is. It's impossible to tell their ages by his voice (or by papa's sighing), but I'm not about to turn around and look at them.

"I like Paris Hilton!" the son says. "She's a role model! *And* she's popular!"

He's teaching himself to read Egyptian apparently, and from time to time in the middle of his monologue, his increasingly fractal and deranged monologue, he pauses to speak some lines of poetry in translation.

> "I have been roasting
> Since the beginning of time
> But it is only now
> That I have seen such a goose!"

The Garden State Parkway is a little two-lane affair down here. We are five automobiles, five sets of taillights moving silently through the darkness.

"I like cell phones!" the son says. "I think whoever invented them is a pretty good man!

"Did I ever tell you a joke? You know what else Donald Trump gives you if you get a royal flush? Toilet paper!"

Someone might have just tried to shush him. Papa just sits there in silence.

"I know Lenin messed up a lot of Russians," he says. "No, he tried to do something *different*—electromagnetic brainwaves into space. We're givers as well as receivers."

Atlantic City is the third-busiest bus destination in North America, behind only New York City and Toronto, according to Greyhound's website,[95] which used to give an estimate of the median salary of its passengers, though I see they've now taken that data down. I remember I was a little below the median during this period.

They recently started referring to their Atlantic City route as the "Lucky Streak" which seems to me a singularly ill-advised way to describe a coach-load of desperate cases, barreling down the Garden State Parkway with a stranger at the helm, but I guess they know their business.

He has moved on to New Year's Eve plans now. He says he's not drinking this year. The father sighs again. Maybe just for half an hour. Maybe just a little champagne. Now he's promising to give papa a massage when they get home ("Tiger Balm—Ben Gay doesn't work for you"). He promises they'll take a car service from the Port Authority back to Brooklyn, then rescinds the promise.

"I have to smoke a cigarette first, so I'll leave you downstairs. The bus is warm this time of night. The cab—you don't know if the guy is going to leave the window open and turn the heater on. People get sick that way, papa."

As we exit the Lincoln Tunnel, he starts singing, "What a

Wonderful World."

"All men are created equal but are not the same," he says. "That's the only thing I know that's written in the Constitution Declaration of Independence."

"All right ladies and gentlemen, this is New York City," the driver says. "Last stop, New York City Port Authority, Forty-Second Street."

And they leave my life forever.

TWENTY-SIX

I am offered Combos

Some months elapse.

July – Bus back to New York City from the Hilton, which used to be the Golden Nugget. When I was a kid, my grandmother (MeMom not BeBop) would walk me up here in the evenings to see the mechanical parrots that sat in a big gold cage in the lobby and sang in the voices of the stars of yesterday. There was a Judy Garland parrot and a Bing Crosby parrot, I think, and maybe a Sinatra. Sinatra himself sung at the Golden Nugget in person for a few years on a regular contract during the early Eighties, but I never saw the real Sinatra. Only his robot parrot voice-double.

There are fourteen passengers aboard the bus here tonight, including a woman with a clip-on necktie that is clipped to her tee-shirt. We stop at another casino (unnamed in my notes) and a group of gypsies boards the bus, among them two children in bathing suits with towels wrapped around them. There's also a young man who looks a little bit like Flea from the Red Hot Chili Peppers and who sits down next to me.

His voice is hoarse, like he hasn't slept in a while. From a knapsack, he produces a ziplock bag full of gummy bears, sets them in his lap and begins snoring.

"It's cold," someone says, and the driver kills the air con.

"No it's not. It's *hot*," Flea says and falls asleep again.

Even before he offers me a gummy bear, I've decided I like Flea. His manner is polite but defeated. He apologizes when he sits down and again when he wakes up with his head on my chest because he has toppled over in his sleep.

I agree with him about the bus temperature too, and so, I suspect, do most of the other passengers, since it's easily in the mid-eighties in here. The only people complaining are the ones sitting up there in their bathing suits.

Somewhere around New Gretna, Flea approaches the driver to ask the whereabouts of a trashcan—an unusual request, under the circumstances, but one born out of concern for the general welfare—and on the way back, one of the gypsies, with whom he's now fighting, says something I can't hear.

"I'm not making a mess," Flea says. "You shut your fucking pie hole."

But now he is asleep again and breathing into my face. Or I am breathing into his face. We are all of us breathing into one another's faces, I suppose. Not that you can even tell anymore, it's so sickeningly hot on this goddamned bus.

I can no longer feel my own breath. I experienced this phenomenon once before, while hiking in the Yucatan. The temperature and humidity of the ambient air corresponded so precisely with the air inside my lungs I could no longer feel the difference. With each indraft, there was mounting desperation.

"This is the way to travel," I think, "asphyxiating on a Greyhound, next to a disgraced bass player, who's coming off a three-day bender, who's beleaguered by gypsies, who are freezing in their bathing suits."

Finally someone in the back speaks up. "EXCUSE ME SIR. PLEASE PUT A.C.," and the condenser coil springs to life and we are spared this humid death.

In the Lincoln Tunnel, Flea opens a bag of Combos and offers me one. He is drinking an Arnold Palmer now.

"No," I say, showing him my hand. "Thank you though."

"Is Atlantic City a moral place?" I wonder. I wish I had asked that question of Boo.

"Breakfast of champions?"

"Yeah," he says. "That and the gummy bears." And he laughs his world-weary laugh.

"Actually, it's just really shitty food."

TWENTY-SEVEN

The 1909 Jabberwocky invasion

On the morning of Sunday, January 17, 1909, the residents of South Jersey awoke after an overnight snowstorm. It had not been an especially powerful storm, but it lay down a fresh covering of snow, in which, some residents would later say, were found the tracks of an unidentified animal that had run through people's yards, across their roofs, and across, in some instances, the tops of fences. A man named Thack Cozzens, a resident of Woodbury, would claim that he saw a strange creature crossing the street as he (Cozzens) was leaving the Woodbury Hotel in the early morning hours.

"I saw two spots of phosphorous," Cozzens reportedly said, "the eyes of the beast."[96]

That same night in Bristol, Pennsylvania, two civilians and a police officer said they saw a large bird hopping around down by the river. Several Philadelphia papers picked up the story and soon more monster reports were flowing out of the Delaware Valley. A paper called The Public Ledger ran a story on Wednesday headlined, "'Monster' Prowls in Jersey Towns—'Leeds Devil,' Mule, Stork or Just Plain Joker, Rouses Countryside."

Meanwhile, The Trenton Evening Times, in a story about the "Leeds Satan," quoted an employee of the United Revolving Door Company, William McElmoyl, who said he found tracks in his yard. "I recognized the tracks from those reproduced in the papers, and there is no mistaking them," he said. "They look to me as if the hoof was that of a young colt, not a cloven hoof, as I've heard its being described, and there are spaces for 100 feet or more between the regular steps in the snow, suggesting beyond doubt, that the visitor flies."

The paper said it was getting letters from all over the region from people caught up in the scare. "Old men, who remember

---

[96] Quoted in McCloy and Miller, Jersey Devil

the day when the 'Leeds Devil' scared lonely communities of the county believe this terror has returned, while in the colored settlements the negroes regard the marks as those of what they term the 'flying death.'"

On January 20, The Philadelphia Inquirer too ran a Jersey-Devil-track story, stating that the proliferation of mysterious footprints in the region suggested the presence of a "whole troupe" of devils. "Old residents" remembered the Leeds Devil, the paper said. "Old Negroes," panic stricken, were barricaded in their houses.

About the same time the Trenton Times quoted a man named James Fleson who said that he had tracks on his property. "I'll take you to a place where these hoofprints cross the top of a broken-down chicken house that wouldn't bear the weight of a sack of flour," Fleson said, "and I'll show you where the creature walked on the roof of a house, along the top of a fence eight feet high, and then through a hole in a close board fence, a hole just four inches across."[97]

In a story with multiple datelines—Mount Holly, Burlington, Bordentown—the Trenton Times said the first alleged sighting of the actual monster had occurred in Skillman. The paper offered the testimony of two men who claimed to have followed the beast, referring to the men (two "Negroes") in quotation marks as "Hank" White and "Tom" Hamilton, as if to signal its surprise that such beings should have actual Christian names. The men's quotes were reported in dialect as if to emphasize the race of the speakers.

"It's an air hoss," White supposedly said, "an' I ain't a-gwine out no mo' without my gun.

"Tom, he told me that down in Georgia there is an air hoss, what flies at night in de woods and wheezes and snorts."

In a short period of time, the story had gone surprisingly national. The San Jose Evening News of January 30 ran an image of the monster beside the headline, "Is this the Flying Death that Hovers over the Village of Burlington?" Again it was alleged that "Negroes" were in a panic, though this time strong men were also suitably "terrified." Descriptions of the

[97] Trenton Evening Times, January 20, 1909

beast ranged from "a winged kangaroo" to a "four-legged ostrich." Hounds would not follow its trail, it was said.[98]

The Tucson Daily Citizen meanwhile reported that South Jersey was in a "quandary of excitement" over the appearance of the Leeds Devil, which had last been seen thirty-five years earlier in Leeds Point, Cumberland County [sic].[99] The Fort Worth Star-Telegram ("Only Six Men in Big Colored Colony Go to Work") told the story of one Nelson Evans, a "paper-hanger" from Gloucester whose story would be repeated throughout the week. Nelson's wife, Belle (identified as a "negress"), woke him up when she heard a strange buzzing sound in the backyard.[100]

"I poked my elbow into Mr. Evans' side and whispered to him: 'Nels, get up quick; something is wrong in the yard!'"

The Star-Telegram called the monster the "*Jersey* devil" (the earliest use I'd seen of that term), claiming it was a "Fearsome Winged Critter" that produced a sound "like the muffled sound a wood saw makes when it strikes a rotten place." The Jersey Devil's breath was hot enough to scorch asbestos, the paper said. "The negro colony at Mount Ephraim was in such a state yesterday that it was said but six men went to work." The Evanses were solid church folk, the paper said, and "neither of them ever even tasted applejack."

Meanwhile, The New York Sun re-ran a first-hand account of a sighting by an engineer on a New Jersey rail line who'd quit his job after an encounter with the *Leeds* Devil, the "Ever-Living, Owl-Faced Fiend o' the Jersey Lightning Region," as the headline proclaimed (Liquid Jersey Lightning being a term for the regional moonshine). This same story had first run in the paper in 1893.[101] The engineer said the creature had stuck its head through the window of his moving train as it sped through the Pine Barrens around sunset. Friends had laughed at the man when he told the story but "old residents" recognized it as the work of the Leeds Devil.

[98] *San Jose Evening News*, January 30, 1909

[99] *Tucson Daily Citizen*, January 25, 1909

[100] Fort Worth Star Telegram, January 23, 1909

[101] See for instance, *The Sun*, January 22, 1893, "The Engineer Quit His Run"

"There ain't an old family in Burlington county that don't know of the Leeds devil," the engineer said. "It was the boogy-boo they used to scare young ones with when I was a boy."

The Great Jersey Devil scare of 1909 marks the beginning of the modern history of the story. In some ways it *is* the modern history of the story, the single indispensable episode from which all subsequent Jersey Devil nonsense derives. McCloy and Miller devote thirty-five pages of The Jersey Devil (more than a quarter of the book) to the "Phenomenal Week" in 1909 when the monster "emerged from his natural lair" in the Pine Barrens and made appearances in thirty towns across the Delaware Valley. The Jersey Devil "or his footprints" (a rather big *or*) were seen by thousands of people, they say.

Wikipedia refers to the "panic" that gripped the region at this time. When I was home one January a few years ago, NBC 40 Nightly News (the local affiliate) ran a feature story commemorating the centenary of the incident. Whenever some newspaper or online magazine refers to the many sightings of the monster by New Jerseyans who live in fear of the beast, they're probably making reference, whether they know it or not, to 1909.

Four years prior to the incident, the Trenton Times had run an account of the monster's origins under the headline, "Leeds's Devil was Bordentown Born." Although the legend was well known in South Jersey, the paper said, few people were aware that it was based on a real event. The story concerned a certain Captain and Mrs. Leeds, the parents of the beast. It was said that the captain had fought in the Revolution and had a scar over his eye from an encounter with a Hessian. Mrs. Leeds was said to be from a respectable family though "queer," and she was suspected herself of witchcraft (to have "associated her name with beings of the other world").

As was standard in these stories, the Leeds mother had not wanted more children, and, after the customary imprecations, gave birth to the notorious monster, which the family kept disguised in a piece of fabric. As it grew, it was kept indoors, sometimes chained. Unlike other babies, it never cried. Soon after its birth, it had perfect control of its limbs and could walk. "In several respects it resembled a monkey," the paper said. Although it scared Mrs. Leeds, she loved the child. The neighbors were tactful but curious.

One evening, as the family sat around the hearth fire, the child flew up the *lit* chimney and disappeared into the forest. It returned a few days later to rest on the lug pole, but then it disappeared again. After that it would come and go regularly, disappearing for days at a time then returning, and then, one day in early November, it left and never came back.

After that, there would be reports of sightings out of the Pine Barrens. One year it attacked a train on the Southern Railroad to Toms River, flying into the cab window and sticking there, like a screeching bat, for a mile or so before disappearing into the scrubland. A hunter (an "ancient inhabitant") had shot it several times to no effect. Nowadays it was rarely seen. "Like Siltrim, the Arabian demon of the waste, it now confines its visitations to haunts least frequented by human beings," the paper said.

The Leeds Devil story seemed to pose a special problem for newspaper editors, many of whom were simply *on fire* to publish stories about the monster but who didn't want to appear batshit crazy before their own reading public. One solution, judging by the stories that were produced, was to attribute a general belief, even panic, to old-timey locals, African-Americans or the perpetually drunk—ideally some combination of these three. If an actual eyewitness could be produced to enliven the story with a credible statement, so much the better, but surprisingly few of these were required to sustain the story's momentum for an entire week.

Throughout the episode, papers themselves found ways to signal their cynicism in their own coverage, to hint that they thought the whole thing was nonsense. A few newspapers made explicit reference to the "joke" but most employed more discreet means. One paper ran a series of drawings of the monster—in a top hat, smoking cigarettes, holding a parasol and reading a newspaper ("ALL ABOUT ME"). In one image, the creature was depicted, apparently pie-eyed, holding a balloon and standing over an egg (a striped egg) that it had apparently just laid. What to make of this? I'm not sure. But it doesn't really suggest a condition of statewide panic.

An illustration accompanying the Trenton Evening Times' story of January 20 showed a man collapsed on the ground beside a bottle of booze, out of which emanated fumes that coalesced into the shape of the Leeds Devil. "It's been a year since I've seen them things," the drunk man says. "Never again for me!"

Maybe the most fearsome depiction of the monster was also the most tongue-in-cheek. In the middle of the crisis, the Public Ledger ran a drawing of a snarling, be-winged Leeds Devil next to the caption, "Jabberwock in Mortal Combat." Not only was the nickname a reference to Lewis Carroll's famous poem *Jabberwocky*, but the drawing itself was a copy of the John Tenniel illustration that had accompanied that poem's publication in *Through the Looking Glass* in 1871.

The Public Ledger said that the monster scare was "probably the thoughtless trick of a practical joker" but the facetious nickname Jabberwock had already entered the water supply, to be repeated as a real nickname for the monster by generations of people who didn't seem to know the nonsense poem to which it referred.

In a story that took this logic to its conclusion, a paper called The Evening World ran a big picture of a bat beside the headline, "JERSEY'S DEVIL IS CLASSIFIED AS A 'BOM-BAT.'" [102]

Per this story, the monster (aka "South Jersey's What-Is-It") could fly, swim, eat hay, chew cud and lay red-white-and-blue eggs. Also, they were explosive, the eggs ("Full Moon Bursts 'Em, so the 'Thing' Makes its Nest in Extinct Craters").

According to The Evening World, the outbreak had been at least partially the fault of a Philadelphia animal dealer who had been putting out descriptions of an "Australian vampire" to drum up business. Though the man had been ordered to cease and desist amid charges of "criminal mendacity" the paper said "there still poured into the Quaker City today a multitude of hot-scented, weird, lurid, hallucinatory, phantasmago-

---

[102] *The Evening World* (New York), January 22, 1909

ric and preternatural descriptions of the 'Thing' that is loose in the applejack belt of South Jersey and the schnapps district of Pennsylvania."

A bombat, incidentally, was defined as a "truncated effulgium of the genus hoptoadorium. Ornithologists claim that it is basically a bird, possessing bat-like wings of iridescent hue and the legs of a crane with pony hoofs."

The allure of the monster was so strong that even stories with no connection to the Jersey Devil went out of their way to make for themselves a connection to the Jersey Devil. In a small item that ran in The Trenton Times about a talk given by the state economic zoologist on the subject of the brown-tailed moth—an agricultural pest that threatened the region's deciduous shrubbery—the presiding scientists announced that they considered the pest more dangerous than the San Jose scale. "I guess it would fall nearer in class with the 'Jersey devil' or 'air hoss,'" one scientist said.

Two days later, in the society pages of the same paper, there appeared a rundown of neighborhood social events (multiple surprise parties) including one event hosted by a Mr. and Mrs. Allan Wilson, at which the entertainment included performances by Charles Ashmore Jr. (who sung "When the Candlelights are Gleaming" and "When the Sheep are in the Fold") and by William Wood, who gave a short talk on the "Jersey Devil." Afterward games were played and refreshments were served.

The Philadelphia Inquirer ran an item on the trial of one Patrick Bowes, accused of striking a small child, a Ms. Annie Flynn, age seven, of 2721 Manton Street in Philadelphia. When the presiding judge asked the child if she knew what would happen if she lied, she said yes. She would go "to the Jersey Devil, and he would eat me."

"You're mistaken," the judge said, "but I think I know what you mean."

Early on in the alleged panic the Trenton paper ran a classified ad from a troupe of vaudeville entertainers that was passing through town.

A Chorus Girl from The Vampire Aerial Ballet

The missing dancer had supposedly disappeared a week earlier from New York while wearing "green tights, high heel suede slippers" and "a pair of green wings highly feathered." She was said to be wandering New Jersey in search of her sister and to resemble the "Australian Vampire erroneously described as 'The Flying Hoof,' and 'the Jersey Devil.'"

"Last seen sitting on a farmer's chicken coop a short distance from Burlington."

"If you see her, catch her in a net."

A week later, another vaudeville troupe (the RFOM Girls) was in town delivering a "spicy" performance of their act (which included minstrel "stunts" and "coon songs") before a packed house. A review of the show said that as part of the evening's program, Miss Annie Fisk, dressed as P.T. Barnum, led a procession of curious beings onto the stage, including the Tall Man, the *Shote* Lady, the Three Grotesques, Reggie the Flexible Giant and something called "the Midnight Screecher." But "funniest of all" with a "horse head, feather duster tail, flippers and wings of brown cambric was the only original 'Jersey Devil.'"

"This conglomerate creature which nearly sent the audience into hysterics, was led about the stage by a rope and answered to the name of Mary," the paper said.

The 1909 episode is still cited by contemporary Jersey Devil advocates as evidence of the South Jersey region's longstanding preoccupation with the monster. The number of newspaper reports and alleged sightings is recorded, but the humor—not to say outright sarcasm—that accompanied those reports is sometimes lost in translation. McCloy and Miller, in their first book, say schools were closed, factories shut down and people "quaked in fear behind closed doors" as "posses scoured the region to no avail."

In Phantom of the Pines, they say the 1909 incident was "one of the rare instances in modern times when a supernatural creature alarmed an entire region." According to Wikipedia, in January 1909, newspapers "published hundreds of claimed encounters with the Jersey Devil from all over the state." A group called the Devil Hunters (the "Official Researchers of the Jersey Devil") who are on television a lot say the "entire state of New Jersey was in a panic" during this "week of terror."[103]

But while statements like this may get the words right, they seem to get the music wrong. There *were* lots of stories in the papers. None that I read seemed exactly serious. There were a lot of tracks in the snow, but the number of sightings of an actual monster attributed to actual people was quite low.

What there were instead were many sweeping statements that seemed to be based more on ancient biases than on any kind of genuine reporting. The journalistic standard seemed to be: What can we get away with? Because no one is taking this seriously anyway. And the attribution of mass panic to old-timey locals, "Negroes" and applejack devotees was unlikely to result in many angry letters to the editor.

Out-of-state editors, meanwhile, didn't need to reference some marginal population of surrogate believers to attribute fear of the monster to. They had a marginal population immediately available in the form of New Jerseyans themselves, and this seems to be the set of circumstances under which Leeds Devil was turned into New Jersey's Devil and finally into the Jersey Devil itself—with all that the term *Jersey* seems to imply: a familiar, faintly comic epithet, an abbreviation, suggestive of a false familiarity and presumed bad taste, the painted kangaroo in the sequined jumpsuit beside the grand empress New York and the society belle Philadelphia.

Soon after the RFOM Girls left town, Dumont's Minstrels, another vaudeville troupe, was satirizing the Jersey Devil, their act running alongside a performance of Hedda Gabler, Ethel Barrymore in Lady Frederick, a performance by the Percy Troupe of English Acrobats and Lew Dockstader and his "big company of seventy minstrels."

---

[103] on their website, www.njdevilhunters.com/1909.html

Meanwhile a museum in Philadelphia claimed to have captured the beast. According to a story in The Philadelphia Inquirer, the "Leed's Devil [sic]" was the main attraction at the Ninth and Arch Museum, where it was chained to the floor, and where other attractions included an Egyptian magician, something called the "Human Ostrich" and an assortment of black-face comedians, comic acrobats and sharpshooters. The monster was said to have been donated to the museum by a Mr. Charles Leonhardt who had captured it, which was news to Mr. Leonhardt, news that he learned after the story appeared in the paper and he began getting phone calls.

"Mr. Leonhardt was disposed to be irritated at first, but soon realized that he was being made the victim of a joke by some of his friends," the paper said.

By February, when the episode had peaked and was beginning to subside, The Trenton Evening Times delivered a lecture to readers on the dangers of the story that the paper itself had done so much to perpetuate and that it now said had originated with some clever publicity agent (no known motive) and had been carried forward by a cynical or credulous press corps. The Leeds Devil had been a great topic of conversation on street corners, in the saloons and mills and shops, the paper said, but it was the women and children who were the real victims, with so many afraid even to go out at night, "lest they might encounter the freak."

In late October, the High Holy Days for Jersey Devil reportage, there was a brief relapse as a second round of stories appeared. The Fort Worth Star-Telegram reported that the Jersey Devil, "whose footprints in the snow last winter caused so much excitement in southern New Jersey," had been found dead in the woods near Kinkora. Its body, covered with red fur, was scheduled to be stuffed and mounted under the direction of Professor Henry Moore, curator of the state museum. The Columbus Daily Enquirer, in essentially the same story, said hundreds of citizens had examined the bones of the monster, which had been discovered by two young men—Morris Sapovits and Charles Maybury—who were out "chestnutting."

The Grand Forks Herald (North Dakota), in another corpse story, said the dead body was proof that the animal was

"Not Listed in Natural History" and that the previous winter's scare was "never due to highballs."

Easily the best of the aftershocks appeared in the July 11, 1909, edition of The Daily Oklahoman, wherein it was baldly asserted that residents of the City of Trenton were in a new panic, this time due to an infestation of dynamite-filled rats that were swarming the city. The warden at a prison in Mercer County had turned up to work days earlier to discover that a sack containing the dynamite ("used for quarry purposes") had been broken into and most of its contents carried away. A cursory investigation proved that no human agent could have performed the theft. The only possible explanation was that rats had eaten the dynamite and must now be wandering the streets, their bowels packed with high explosive. "Trenton has only just recovered from an awful fright, due to the visitation of the imaginary Jersey 'devil bird,' when a new scare is caused by a plague of explosive rats," the paper said. [104]

Officials were terror stricken. Extra police and fire personnel were on duty to help prevent explosions, but little could be done in a city of one hundred thousand people to stop "something happening that might cause several of the loaded rodents to explode." In the meantime, "Housewives have unbaited and locked up the rat traps and cats and dogs are being kept under restraint."

More Jersey Devil stories would follow, but never with the same intensity as 1909. A Philadelphia Inquirer story from 1918—dateline South Seaville—reported on new developments in what was then being called the "Jersey Chicken Mystery." The previous evening a Mrs. Rose Hilton ("who takes great pride in her chickens") had heard a "commotion" in her hen coops and had run out to discover several deceased birds. The week before, Edward Hallman had lost eight chickens. Then seventy-five chickens belonging to William Tozer were "killed in this mysterious manner," the paper said. People remembered Leeds Devil.

In February 1919, Dumont's Minstrels were back in town performing their "Lively Satire on 'The Jersey Devil.'" The act,

[104] Daily Oklahoman, July 11, 1909, "City is in Terror"

a burlesque, purported to "depict the beast which has created so much consternation around Woodbury and Gloucester," The Philadelphia Inquirer said. There were reports of audience laughter throughout. A few weeks later, when the bell in the Gloucester firehouse began ringing one night for no obvious reason, the same paper declared that the "Jersey Devil" had returned, "or else some other ghost appeared frequently during the night and mesmerized the big fire bell in the City Hall tower, causing it to ring."

A March 1922 story on the discovery, by scientists in Patagonia, of a living plesiosaur was met not only with snickering but also with hoots of derisive laughter by scientists in Philadelphia. "We haven't heard anything about it since the Jersey devil scare of ten years ago," one of the Philadelphia scientists said.[105] "I really thought it would die out completely then, but, as one of the philosophers has it, history will repeat itself."

In a charmingly condescending story, with many elements of incipient classism, The New York Times of August 5, 1930, stated that "berry pickers in Leeds Point and Mays Landing" believed the Jersey Devil was back. The Times described the monster as the "son of the wife" of a South Jersey fisherman who had borne twelve children and who'd hoped that her thirteenth would be a devil. "He always appears in early August, when berries are ripe and applejack takes on its mellowest flavor," The Times said. "Sometimes it sings bass solos in the berry patches of dark woods at midnight and sometimes it chases motorists."

According to The Times, the theory was that the beast's return had been invented to scare off rival berry pickers, but it had succeeded instead in attracting federal law enforcement. "This time the persons who seem to be the most interested in the phantom's appearance are the prohibition agents, practical hard-headed men who argue that devils—especially the kind that have not only cloven hoofs and tail, but feathers and claws and a hoot like an owl, can originate only where the Volstead act is flagrantly violated."

***

[105] Philadelphia Inquirer, March 8, 1922, "Poor-Pooh Chorus on Plesiosauras"

It's sometimes said that the Leeds Devil turned into the *Jersey* Devil around the time that the creature was named the Official State Demon, but the Jersey Devil occupies no such office. *The WPA Guide to 1930s New Jersey*—a Depression-era publication compiled under the auspices of the Works Progress Administration—merely stated that, "By default the title of official State demon has rested for nearly a century with the Leeds Devil, a friendly native of Atlantic County who has traveled extensively throughout southern New Jersey."

In an essentially comic essay, the WPA Guide said the monster tended to appear on the eve of war or natural disaster, noting that a recent outbreak of hostilities in Ethiopia coincided with a sighting by William Bozarth in Batsto.

The Guide said that Leeds Devil was the child of a Mrs. Leeds of Estellville who had, in a "petulant" moment, cried out that she "hoped the stork would bring a devil." What emerged was "cloven-hoofed, long-tailed and white" with the head of a collie dog, the face of a horse, the body of a kangaroo and the "disposition of a lamb."

Also included in the WPA Guide were the by-now-customary remarks on Negroes and the elderly. "Practically everyone in southern New Jersey knows of one or more persons who have seen the devil," the Guide said, "but very few will acknowledge personal acquaintance." But one person had been found, Philip Smith, a "Negro" who worked in a slaughterhouse in Woodstown (his reputation for sobriety and honesty unimpeachable) who said that he had seen the beast walking down the sidewalk. It "looked to me something like a giant police dog," Smith said, "kind of high in the back. He walked past the grocery store and disappeared."

The Leeds Devil was peaceful, harmless and curious, the Guide said. It had never harmed a soul or even violated a local ordinance, and it was presently writing a thesis ("A Plutonian Critique of Some Awful Aspects of the Terrestrial Life") in anticipation of a doctoral degree from the University of Hell. Any recent run-ins with the innocent had been a result of this research, but the beast did have a regular audience with one human counterpart, a certain Old Judge French, with whom it breakfasted each morning, discussing politics over South Jer-

128

sey ham and eggs. Judge French was a Republican, naturally.

Old Bill Bozarth's obituary ran in some disintegrating newspaper I found in the Leap Collection at the Stockton College Library in Galloway.[106] He was seventy-nine when he died and he claimed to have met the Jersey Devil one night in 1928 while walking beside the Mullica River. The Jersey Devil had come scampering up to him in the darkness, he said, and then it had scampered away and that was that. Bozarth had operated one of the few water-driven sawmills left in the county, the paper said, and had been the caretaker of the Wharton Estate.

TWENTY-EIGHT

Folkroulette, and Mabel yells 'Crackers'

If the Jersey Devil was indeed a regional story, as was assumed, one might expect people in New York or Philadelphia to be less fluent in the particulars of the legend than their South Jersey counterparts. Why not pretend at least to test this hypothesis?

From a base of operations in Alphabet City, I wandered around Manhattan looking for people to talk to about the Jersey Devil, trying to add to the dataset. I would travel on foot uptown or downtown, as the spirit moved me. I spent some time seeking counsel from the many Psychic Advisors who still eke out an existence, operating from various storefronts across the city, but I found none whose confidence I could gain. The Spiritual Advisor above the Dunkin' Donuts on Second Avenue ejected me from her apartment when my assiduous note-taking excited suspicion. It's like they thought I was an FBI agent.

I would approach strangers, in the streets, and ask if they'd *heard* of the Jersey Devil, and if so, what they knew about the beast. It was exhilarating in a way, like operating under a whole new social contract. I actually talked to people on the streets of

---

[106] I couldn't tell which newspaper

New York City for once.

We would have conversations—five seconds or thirty seconds or five minutes—or we wouldn't have conversations. I didn't care really. There was always someone else to talk to. It was like Chatroulette, internet conversation bingo—only folksier and face-to-face—a kind of *Folk*roulette, if you will.

I met a Hare Krishna from Michigan who had not heard of the Jersey Devil. He was padding around Union Square in his sandals, handing out copies of the Bhagavad Gita.

"How much for one of those?" I said.

"We don't sell them, but we do accept donations."

Somehow, I ended up giving him a high-five but no donation.

At a shop called Vampire Freaks ("Fuck the Mainstream") on Avenue A, the clerk *had* heard of the Jersey Devil "of course" (his words). He had read about it in a book "that was a folklore book." He was from the New York area, he said, but declined to be more specific.

His coworker, who was even less interested in talking to me, said she hadn't heard of the Jersey Devil.

"New Yorker all my life," she said. "I don't watch sports."

A three-hour stint in the Port Authority Bus Terminal resulted in no data, owing to a sudden anxiety about approaching strangers with my question list. Instead I sat on the floor, on the mezzanine level, and plugged my laptop into a wall socket and did my day job, which involves writing summaries of mutual fund news, expecting all the time to be handed a summons for loitering and instructed to move along. But of course the Port Authority is one of the few extralegal zones left in Manhattan. I could have sat there all day.

The mezzanine level was full of Eastern European teenagers with suitcases full of I-Heart-New-York tee-shirts, which they packed and unpacked on the Port Authority floor. They were young and lovely and looked like they could murder you without remorse.

At Penn Station, I had better luck. There you could sit in one of the plastic seats in the big atrium where passengers on the

New Jersey Transit trains waited for their track assignments to be announced. Each time a track was announced, one group would get up and run for their trains while another group would sit down, meaning I could just chat up whoever sat down next to me. Penn Station practically folkrouletted itself.

After one or two rounds of this, an older woman sat down next to me—Mabel Olive from Brick, New Jersey, who *had* heard of the Jersey Devil, naturally. She was traveling with her niece, who lived in Chicago, and who had also heard about the Jersey Devil, though I'm not sure I ever learned how.

When I asked Mabel where she thought the story came from she said probably from the Pineys.

"You know like the Crackers in Florida and all that? You know we have the Pineys here. So that's probably where it got its start. I would imagine."

Straight-shooter, Mabel.

"What he did or how he came about, I have no idea. Why don't you Google it?" she said.

"That's not what he wants to know," Mabel's niece said.

"Now you got me interested," Mabel said. "I'm going to Google it when I get home.

"Is he a bad guy?" the niece asked.

"I think so. Why else would he be a devil?" Mabel said.

"When I was a kid, my grandmother told me I was related to it," I said.

"Oh really! Well you must have been a pretty bad little boy!"

"He couldn't have been too bad, if he ended up like he is now," the niece sad.

"Well hey. Maybe he had therapy."

"Eighty percent is genetic."

"He's probably trying to find his roots," Mabel said. "Instead of Kunta Kinte, your name was Beelzebub! That's my theory anyway!"

She seemed pleased with this analogy.

"Do you think it might be real?" I said.

"You're actually *asking* us?" the niece said. "Lord bless us."

"Some people say they've seen it," I said.

"Without pharmaceutical assistance?" the niece said.

There was a piece of installation art in the atrium, a big mobile depicting all manner of Jerseyana. It was divided into North and South Jersey and on the South Jersey side were Mr. Peanut, Miss America, an Atlantic City Beach Patrol lifeguard boat and various other objects appropriate to the region, including a little statue of the Jersey Devil itself.

I told Mabel about the statue, so she ran off to check it out.

"Speaking of regional," the niece said, "I didn't even know things like jughandles. Where I'm from, in the Chicago area, we have Resurrection Mary, a woman, whom they see appearing on the highway outside Resurrection Cemetery."

Mabel came back. She seemed to disagree with the depiction in the mobile. "He stands there with that three-pronged thing that he's got in his hand, and there are horns coming out of his head," she said.

"Everybody's got a different interpretation probably."

"You ought to travel through New Jersey and take Route Seventy," Mabel said, "because it's on both sides, by the Pine Barrens. That's where the Jersey Devil is."

Their track was announced. "Fourteen! Fourteen!" they yelled, and off they ran. "I guess you won't forget us!" Mabel said, looking back.

"Nice to meet you!" the niece said, and she laughed as she ran.

TWENTY-NINE

A cabinet of curiosities, and 'We *had* older heads'

I walked into a shop on Tenth Street in the East Village—Obscura Antiques and Oddities—next to a Japanese curry place where I used to get takeout. It had always piqued my curiosity, but I'd never been inside.

It was a small storefront. The sensibility seemed to rest somewhere between the Mütter Museum of medical anomalies and the dressing room of a nineteenth-century carnival magician. On the day I was there, they had for sale, among other things, a set of Nazi poker chips, a sea urchin encased in Lucite, a set of human teeth under glass, a vase made from a World War I artillery shell and a stuffed alligator that had been turned into a lamp ("Early Mounted Standing Alligator With a Light Bulb in its Mouth").

There were arcane uniforms of obsolete armies. There was a set of giant paper mâché animal heads—a donkey head, a rabbit head, etc.—that were accompanied by paper mâché children's heads. They loomed off a wall with their giant, nightmare eyes. These were costumes worn in parades, someone said. There was a mummified human head (a prize item) with the ears removed (it had once belonged to an ear doctor). If the Jersey Devil had ever been stuffed and mounted by Professor Henry Moore back in 1909, I felt like it would have ended up eventually on a wall at Obscura.

The on-duty clerk—a punk rocker from Ohio—said she *had* heard of the Jersey Devil but only recently and only because Whimsy's wife had come to the Halloween party dressed as the creature, prompting Mike (one of the owners) to tell the story. "Mike gave me a half-hour explanation of what the Jersey Devil is." She said I should come back the next day when Mike would be there, and he'd tell me all about it, so that's what I did.

Mike had grown up in Neptune, (the Jersey Devil "wasn't too popular back there") and now he lived in Princeton, (alas, also not big Jersey Devil territory either) but he had a professional interest in cryptozoology and in weird shit in general, so he was well acquainted with the story.

His response to my standard icebreaker ("Have you ever heard of the Jersey Devil?"), was "Yeah," it was "someone born with born with *hypotrichosis* or something." I had to look that up, but apparently it's a medical condition involving abnormal hair growth. Whimsy's wife's Jersey Devil costume had been humanoid and fur-covered, apparently. I think Mike was kind of kidding.

It was the dinner hour, and the after-work crowd was shuffling into the shop, even as Mike discussed its role as a locus of neighborly interaction. And in fact people were stopping in, not to buy things but just to say hello, or to chat about the Mets, or to chat about the Jersey Devil or to chat about the

German organ-grinder's hat that was being worn by the puppet on the wall ("How could they keep it on at such a rakish angle?") or to chat about the earless mummy head ("We *had* older heads") and so forth.

Mike said that he saw his shop in the grand tradition of the *wunderkammer*, or Cabinet of Curiosities, which "goes back hundreds, if not thousands, of years. For ages people have been collecting really weird, creepy shit," he said.

We pondered this for a second.

"Not everyone, but certain people."

Mike said that the man I really needed to talk to, the true expert in these matters—Jersey Devil as well as South Jersey matters—was Whimsy. Whimsy was properly South Jersey and spent a great deal of time in the Pine Barrens. Mike himself had once spent ten hours wandering around in the Great Swamp (something I'd never heard of) looking for a particular stand of virgin cedar trees in the company of Whimsy. He gave me an email address and I wrote to Whimsy.

THIRTY

Lord Whimsy proposes an investigation

Lord Breulove Swells Whimsy was the alter ego of Victor Allen Crawford, a graphic designer and artist and friend of the shop. He described himself as a "failed dandy, bushwhacking aesthete," and "parenthetical naturalist." He had grown up in Somers Point and gone to Mainland Regional High School, a fact I found almost as amazing as any of the other amazing facts about Whimsy. Mainland, whose marching band was audible from our front porch in EHT, was the quintessential New Jersey suburban high school, in my mind anyway. Half my family went to Mainland.

Whimsy and his wife Susan designed the identification art for the Milstein Hall of Ocean Life at the American Museum of Natural History on Central Park West in New York City—

lovely little watercolors[107] of sea polyps and sea turtles and raccoon butterflyfish and so forth, but he seemed to subscribe to Oscar Wilde's dictum that one should either *be* a work of art or *wear* a work of art.

He had lived in New Egypt and now he lived in Mount Holly. He was not a writer, he said, though he had written one book, *The Affected Provincial's Companion Vol. I*, and was at work on another, an illustrated edition of Walt Whitman's *Song of Myself*.

"I'm just busking," he said.

When Whimsy was *not* not doing these things, he sometimes rode his velocipede around in the Pine Barrens or wore a cravat. His idea of an exotic diversion was go *out* of the Pine Barrens, a refreshing reversal of the usual situation. He would take long canoe trips down the Rancocas River or the Delaware River, through the post-industrial landscapes of New Jersey and Philadelphia, traveling on the *terrain* rather than on the infrastructure, as he put it, the better to experience the pockets of the city that were being reclaimed by the forest. But he spent a lot of time in the actual Pine Barrens too, doing volunteer conservation work, conducting wildlife tours and performing assorted bushwhacking activities. "I've had my Lyme's disease card punched twice," he said.

Whimsy's family was from Kentucky, but they'd moved to South Jersey in 1961. His father had been a school teacher in New Gretna. "My father—I doubt he knew even one kid that didn't have some sort of tale, out there, running with the Jersey Devil. All of them swore they'd seen the Jersey Devil at one time or another, all those old New Gretna kids."

When I told him I was distantly related to the beast, he suggested I should see a doctor immediately, to "get that checked out." When I asked him for his earliest memory of the Jersey Devil he said it was "the poster you'd get in Smithville, the little q-tip looking guy with the dapper looking vest in the moonlight. He looked like this little monster from Dairy Queen or something. It had absolutely nothing to do with the original renditions."

---

[107] (I think they're watercolors)

I had been hoping that Whimsy might introduce me to an actual Piney (I'd never met one) and we planned to go out hiking in the Pines but it never came together. He said there were very few actual Pineys left anyway, and I trusted his judgment in these matters.

"The old stock is almost…They're out there but they're mall rats like everybody else now, working for the local townships, superintendents. Not the people they were fifty years ago.

"There's maybe about twelve families that probably have any real claim to the title," he said. "I do think there are people out in the Pine Barrens who may have self-selected in some ways. They like the area. They live out there. They consider it home. They appreciate the history. They know the wildlife. They hunt out there. They raise their kids out there. Whether or not they're Pineys or just residents of Southern New Jersey is up to the individual's judgment.

"There's one guy I run into all the time out in the deep areas. He's old-school. I'd say he's a Piney. The guy's got three teeth in his head. Every time I see him, he's got a cigarette in his hand, and he's got a ball cap on his head, a white tee-shirt that he probably wore in the war, and he's carrying around a machete. The guy doesn't hunt bear because he finds them too easy. He likes going after rabbit—an interesting guy."

The classic Pineys who worked the old subsistence cycle of blueberries, cranberries and charcoal, were basically extinct, Whimsy said. "You've got a crew of seven guys working an entire cranberry bog now, a combine, people coming in the summer to work. Who does that now? You have migrant workers maybe. You have Haitians and Jamaicans and Dominicans. Maybe they're the new Pineys, because they're the ones I see out there picking in the summertime."

It was Whimsy's considered view that the Pine Barrens had always been more maritime in nature than is generally acknowledged. In the nineteenth century large sections of the woods had been cut down to make charcoal for the furnaces. Cedar and iron were used in shipbuilding. Privateers travelled up the waterways to trade and get fresh drinking water.

"A lot of those families went back and forth between the

furnaces" and the sea. They had "one foot in the ocean and the other deep in the bogs.

"It's a maritime culture," he said. "Pine Barrens culture in general is all maritime really when you get down to it. The shore is the business end, but the back end is the Pine Barrens."

Throughout their history, Pineys had been depicted as drunks, degenerates, "toothless monsters" and so forth by communities on the woods' periphery, where the economic prospects were brighter and the "rectitude factor" (Whimsy's term) was higher.

Summarizing the conventional view of Pineys by outsiders, he said, "I think a lot of it is like urbanoia—a genre of horror films—the trope of people from civilized, you know, parts of the world, cities or suburbs, coming into a rural area that is home to mutant cannibals, or something like that, portraying country people as the *Other*, demonizing them, making them into monstrous things. It's a classic trope.

"It's almost like Pineys and the Jersey Devil almost melded into this hybrid monster."

Whimsy floated the idea, not uncommon in Jersey Devil circles, that the legend might have originated with an old Lenape myth about a forest spirit called *Massingw*. Massingw was said to be between eight and ten feet tall, with a face that was half-red, half-black, and he was attended by a legion of forest dwarves whose name I'm not even going to try to Romanize.

"There's speculation," Whimsy said, that Massingw was "partially responsible for the Jersey Devil, that this forest spirit was deemed a pagan, heathen entity, so the early settlers saw it as evil and projected European preconceptions on it and it became the Jersey Devil. I don't know how true," it is, he said, but it "could be a fun investigation."

THIRTY-ONE

Beck's romantic Jersey Devil

In the 1920s and 1930s, Henry Charlton Beck went into the Pines. Beck was a newspaper reporter for The Courier-Post of Camden and later for The Newark Star-Ledger, and he wrote a series of popular books on the rural areas of New Jersey and the relics of the lost civilization that he encountered there, which he perceived to be in need of preservation.

In 1936 there was *Forgotten Towns of Southern New Jersey*. Then came *More Forgotten Towns of Southern New Jersey* (1937), followed by *Jersey Genesis* (1945), *The Roads of Home* (1956) and finally *Tales and Towns of Northern New Jersey* (published posthumously in 1964). If Pine Barrens writing post-1935 can be seen as an attempt to live down the legacy of Mayers, Goddard and Kite, then Beck was the first Pine Barrens apologist.

Beck was born in Philadelphia in 1902, but his family had moved to Haddonfield by 1911. In addition to his newspaper career he was also an Episcopalian minister, a concert violinist, a schoolteacher, a writer of detective novels and eventually the first president of the New Jersey Folklore Society.

He seems to have discovered the Jersey Devil sometime between 1936 and 1945. He mentions the creature ("that uncertain monster") only once in Forgotten Towns of Southern New Jersey and not at all in More Forgotten Towns of Southern New Jersey,[108] but he devotes an entire chapter to the beast in Jersey Genesis.

Beck's account, which seems a kind of synthesis of interviews, secondary sources and his own imagination, is mostly derived from a copy of a newspaper article ("On the Trail of Leeds' Devil: The Dread Monster of Jersey's Big Forest") that he says was written by J. Elfreth Watkins in 1905. In fact a version of this same story appears to have been in syndication

---

[108] That I saw

138

nationally as early as 1899.[109]

The Leeds Devil, as Watkins (and then Beck) describe it, possessed the same powers as the "black witches of English folklore." It turned the milk sour in the pails, lamed horses in their stalls, dried up the cows in the "clearing pastures" and "sered" the corn in the fields. It was an inevitable "forerunner" of disaster and "harbinger" of dire calamity, having "warned the Piners of the coming of the Civil War." Its favorite pastime was to sit on the dunes by the seaside and laugh at ships that wrecked on the shoals of Barnegat.

Watkins said the Leeds Devil kept company with a "beautiful golden-haired woman in white" and the headless ghost of a pirate, decapitated by Captain Kidd. Joseph Bonaparte (the older brother of Napoleon) was said to have seen it while hunting in the Pines. Commodore Stephen Decatur shot at it when he (Decatur) stopped to buy cannonballs at Hanover Furnace. The missile had passed through the monster harmlessly, "without halting its mad pace."

Sometimes the beast was "seen to hover, like a giant bird of prey" above the swamps, Watkins said. "On such occasions its foul breath blasts the lives of hundreds of fishes, found floating the next day upon the surface, tainted and unfit for food."

The story had everything, Beck said, "A monster that combines the worst of the animal, bird and reptile kingdoms, notable witnesses of its frightfulness, the original touch of trying to shoot down a ghost with a cannon—and even a blonde."[110]

Watkins' account of the Leeds Devil's birth adheres closely enough to the account given by W.F. Mayers in The Atlantic forty-five years earlier—using much of the same language— that I think we can assume he read Mayers' original story (or some subsequent copy) and used it as source material for his own writing. Like Mayers, Watkins ascribes the monster to a Mother Leeds of Burlington, a Quaker ("accused of amateur witchcraft") who had given birth to Leeds Devil in 1735. Like

[109] See for instance *The St. Paul Globe* of July 16, 1899, "Leeds' Devil Returns" by John Elfreth Watkins Jr.
[110] Beck, *Jersey Genesis* (1945)

Mayers, he says the father was "none other than the very Foul Fiend, the Prince of Darkness." And Watkins too calls the Pineys "Pine Rats" (though he also calls them "Piners"), and he attributes to them a widespread belief in the Leeds Devil.

"Leed's Devil [sic] is as firmly believed in by many of the better class of Piners as by the 'Pine Rats,'" he says, noting that recent sightings by Joel Harrison of Sooy Place and Martin Giberson of Burrville had convinced the local population that the monster had finally returned to the region after a long hiatus, causing people to keep indoors at night.

Beck himself made two trips to Leeds Point as part of his tour of South Jersey's forgotten towns, his term for places like Batsto, New Egypt and Ong's Hat, places that had lost population or disappeared altogether as the iron and glass industries abandoned the Pines. On his first trip he was either unaware of or uninterested in Leeds Point's connection with the Jersey Devil, devoting himself instead to a digressive search for the remains of an old hotel.

He knocked on the door of the big stone house at the end of Leeds Point Road (sometimes referred to as the Leeds House) and demanded loudly (his words) to know if anyone was at home, whereupon Jesse Mathis, the owner, emerged from a nearby field. Mathis, whom Beck calls a "lineal descendant of Daniel Leeds, author of early American almanacs" and a descendant of "Great John Mathis, pioneer shipbuilder," told Beck that there had been two families of Leedses in the area, and that he was somehow related to both of them.[111] On one side were David, Brazilla and Samuel, Mathis said, and on the other were William, Henry and Jesse. But, "We're all Quakers," Mathis purportedly said, "all the way back to Danny Leeds and the first settlers," an odd statement in light of what is known about "Danny" Leeds and his relationship with the Quakers.

Beck seemed to have had an instinctive need to charm-up the simple downcountry folk he encountered on his journeys, but Mathis did not even meet his standards for bumpkinly charm. "We couldn't pin the old chap down to details," Beck

---

[111] Beck, *More Forgotten Towns of South Jersey* (1937)

said. "He seemed to be one of those to whom one day is as good as another, nothing very interesting, everything in a kind of fog."

A minute after that, Beck met William Leeds, my great-grandfather.

BeBop's branch of the family had left Leeds Point by this time, and they were now living in Oceanville—just a few hundred yards up Shore Road but a huge psychic break for BeBop and Aunt Dottie—but William Leeds had apparently returned to the ancestral plantation to go fishing.

He and Beck talked about harvesting oysters in Hummock Cove and who owned the shell-fishing grounds (the Wharton family) and the old hotel that seemed to preoccupy Beck. And then William Leeds said something characteristically Beckian about what a fine life it was indeed to be a subsistence fisherman in Leeds Point.

"There's plenty down here to do but there's plenty of time to do it in. And you've always got the sea and the salt tang of the air to make up for what you don't get."

William Leeds—aka William the Famous, aka Our Illustrious Father, who smuggled rum up the Mullica River in his spare time and couldn't wait to get out of Leeds Point and loved his car more than anything else in life (my mom's account)—supposedly said these things.

After Beck's first Leeds Point story was published he received a letter ("a highly informative scolding") from a woman named Carrie Mathis Bowen who lived in Leeds Point and who claimed to be a Leeds relative. Bowen apparently felt that Beck had written disrespectfully about the family and wished to correct the record. Beck said he responded to Bowen's initial complaint and then more or less forgot the whole incident (since he had "no intention of dawdling further among the Leeds"), but then he received a second letter from Bowen that ended with the words, "Of course you knew that The Jersey Devil was born here!" Beck had not known, apparently, and so he went back to Leeds Point to investigate.

On this second trip, Carrie Bowen led Beck on a tour of

Leeds Point, including the ruins of the house where, it was said, the Jersey Devil had been born ("Not The Jersey Devil! Leeds's Devil!" someone said). Jesse Mathis, by this point, had died. Beck described sound of seagulls over the bays. He noted the electrified fence at Oyster Creek that zapped insects as they tried to enter the restaurant. It, or one of its descendants, was still there when I was a kid, an object of enormous fascination.

Bowen also gave Beck a capsule history of the Leeds family, saying that Daniel's marriage to Ann Stacy had been a "respectful" two years after the death of his previous wife, Dorothy Young, another odd comment given that the Quakers seemed to believe the reverse about the timing of Daniel's remarriage.

She then took Beck down to see the ruins of the old house.

Bowen hadn't been down there in a while, and she couldn't immediately find the place. Beck grew frustrated. They passed one location ("a perfect ruin of a place") that Beck thought must be the Leeds Devil house but wasn't. Bowen may have been briefly lost. Beck made disparaging remarks about her sense of direction. Bowen got her bearings and eventually they found the hole in the ground, which had been only a few feet away from them the entire time but had been invisible from the road.

They plunged into the underbrush and there, "in the midst of a tangle of weeds and honeysuckle and brambles which had grown up through the years" (Beck's words) and amid the "fallen timbers and the old bricks of a chimney, tumbling in the rubble of a filling cellar hole," Bowen told her story.

The matriarch of a large family (Bowen calls her a Mrs. *Shourds*) had grown weary of motherhood and announced that if she ever gave birth to another child, she hoped it would be a devil. In consequence she gave birth to the baby, a "poor dwarfed misshapen being" (words attributed to Bowen) that became known first as the Leeds Devil and later as the Jersey Devil. The child "grew painfully in size," Bowen said, until "the time came when it could move clumsily about in the house in which it was born and where, from most accounts, it was sheltered mercifully from the curious who came to peep in at the windows."

In general, Beck was displeased with Bowen's account. He complained of her "sketchy recollection," and he wrote to associates seeking something more *upbeat* perhaps than Bowen's version, which seemed to be a prototype of the darker, more starkly realistic version of the story that I remembered from the Chelsea Village courtyard.

If there's one thing I did genuinely learn from my folkroulette research, it's that this darker version (what Beck calls the "modern derivation") involving a sick or mistreated child locked away in a house was the one you heard over and over again when you actually *talked* to people about the Jersey Devil, in contrast to the kind of comic fairytale involving the flying-kangaroo bat that you read over and over again in written accounts.

Beck preferred the fairy tale. Bowen's version "it becomes evident at once" had "lost much more than names in years of retelling the story," he says.

In response to his request for stories, Beck received many letters and was ultimately led to the Watkins' story involving cannonballs, pirates and blondes. He was also led to an old story, recorded by a Warner Hargrove, in which it was claimed that children along the Mullica River who were born "half-witted" (Beck's words) were said to have been "touched" by the Leeds Devil.

A letter from a Mrs. Blake in Pleasantville claimed the Jersey Devil story had a number of different origination points but that in each case the circumstances were the same: the "unwanted child, the home already filled with numerous offspring from the poor feeble-minded parents. The mother wishes the child may be a devil when born; the child has a cloven foot and hands like claws."[112]

Blake's theory was that, "Possibly a deformed or degenerate child" had been born into one of the communities along the shore. "The child may have run away, either perishing or dying when attacked by wild beasts." After that, "parents and neighbors imagine all sorts of stories."

---

[112] Quoted in Beck's Jersey Genesis

Beck seemed to typify a certain romantic strain in Pine Barrens writing. Next to Watkins' fantasy, the nasty tales of a sick or abused child were "feeble and forlorn."[113] And he was apparently unmoved by the echoes of domestic tragedy that the story, whichever version you favored, must contain.

"How would you have acted," he asked, "if the story had come to you," of Mrs. Leeds and her child, locked in the house at the end of Leeds Point? "Wouldn't you have sidled by of an evening, on one imaginary errand or another, to see what you could see?"

Leeds Point was not the only stop on Beck's Jersey Devil reality tour. He visited also Hanover Furnace, which had now become part of Fort Dix Army base. The town itself was completely gone. A photograph showed no sign of the village, the schoolhouse or the church and no trace of the manor house that had once overlooked the lake, though strawberry bushes and rose bushes showed the outlines of where the garden had been. The only evidence that iron had once been produced there was the slag pile, and even that was eroding, dug up piece by piece for use in the paving of nearby roads. The last resident, Hannah Foulks, had operated a roadside stand near Pemberton and had been evicted from her home during World War I.

Beck also visited New Egypt, Mayers' jumping-off point for his journey into the Pines. New Egypt had not turned into a forgotten town but instead contained one thousand people, electricity, running water, a bank and a daily newspaper. The movie theater was named after the goddess Isis. The Masonic Lodge was modeled on the great pyramids. The town itself was famous for its giant hogs.

Beck said that his calling was preservation and he spoke often of his fear that the people and places in his books would be forgotten unless made permanent through his storytelling. He seemed to address the same question that had confounded Mayers—and to an extent Goddard and Kite—so many years before: Why had certain elements of the local population re-

---

[113] It's tough to tell if he's being cute here with the word "feeble."

mained in place for generations, even as entire villages, industries, and an entire way of life, abandoned them?

For Mayers, Goddard and Kite this stasis had been due to some inborn moral failings on the part of the Pineys, but for Beck it was simple affection for their surroundings. Pineys stayed in the Pines because they had made a conscious decision to reject what they understood to be the superficial progress offered by society at large.

In Jersey Genesis, his book on the Mullica, Beck wrote of the people of the region, saying, "They would not have remained beside the river, in such obvious contentment as long as they have if anything about them were ordinary. Through generations they've held on, unspoiled by the word outside, entirely uncontaminated."

"You forget," a friend challenged him, "that the Mullica River was once very much a part of the world and that the grandfathers and great-grandfathers of these people had a part in world trade and bustling community life not very different from the industry and living you claim to despise now. They didn't measure up to it, probably. Certainly the world passed them by."

"The world didn't give them up at all," Beck said. "They gave up the world. They discovered they had something infinitely more important than all the world could give them. They decided to hold on to it, to make it serve what they needed from life.

"In spite of wars and chaos in the world outside, towns and people along the Mullica have maintained their own equan-imity, their own refinements, their own essentially American resourcefulness," he concluded.

For Beck, society itself was the contagion.

THIRTY-TWO

Halpert's Piney testimonies

In the 1930s, Herbert Norman Halpert went into the Pines. Halpert was a folklorist and anthropologist, collecting material

145

for his doctoral dissertation, *Folktales and Legends of the New Jersey Pines: A Collection and Study*, which he would submit to the English Department at the University of Indiana in 1947.

He traveled the woods in the summer of 1936, on foot, by bus and in "cars of ancient vintage" that had "the disconcerting habit of coming to a dead stop" in the "sandy wastes," he said.[114] The Pine Barrens he described were an island of acidic sands between the rich, truck-farming soils along the Delaware River and the busy resort towns of the coast. The trees were scarred and stunted, secondary-growth pines mostly, with some oaks mixed in. The residents had been looked on as an alien race by the people on the woods' periphery since the middle of the eighteenth century. He quoted Thomas Thompson, an Anglican missionary, who toured the region in the 1740s, and who had said that some Pineys were decent people, but many of those born and raised in the region had "neither religion nor manners, and do not know so much as a letter in a book."

Halpert's chapter on the Jersey Devil—a secondary Piney myth, in his view—relied on interviews conducted in 1940 and 1941. His research was sponsored by the Columbia University Department of Anthropology and the vaguely sinister-sounding American Council of Learned Societies. He said working in the Pine Barrens was the most difficult experience of his professional life because Pineys were so distrustful of outsiders that winning their confidence was nearly impossible. Relations between Pineys and neighboring farmers were characterized by "sharp antagonism." Relations between Pineys and itinerant academics were probably similarly strained a mere two decades after Goddard and Kite had suggested that Pineys be sterilized.

Still, Halpert worked to build up a group of informants and eventually he came to be on speaking terms with about forty people, he said. He limited his fieldwork to the terrain north of the Mullica River (north of Leeds Point) a region characterized by the predominance of the *Lakewood* soils. The *sassafras* soils, south of the Mullica, were harsh and acidic, but the Lakewood

---

[114] Halpert, Folktales and Legends

soils were even harsher, and more acidic, and the communities that developed there were distinct, he said.

Despite an apparent work ethic—and Halpert collected many stories of champion workers—the woods had very little agriculture and a great deal of poverty. Hanover Furnace, by this time, was gone. As were the glassworks at Lebanon. Halpert's Piney subjects were mostly the children and grand-children of people who had lived in those places and who were now scattered throughout the woods, from New Egypt to Buddtown to Waretown to Tuckerton.

The most common folk stories in the Pine Barrens—as everywhere else in the world—were witchcraft stories, and the two most important legend cycles in the Pines were those of Sammy Giberson, a famous fiddle player, and Jerry Munyhon, the "Wizard of the Pines." Giberson lost his soul in a bet with the devil (not the Jersey Devil) and was saved from eternal damnation only when he played a song that the devil had never heard before, a melody that came to him on the night air and that was known ever after as "Sammy Giberson's Air Tune." Munyhon was famous for his inclination for strong drink and his disinclination for work. Among his numerous accomplishments, he once removed his own head to better give himself a haircut.

Beside these two superstars, the Jersey Devil was a minor sub-deity, Halpert said, but it enjoyed an outsized reputation outside the Pines due to disproportionate press coverage. There were two basic versions of the story.

In the first, a preacher was badly treated by a member of the Leeds family and told the mother of the family that the child she was carrying would *probably* be a devil. In the second, a woman with a large family cursed her own unborn child. In some versions the child was born a monster and in others it was born normal, then transformed and attacked the family. The most common version of the story, though he'd never seen it published anywhere, Halpert said, was one in which the Jersey Devil was a twin.

On December 19, 1940, a Piney named Elven Sweet told Halpert that Leeds's Devil had been born on the road that ran from Bowker's Corners to Buddtown.[115]

"I've heard about him," Sweet said. "I've heard they had twins, and they was devils for fair."

Mary Parks, another Piney, also told Halpert that the baby was a twin. Parks said the mother of "Leed's Devil" had prayed that her child would be a devil and when it "landed" (Parks' word), it was. The child's "fingernails was kind of clawy."

"They couldn't hold it. They couldn't do a thing with it. Said when it was a-dyin' they couldn't do a thing with it," Parks said. "And they all thought it was a thing come on her for the expression she made."

Halpert said he transcribed the testimony of his Piney interlocutors longhand, often slowing them down or asking them to repeat things when he was uncertain of their meaning, a process that annoyed the Pineys ("You can't get a story together right when you have to wait 'till *you* get it down!") but that at least gives his account the feel of authentic speech.[116]

On January 23, 1940, Charles Grant told Halpert that the child's parents were Leedses, and they "was both pretty ornery, these people." When a preacher tried to convert them, "they run him out." When Leeds Devil was born it had a cloven foot. When it was four, it killed both its parents. It would kill horses, sheep, hogs and sometimes other children.

"So every outrage that was committed like that, was laid onto Leeds's Devil," Grant said. "Everybody was afraid of it." It was "an awful lookin' varmint—half man, some kind of beast; had wings—could fly too."

Jerry Munyhon had told Pineys to carry silver bullets as protection in case they met Leeds Devil, Grant said.

Another Piney, James Estlow, told Halpert that the monster had been cursed by its own mother, and that it was a twin. "One was smothered to death 'atween a feather bed, and the other one he got away. The one got away that's the one."

"They used to hear it hollerin' around different places, but they couldn't get it. That's the first I ever heard it. Since then

[115] Named for the Keithian Thomas Budd
[116] His own account, Folktales and Legends of the New Jersey Pines

I've heard—they had newspaper talk."

In context, the Leeds Devil did not in fact seem especially colorful or noteworthy. Among the other tales Halpert collected was one about a man who killed a hippopotamus with a coal rake and another involving two mosquitoes that carried a cow across a meadow. Halpert was also told the story of Cracky Wainwright, who began to jump across a river, and then, realizing half-way that he wasn't going to make it, turned around and jumped back. He didn't want to get his feet wet. Halpert wrote about one woman who told a preacher that she didn't know Christ had died, because they didn't get the paper back in them woods.

To Pineys, the Leeds Devil was sin incarnate, Halpert said. Its most important function was to reinforce the standards of the community by serving as a warning to potential transgressors. In some versions of the story, the Leeds family reformed after being punished for its sins.

Halpert said he had been inspired to collect Piney stories after studying the folklore of Tennessee. Like "most isolated rural areas in America" the Pine Barrens region was "gradually losing its individual character before the encroachment of cars, phonographs, radios and other appurtenances of our machine civilization." But Halpert's wish was not to retard human progress, he said, only to recognize the human values worth preserving.

THIRTY-THREE

'Attitudes and ambitions'

When John McPhee's *The Pine Barrens* was published in 1968, it seemed like the literary mythology of the woods might be put to rest for good. The Pineys that McPhee introduced were straightforward individualists, who placed great value on self-reliance and had traditional ties to the land.

"They have a strong sense of regional pride," McPhee wrote, "and, in a way that is not at all unflattering to them, they *are* different from the run of the people of the state. A visitor who stays a while in the Pine Barrens soon feels that he is in another country, where attitudes and ambitions are at variance with the American norm."

McPhee was a staff writer for *The New Yorker*. He had grown up in Princeton, on the periphery of the woods, and he spent some years driving around the Pines, making "outlines of the integral woodland on topographic maps" as a way of getting to know the region and then portraying it in print.

He began his book with a description of the view from the top of the fire tower on Bear Swamp Hill in Washington Township, Burlington County, noting that the vast stretches of unbroken pine and oak forest that were visible from this perspective were so different from "the picture of New Jersey that most people hold in their minds," that the Pine Barrens become, as a result, "as incongruous as they are beautiful."

McPhee addressed the legacy of Mayers, Goddard and Kite, with more skill than Beck had done. And it was a legacy, he said, whose negative effects could still be perceived. "Some of the gentlest of people," McPhee wrote, "botanists, canoemen, campers—spend a great deal of time in the pines, but their influence has not been sufficient to correct an impression, vivid in some parts of the state for fifty years, that the pineys are a weird and sometimes dangerous barefoot people who live in caves, marry their sisters, and eat snakes."

For McPhee, the Jersey Devil was simply a part of a vernacular culture that had developed in relative isolation in the Pine Barrens and that included regional names for the flora and fauna, as well as a roster of fantastic characters, from Jerry Munyhon and Sammy Giberson (who had danced with the devil), to Salt Cesar, who cut ten cords of wood in one day. He put the legend in its proper context, and it was a context to which he was honestly, if also persuasively, sympathetic.

McPhee visited the town of Chatsworth, the "Capital of the Pines," six miles from the geographic center of the woods and surrounded on all sides by deep forest. Unlike people elsewhere in the Pines, the people of Chatsworth were "apparently just a little competitive about the appearance of their houses," he said, and they would bring in topsoil to grow lawns. But at heart they were just as concerned with "individualism and personal independence" as the rest of the Pineys.

He sat on the radiator at the Chatsworth General Store and talked to Kate Buzby, one of the old owners of the shop.

"We're the original pineys," Buzby told him. "People come here and say, 'We're looking for the pineys,' and I say, 'They're right here,' and they say, 'No, we mean the people who live in caves and intermarry,' and I say, 'I don't know of any such people. We're pineys. We live right here.'"

McPhee's writing narrowly prefigured the coming of age of the Pine Barrens preservation movement, when, in 1978, the woods were designated a national reserve. Much of the impetus for this legislation was rooted in the self-interest of a booming population whose future water needs were at stake, but it also signaled a growing recognition that the Pines were a valuable cultural as well as natural resource. This idea was made explicit in the Pinelands Commission's own stated mission, to "preserve, protect, and enhance the natural and *cultural* resources of the Pinelands National Reserve" (emphasis mine).

A decade before the Preservation Act passed, McPhee wrote about a piney named Scorchy Jones, who'd told an interviewer, "Unless these wild areas are preserved, we're going to get to the point where dense population is going to work on the nervous system of the people, and the more that takes place, the poorer neighbors they become."

McPhee said "most people" in the Pine Barrens looked upon the Jersey Devil as "pure legend"—though many others did not—then he instantly produced two examples of this latter type from among his two main Piney companions, both of whom seemed to think there was at least some chance that the Jersey Devil was real.

Bill Wasovwich said that he'd had an encounter with something that could have been the Jersey Devil while out in the swamps one night. "Something screamed," he said. "My hat flew off my head. I ran home, through briars. My arms was all cut up when I got home."

Fred Brown, McPhee's main Piney companion, was even more definitive. "That is no fake story," Brown said. "A woman named Leeds had twelve living children. She said if she ever had another one she hoped it would be the Devil. She had her thirteenth child, and it growed, and one day it flew away. It's haunted the earth ever since. It's took pigs right out of pens. And little lambs. I believe it took a baby once, right down in Mathis town. The Leeds Devil is a crooked-faced thing, with wings. Believe what you want, I'm telling you the truth."

THIRTY-FOUR

The feedback loop, and a 'No-last-name-local'

The last real Jersey Devil scare took place in 1951, when a ten-year-old boy looked out a window and reported seeing something outside "with blood coming out of its face."[117] Additional reports soon followed and a newspaper called The Record ran the headline, "JERSEY DEVIL 'INVADES' GIBBSTOWN." There exists a famous photo from the period showing two Greenwich Township police officers posting a sign to a tree.

"The Jersey Devil is a Hoax," it says.

The Courier-Post of July 17, 1965 ran a drawing of the Jersey Devil, looking kind of like a cow with wings, as it flew over a New Jersey neighborhood, the Man in the Gray Flannel Suit gazing up at it from the foreground. Accurate reportage on the monster was complicated, the story said, because the average native of the region was more concerned with advertising his own skepticism than with discussing what he actually knew about the beast. In a similar story, a librarian was quoted saying that she wasn't afraid of the Jersey Devil., but then she didn't expect it to stop by her place of work. "I don't suppose he cares much for reading," she said. "But I guess he would never dare come into the building as long as we have *The Lives of the Saints* on the shelves."

There have been organized and highly technical Jersey Devil hunts in the Pine Barrens since at least the 1970s. Wil-

---

[117] McCloy and Miller, Jersey Devil

liam McMahon, in his *Pine Barrens: Legends and Lore*, described one occasion, in 1974, when two "research students with electronic gear" spent a few autumn nights in the woods of Leeds Point. "They were driven out by mosquitoes," McMahon said, "whom they concluded were the real Jersey Devils."

By this point, James McCloy and Ray Miller were well on their way to publishing The Jersey Devil. After that, you wouldn't need to look up old newspaper clippings or poke around in historical society archives to read about the beast. Anyone could pick up a copy of their book in any library or bookstore in the state.

A New York Times story from November 1981 called the Jersey Devil, "the pride—or nightmare—of our state," saying that it had allegedly been "flitting or skulking" around in the Pine Barrens for two hundred and fifty years. On the Friday before Halloween, a group of students from Mater Dei High School in New Monmouth had thrown a birthday party for the beast. As part of the festivities, a poster contest and a costume contest were held. Alan Payne, a senior, reportedly drew a six-foot-tall monster with orange horns and a blue tail, "because he's my state monster and because I heard a lot about him in social-studies class."

Thomas Murray, the chairman of the school's social studies department, said he had "instigated" the party because the Jersey Devil was "the Number 1 mythological figure in the state."

That same year, The Times reported on a devil hunt in the Forked River Mountains, led by Shaun O'Rourke, an Ocean County naturalist. Participants were "advised to bring flashlights to help spot the shy creature."

When the Colorado Rockies of the National Hockey League relocated from Denver to New Jersey the next year, a name-that-team contest was held to choose a mascot. Ten thousand votes were cast, and the New Jersey Devils beat out the New Jersey Blades, New Jersey Colonials, New Jersey Coastals and New Jersey Meadowlarks to become the new mascot. The team's principal owner, John McMullen, initially rejected the name due to possible objections from religious groups. A reporter who wrote about the contest received a death threat from a reader who called him "an agent of Satan." The Times said the mascot was based on the famous monster, "a bizarre-looking but supposedly harmless creature" that had roamed the Pine Barrens "from 1887 to as late as 1938."

Maybe the one place in the state that wanted to avoid association with the story was Leeds Point. In 1986, during the yearly round of Halloween-inspired Jersey Devil stories, The Philadelphia Inquirer ran a brief interview with Bob Kuppel, who owned Oyster Creek, the restaurant at the end of the point.

People "used to get pretty worked up over it," Kuppel said of the monster. "I never took any stock into it."

According to the Inquirer, residents were fed up with the stream of unsolicited tourists, college students and television crews, who could often be seen "tromping" around Leeds Point at inconvenient hours, looking for the Jersey Devil.

One "long-time resident" agreed to speak with the reporter only on condition of anonymity, saying he feared reprisals from neighbors. "I don't want my name used," the person said, "people'll bomb my house."[118]

By 2000, it seemed that the media feedback loop had been firmly established. Television shows about the Jersey Devil prompted newspaper stories about the Jersey Devil which in turn prompted more TV shows. The Philadelphia Inquirer of February 9, 2010 ran a review of *Paranormal State*, a television show that ran on The A&E Network and that claimed to have "the most compelling evidence that has ever come out about the Jersey Devil."

The Inquirer, in its review, assured readers that if this were the best evidence for the creature—night-vision footage of a deer standing behind a bush—then Delaware Valley residents had nothing to fear, though there were some locals who disagreed.

After some perishing comments about the "surely inebriat-

---

[118] Philadelphia Inquirer, October 29, 1986, "The Legend of the Jersey Devil Lingers," by Daniel LeDuc

ed" folk who had been afraid of the beast, an example of one such believer was produced by the paper, a certain "no-last-name local Harry," who instructed people, "Don't go out at night. Do not ever go out alone, because there's something out there."

THIRTY-FIVE

A C-list cryptid, and the loss of a certain elemental power

Every day at precisely 5:02 a.m. on weekdays (6:02 a.m. on the weekends) I used to get an email of the day's news headlines from the Press of Atlantic City, and across the top of the message, in what I think is known in the trade as the "banner advertisement," would appear the smiling face of the Jersey Devil. It had rosy cheeks, I remember, and its arms were spread wide, palms upturned, in a gesture either of supplication or apology. Black tee-shirt. No pants.

Some mornings it would kind of bound back and forth across the screen with a pitchfork in its hand, and some mornings it would drive from one side to the other in a red convertible sports car. Apparently some enterprising young salesperson had bought the domain names JerseyDevilHOMES.com, JerseyDevilJOBS.com, and JerseyDevilCARS.com and the Press was now using them to post its online classified ads (an experiment that's since been discontinued).

There was a time, not too long ago, when you could drink a Jersey Devil cocktail—applejack, Triple sec, cranberry juice—at the Jersey Devil Taproom in New Gretna. You can still eat a Jersey Devil burger at JD's Pub & Grille in Smithville, where they also have a "zombie burger" (topped with a fried egg) on the menu. There's a Jersey Devil Cheerleading Academy in Morganville and a Jersey Devil Dietetic Center in Belle Mead and a squadron of fighter pilots (the 177th Air National Guard), whose mascot is the Jersey Devil, based in Pomona.

I tried multiple times to get an interview with the proprietors of the Jersey Devil Doggie Day Care and Training Center in Cape May ("where you drop off your little devil and pick up an angel"), but they never returned my calls.

There are at least three feature films based (however tenuously) on the Jersey Devil story, including one (*13th Child*) that stars Robert Guillaume (TV's *Benson*!) and Lesley-Anne Down. There's an *X-Files* episode about the Jersey Devil, in which Special Agent Mulder chases the Jersey Devil to Atlantic City, where he (Mulder) spends the night in jail, having been locked up by a local police commander who's trying to sabotage the investigation, fearing that any positive evidence of the monster's existence would negatively impact tourism.

"It's my job to protect the city and avoid spreading panic," the police commander says (I'm paraphrasing).

"Oh, is that your job?" Mulder says (I'm quoting), "Or is it to keep the dice rolling, keep the tour buses rolling in? You can't fill those casinos—this town disappears like a quarter down the slot."

There's a Jersey Devil episode of the cartoon *Extreme Ghostbusters* where the monster emerges from an iron forge, which seems like it's supposed to be Hanover Furnace. And of course there's the multiple-Stanley-Cup-winning NHL hockey team, the New Jersey Devils, based in Newark, though nobody in South Jersey knows the hockey mascot has anything to do with the folk story. South Jersey is firmly Flyers territory.

In the videogame "Jersey Devil" it is alleged that the monster was discovered many years ago—in a place called "Jersey Town" (Pop. 382)—by a deranged Scottish doctor named Knarf who spent his days performing ethically dubious experiments on ordinary garden vegetables. Knarf's perpetually harassed assistant (a talking pumpkin named Dennis) presented Knarf with the infant Jersey Devil as a kind of gift, or peace offering. But Knarf, failing to appreciate the monster's cultural significance, immediately announced plans to cut the Jersey Devil into little pieces, "in the name of science, of course."

Sometime later, while Knarf was out running errands, the Jersey Devil detached itself from the clothes hook upon which it had been hung (by its diaper, it looked like) and ran amok in the laboratory, upsetting various beakers and flasks and generally making a big mess. In the chemical chaos that ensued, a race of mutant, anthropomorphic vegetables was spawned, and these subsequently lay siege to Jersey City. In a novel twist, the Jersey Devil was then called upon by government officials to save civilization from these "unidentified terrorists."

The Jersey Devil wages Kung Fu warfare against the mutant vegetables. It defeats its enemies using "jumping tail-swipes." It battles hopping pumpkins and sociopathic tomatoes. It is beset by giant bees. In a climactic scene, it fights a giant bear. About this bear, it has been said, he "looks Japanese, he has a Japanese samurai hairdo, and he's wearing diapers."[119]

The claim is sometimes made, among pundits who care about this kind of thing, that the Jersey Devil has become part of pop culture, but I'm not sure how I feel about this statement, which might obscure more than it enlightens. Certainly the Jersey Devil is for-sale in many contexts across the Garden State. Certainly many people have tried to cash in on the folklore. But whether these efforts have had any noticeable impact on the shape of the story itself is, I think, very much an open question.

The Jersey Devil is a resolutely C-list cryptid. No classic image of the beast has imbedded itself in the popular consciousness. The Loch Ness Monster has its famous black-and-white still photograph ("the Surgeon's Photo") and Bigfoot its grainy, eight-millimeter home movie ("the Patterson-Gimlin Tape"), but there's nothing comparable in the case of the Jersey Devil. One hundred and fifty years after the story first appeared in print, there's still this basic disagreement over what the creature *is* even—whether it's a fire-breathing kangaroo-bat, or a kind of sick or feral human.

Large-scale attempts by traditional big-time media to monetize the Jersey Devil have been met with mixed results at best. The movies are generally unwatchable. The video game, while fun to play I'm sure, is kind of a joke. The story seems to lose some of its elemental power when removed from its traditional context of grandmothers and camping trips and ghost stories told while driving through the Pines.

---

[119] GameFaqs Walkthru

In roughly ten years of highly unscientific but more or less nonstop random polling of strangers on the subject of the Jersey Devil, no one has ever once mentioned Dr. Knarf.

THIRTY-SIX

Instant nonstick folklore

Maybe the closest the Jersey Devil has ever come to a king-hell pop culture breakthrough was in 1998, when two filmmakers from Pennsylvania, Stefan Avalos and Lance Weiler, released a film called *The Last Broadcast*, about the members of the crew of a cable-access TV show who go missing while looking for the Jersey Devil in the Pine Barrens and end up (most of them) gruesomely murdered. During the subsequent trial, found footage said to have been shot by the now deceased crewmembers is played to reconstruct their final moments.

In the winter of 1997, Avalos and Weiler traveled to the Sundance Film Festival in Park City, Utah, to try to drum up interest in their film. They handed out flyers depicting the (fictional) missing filmmakers. They designed a website that supplied interested parties with an elaborate backstory, including interviews with the crewmembers (now allegedly deceased) and a timeline of events. The movie poster was an image of a homicide report with sections redacted. The whole marketing strategy, it seemed, was to present the movie in such a way as to suggest that the events depicted in it might have happened in real life.

The Last Broadcast was a decidedly handmade and *Independent* film. Avalos and Weiler not only wrote and directed it, but they also starred in it. Avalos, a classical violinist, did the music. The film is often cited as the first feature-length film to have been shot, edited and distributed entirely digitally. To save money, the filmmakers never actually converted the footage to celluloid film. To release it, the distributors beamed it by satellite to participating theaters who then projected it onto their screens using digital equipment. The whole thing was done for nine hundred dollars and was a tremendous financial success, the filmmakers have said.[120]

But it was not, of course, *The Blair Witch Project*.

In 1998, Avalos and Weiler went back to Sundance with real hopes that their film would be awarded a screening during a high-profile midnight timeslot, but in the end The Last Broadcast was removed from contention. A year later, Blair Witch would be screened in the same midnight timeslot, picked up by Artisan Entertainment and go on to earn $248,639,099 at the box office globally,[121] spawning an entire industry of spinoffs in the process, including one sequel, one other planned sequel, eleven books, two comic books, a planned remake to be set in Scotland, a videogame trilogy and uncountable parodies, including one amazing-sounding parody from The Cartoon Network called *The Scooby Doo Project*.

Like The Last Broadcast, The Blair Witch Project dealt with a team of young filmmakers lost in the woods while investigating a local legend. It too relied on a marketing strategy that was designed to plant confusion in the minds of prospective audiences about whether the events depicted in the film took place in real life. And it relied heavily on a website that supplied readers with an elaborate (and totally fictional) backstory, including a timeline of events and lots of false documentation, including interviews with the filmmakers (sadly no longer with us). In fact, the two projects were similar enough from top to bottom that Avalos and Weiler said they considered legal action against the makers and distributors of Blair Witch, but in the end they decided not to get "entangled" in legal matters and to "just do films instead."[122]

The phenomenon that was The Blair Witch Project seemed to come together at a particular moment in the history of communication, when the new medium of the internet was perva-

---

[120] Avalos' Wikipedia page (which appears to have been written by Avalos or his grandmother) says that on a budget-to-profit basis, it was "one of the most profitable movies in history" but gives no numbers. The filmmakers have said they made "good money." I've seen estimates as high as $4 million, but really I have no idea how much money they perva.
[121] Per Box Office Mojo
[122] Weiler's words, from, "The Facts about The Last Broadcast: An Interview with Lance Weiler," in dvdreview.com

sive and powerful enough to exert a tremendous influence on the culture at large, but when few people understood the nature of this awful power. To market The Blair Witch Project, in 1999, Haxan Films and Artisan Entertainment used the novel medium of the internet to produce an example of instant, nonstick folklore.

The real-life producers of The Blair Witch Project—Daniel Myrick and Eduardo Sanchez—were genuinely youngish and relatively unknown. The actors too were unknown. The movie was shot in a short time frame on a modest budget (though not nearly so modest as that of Last Broadcast).[123] If it looked like the film was produced nonprofessionally, that's at least in part because it kind of was. All of these factors were used by the marketers to enhance the film's marketability.

Well before their deal with Artisan, Myrick and Sanchez began their sales campaign, *seeding* various internet chat forums with their story about missing film students.[124] When the buzz began to grow, they used their established presence in these forums to direct people to their own website, which was later augmented with capital and expertise from Artisan.

As the Blair Witch marketeers knew, the members of their target audience of seventeen-to-twenty-eight year olds needed to be congratulated on their superior taste and discernment, to feel like the possessors of some privileged information. Conventional, mainstream advertising could be counterproductive in this case. Instead the film was taken on a tour of college campuses. Ads were mostly limited to cable channels, independent weeklies and the radio. Interviews with cast members were *streng verboten* since they were supposed to be dead. Rather than sending advance copies of the film to critics, a promo was leaked to the host of *Split Screen*, a television show on the Independent Film Channel, who then presented it as real,

---

[123] The number $25,000 gets thrown around but Sanchez himself has said "what you saw in the theaters" cost between $500,000 and $750,000); see for instance *Entertainment Weekly*, "'The Blair Witch Project' 10 years later: Catching up with the directors of the horror sensation," July 9, 2009
[124] From an account of the campaign by Roger Darnell, a PR exec who worked in Hollywood but not on the BWP campaign

found footage of a mysterious murder.[125] Before the film debuted, another "documentary" purportedly dealing with the real (fictional) filmmakers would air on The SciFi Channel. When the film was finally released, the number of theaters was limited to preserve the hard-won scarcity value.

Among devotees of ad-industry porn, the whole thing is considered a kind of work of exemplary genius. The Blair Witch website is said to have cost more money than was spent shooting the entire film, and the success the site generated prefigured the way big corporations would use informal media to sell products. People who read through the website thought they were getting an independent education on an obscure historical event, when in fact they were looking at a Hollywood movie executive's idea of an extremely slick commercial. Among the many perverse consequences of this sales tactic was that people who believed themselves to be the most well-informed about the movie were in fact the ones who had the entire thing ass-backwards. If (a big if) we're less vulnerable to this kind of manipulation today, it's due in part at least to the success of the Blair Witch.

Not everyone who read the Blair Witch website or sat through the film ended up thinking that a group of young filmmakers had really disappeared in the Maryland woods (a lot of people seemed to join in just to make fun of the whole thing). But *enough* people believed it. And by the middle of the summer of 1999, when the movie went into wide release, the buzz was loud enough that tens of millions of Americans who otherwise probably wouldn't have bothered (yours truly for instance) shelled out ten dollars to sit through an ersatz Independent film about a man-eating witch just to see what all the fuss was about.

The Blair Witch marketing campaign proved a delightful affirmation of the old adage that any publicity is good publicity. The strategic use of misinformation allowed the marketers of The Blair Witch project to generate a tremendous amount of discussion about their movie in a way that did not resemble conventional advertising, thus preserving an element of au-

---

[125] Interview with Dan Myrick, www.houseofhorrors.com

thenticity and artistic cachet.

Even the most cynical observers might have failed to appreciate where the line between cinematic license and marketing bullshit lay precisely. Unlike the Jersey Devil for instance, the legend that The Blair Witch Project was based on wasn't a *real* legend. It hadn't existed before the screenwriters invented it as part of the movie's plot. Likewise an 1809 book about the legend, titled *The Blair Witch Cult* ("commonly considered fiction"), wasn't a real book. It (or its title at least) was invented by the marketing department to lend an atmosphere of authenticity to proceedings and promote ticket sales. For that matter, this imagined readership of simpletons who foolishly considered the make-pretend book fiction—they weren't real either. No readers existed, so no opinions existed, because no book existed—all were invented by marketeers as part of an elaborate invitation to audiences. The ritual disemboweling of seven children by a reclusive lunatic in 1941 was likewise not believed to be true, not because it hadn't happened (though of course it hadn't) but because denying your own marketing nonsense added another layer of misdirection and enhanced the effect. Hadn't heard of the 1994 filmmaker disappearance? Probably another cover-up.

Perhaps the most succinct statement of the campaign's effectiveness came in 2007, when the website Snopes, which evaluates urban legends, addressed itself to the question of whether The Blair Witch Project was, "based on footage shot by three student filmmakers who mysteriously disappeared while making a documentary about the legend of the Blair Witch."

The conclusion (it certainly was not) was less interesting than Snopes' decision even to take up the question in the first place. The Blair Witch ad campaign, they were saying, had become *its own* urban legend.

Blair Witch went viral, in other words. And it did so in a way that might have had special resonance for anyone interested in the shape that the Jersey Devil story might take—that any piece of folklore might take—in a new era of mass communication. Blair Witch was a blueprint for how finally to monetize the Jersey Devil legend. Under different circumstances, Blair Witch could have *been* the Jersey Devil. But it wasn't the Jersey Devil. But it could have been.

THIRTY-SEVEN

Leut and the Devil Hunters

About the same time that Avalos and Weiler were making The Last Broadcast, another partnership was coming together across the river in New Jersey. A group called the Devil Hunters ("Official Researchers of the Jersey Devil") was the creation of a young woman named Laura Leuter from Toms River who became interested in the Jersey Devil as a child and assembled a team of researchers in about 1999 with the stated mission of looking for the monster in the woods of central and southern New Jersey. "I think there is too much evidence for it to be just a story," Leut has said.

The Devil Hunters described themselves as "a professional research organization dedicated to the legend" of the Jersey Devil. Like the characters in the Blair Witch, they made regular forays into the Pine Barrens in search of the Jersey Devil. They had their own website, which they used to document their experiences, collect Jersey Devil stories and accounts of sightings, lay out their theories on the monster and their reasons for looking for it and field questions from around the state. If they ever found the Jersey Devil, their intention was not to harm the creature in any way—their motives were too altruistic for that. They simply wanted to document as much of the encounter as possible and maybe take a few pictures.

By 2000, the group had made four trips to Leeds Point to look for the remains of the house where they believed the Jersey Devil had been born. When they made these trips they carried with them audio and visual recording equipment, night-vision goggles, a loran global positioning system, various pieces of hunting equipment and a laptop computer on which to record the day's events.

On one such trip, they found the ruined walls and sunken basement of an old house, set back in the woods some distance from the road, and they identified the ruins as the remains of the Shourds House where they said the Jersey Devil was born to a Mrs. Shourds in 1735. When Leut and the Devil Hunters were there, they reported hearing a series of strange growls and a mysterious hissing noise. They also saw a set of footprints, "like a hoof with toes."[126]

During another hunt in the woods near Jackson, the Devil Hunters had an experience they said they couldn't explain. While walking east, surveying a section of forest, they heard a rustling sound ("which could have just been squirrels") followed by a high-pitched screeching noise ("similar to a woman screaming but without the human aspects of the voice"). The sound lasted a few seconds, but none of the Hunters present could identify it. When they went off to investigate, they found nothing.

"Now we aren't jumping to conclusions, immediately claiming to have heard the Jersey Devil," Leut later wrote. "But we will say that we heard something we have never heard before, and that we can not come up with any logical explanation for it."

"We're dying to know if anyone else has any logical explanation for that noise."

The Devil Hunters seemed to keep up a regular presence on a number of internet chat forums about the Jersey Devil, including one run by New Jersey Online, where their postings seemed to generate a lot of commentary, some of it friendly, some hostile. Theories and interpretations flowed freely.

Perhaps the Jersey Devil was a muntjack, someone would offer. Or maybe it was a windigo. Or maybe it was a chupacabra, the famous Latin American vampire monster that was making headlines at the time. Something strange and unidentifiable had been seen in Somerset. Something—the Jersey Devil itself maybe—had been seen in Hunterdon. "Had the Jersey Devil ever been seen outside New Jersey?" someone would ask. Yes, people would answer, plenty of times.

Not all the postings were pro-monster, of course. ("You people in the sticks need to stop smoking grass!" one read.)

---

[126] From the group's website, www.njdevilhunters.com

But they didn't seem to have to be. Even the insults kept the discussion going.

Maybe visitors to these forums didn't use their real names. Maybe they were neighbors, but maybe they didn't even live in the same country. But I got the feeling I was looking at a kind of postmodern analog to a very premodern process that has probably surrounded this story—any story really—from the beginning. Some piece of news or a reported sighting would set off waves of discussion, among believers and nonbelievers alike.

Leut's position at the nexus of a lot of Jersey Devil gossip allowed her to act as a kind of unofficial spokesperson for the beast—a kind of new-media version of Harry Leeds—and the Devil Hunters kept a list of Frequently Asked Questions on their website.

Q: "Where is the best place to find the Jersey Devil?"

A: "There are several towns in New Jersey that seem to be 'hot spots' for Jersey Devil activity. These areas vary throughout the years. Right now, I would say that the current hot spots for the 90's have been Bamber Lake (there have been a lot of recent sightings out there!), Jackson, and the inevitable Pine Barrens…"

Q: "What are other names for the Jersey Devil?"

A: "There's a bunch. The original name of the beast was the Leeds Devil, named obviously after its supposed family. Other names have been Jabberwock. I know there's more, I'll get back to you on that."

Q: "Does the Jersey Devil still exist?"

A: "I would say yes. I have been continuously bombarded with sightings, including very recent ones. And our Devil Hunts have become filled with odd things. I think he's still out there."

Q: "Do you think that a lot of the sightings are because of the 'Devil Hunters' group that you started…it's a way to keep the legend alive?"

A: "Good question, and it's definitely something we worried about. But after this page was put up, suddenly all sorts of people began coming out of their silence, and although I get some recent sightings reports, I also have many people who saw something years back and thought they were crazy. I think that the Devil Hunters have brought back the Jersey Devil 'stir', but I don't think that we are the whole reason for the recent sightings."

The Devil Hunters naturally drew comparisons to The Blair Witch Project and The Last Broadcast, but Leut has said her group predates both movies. Still, it was tough to imagine she really minded these comparisons. The Devil Hunters' website was full of grainy, green-and-black night-vision images that looked like they could have been still photos from Blair Witch.

The Devil Hunters and The Blair Witch Project seemed to belong to the same cultural moment, the same intersection of premodern tradition and postmodern communication. They relied on the same mild distrust of the mainstream culture, the same hint at occult wisdom. Leut herself said she thought the Jersey Devil was an "unclassified biological entity" hinting either at the limits of scientific inquiry or an active conspiracy of suppression.

But while the Devil Hunters were the product of a group of sincere, amateur young people who did this stuff as a sideline, The Blair Witch Project was the product of a sophisticated entertainment joint venture, with a marketing budget in the hundreds of thousands, if not millions, of dollars, seeking to tap audiences for fun and profit.

A hundred years ago, the folklorist Charles Skinner predicted that electricity and paved highways would kill off the Jersey Devil, but in the event, technology had had an altogether more ambiguous effect. Today anyone in Sweden with a computer could read about the Jersey Devil on Wikipedia. Anyone with a camera could wander about in the Pine Barrens and put a documentary up on YouTube. It wasn't necessarily folklore, but it was something.

In 1941, Cornelius Weygandt had written that no one believed in the Jersey Devil. This was not literally true in the 1940s, and it's not true today. There has always been, and there remains, a population of New Jerseyans who think the monster is a real creature and that it haunts the backyards and byways of their state, but with the advent of mass internet communication it was possible to see this community in a new way. Its members were allowed to speak for themselves, and to each other, for the first time without the intermediation of a condescending and cynical press apparatus. And by all appearances they were literate and technologically savvy and capable of critical thought—a long way from the Pine Rats anyway.

THIRTY-EIGHT

BeBop and I go into the Pines, and a memory of shad roe

One afternoon in early spring I went for a drive with BeBop across the Pine Barrens to visit Aunt Dottie in the improbably named suburb (Hamilton Square) outside Trenton where she lived. I'd never been there. In fact I had no memory of ever meeting Aunt Dottie before. It was only an hour and a half away, seventy-two miles by car, but it was a different world.

There was some debate later over how we got there. I think we took the Black Horse Pike to Route 206, my blind grandmother giving directions from memory as we went. We passed classic Pine Barrens non-places—Shamong, Atsion, Indian Mills etc—though there's very little to distinguish them from the surrounding forest. Somewhere in the woods we must have passed the headwaters of the Mullica. Somewhere outside Tabernacle we must have passed the Carranza Memorial, written about by McPhee in 1968. I remember, unbelievably, a series of barns and what looked like pastureland, the smell of defrosting turf and the feeling that I couldn't possibly have been in New Jersey.

Aunt Dottie lived in a little suburban bungalow on a street with a crazy name—Shackamaxon—an old Lenape name, it turned out. I think we ate lunch at a little diner around the corner from her house. By little I mean gigantic.

She was two years older than BeBop. They were really funny little old ladies, great company, though again I'm at a loss to give examples. Each of them could be counted on to forget her false teeth from time to time. When they got together they would sit side-by-side on the couch and swing their feet and tell stories and laugh for hours.

Aunt Dottie's nickname for her husband was Briar. Her oldest child's nickname was Snookie. Somehow the subject of midwives came up, and she said, "You know something? I'm going to tell you something personal. I had my first child—Snookie—by a midwife. She was as good as any doctor I had since. She was outstanding. Yup, yeah. Her name was Annie T., and everybody knew her. I don't know of it was the letter *T* or *Tee* or what."

Annie T.'s delivery fee was ten dollars. "And my husband worked like a dog to get it."

Snookie had been born at home in a beautiful old four-poster bed. "Mother had that bed for the longest time. Don't know what happened to it. Old-fashioned, wooden bed. Beautiful."

Aunt Dottie had a coffee cup with a picture of the Jersey Devil on it, and every so often it would hit her, she said, the absurdity of this situation.

"There's my relative on that cup!" she would say. At Halloween, the kids would joke about it. "Mom, come and see this! That's your relative on television. Ha ha hahah!"

She had an antique rifle hanging above a wood-burning stove in her little suburban bungalow. Years later, I called her on the phone to ask about it.

"Do you remember that rifle you told me about?"

"I'm looking at it now," she said. "It had belonged to my grandfather Charles."

She said Charles told her that ships frequently wrecked themselves around Barnegat and the hazardous inlets leading into Great Bay. After one disaster, the dead washed ashore near Leeds Point and were buried at a place called By's Hill.

I thought there may have been some connection between the rifle and the shipwrecks, but Aunt Dottie said no. "Thank God.

"It's old, old, old, really old," she said. "And it's hanging over the fireplace. My husband put it up there. We got pictures underneath it.

"And none of my boys wanted it. Isn't that something?"

and she laughed.

"If it could talk, it would really tell some tales."

My grandmother's family left Leeds Point during the Great Depression. There are a variety of theories about the causes of this disaster, but in each case William Leeds, the Captain, seems to play a prominent role. In one version, after Charles died, William convinced the family to take out a mortgage on the house (Charles hadn't believed in banks) and then he used the proceeds to buy a car. As part of the deal, William promised to teach Grandma Sally how to drive, a promise he kept. According to BeBop, Grandma Sally enjoyed the car very much and was regularly seen barreling around Leeds Point, taking corners on two wheels.

Not long after they bought the car, the Depression hit. The family had never had much money. Now, with new debts and even less liquidity, they couldn't meet the mortgage payments, and the bank foreclosed.

In the other story, Captain Leeds either forgot to pay the taxes or intentionally decided not to pay the taxes on the family land. When the Depression hit he languished in unemployment while his wife made pot-holders and sold them door-to-door. Either way the result was the same.

"The Depression came, and, 'woop,' lost the house," Be-Bop said.

It had been two hundred and thirty years since Daniel Leeds moved his family to the little peninsula by the mouth of the Mullica River, but there it was—one *woop* and it was over.

After that, they moved around a lot. BeBop and Aunt Dottie had always talked about Leeds Point like they'd lived there all their lives, but they must have been young girls when they left. They would talk and talk about their childhoods in that place, but when I asked them about the aftermath, their minds seemed to close up. Aunt Dottie once referred to these as the "tough years" but that was about it. Not that they refused to talk about it, they just couldn't remember really. Or couldn't make the effort required to remember, for some reason. After all, seven decades had elapsed since then, and life had intervened.

At some point Dottie married Briar and moved across the state, and BeBop married an Irishman, James Patrick Walsh, and ended up on Vermont Avenue in the Inlet in Atlantic City. She was a seamstress for a while. James Walsh, my grandfather, had been an apprentice shoemaker in Ireland, and when he moved to Atlantic City he worked as a carpet-layer in the old hotels. In this way Mildred Helen Leeds, of one of the first Quaker families of West Jersey, raised six Irish-Catholic Walshes who went to Holy Spirit High School and went to mass at Our Lady Star of the Sea or St. Bernadette's every Friday during Lent. And had grandchildren who went to the St. Patrick's Day parade on the boardwalk, and went to Bag Day at the Irish Pub the day after the St. Patrick's Day parade, and so on. A generation later and we were in the suburbs, BeBop's grumbling about Harry Leeds, and her stories about our fire-breathing relative, the only links to a family history that no one really spent much time thinking about.

It was on the drive home from Aunt Dottie's, I think, but it might have been some other trip altogether, that we started talking about shad roe. I'd been reading McPhee's latest book, *The Founding Fish*, about shad fishing in the Delaware River and the unlikely part that *alosa sapidissima* had played in American history.

"Did you ever have shad roe?" I can hear her say. "Oh, it's *good.*"

It was still early in the season, but we resolved to find some-one who would sell us shad roe. It was getting to be close to dinner anyway. We must have called home to let my parents know, and by the time we reached Atlantic County, forces were beginning to mobilize. Maybe we hit Bob's Seafood in Northfield and maybe the Crab Trap in Somers Point and maybe we considered at trip out to Oyster Creek even, but probably we ruled that out as too far away.

We ended up in Somers Point at a restaurant with a big plaster crustacean on the roof, a place I'd driven past hundreds of times and never once considered entering, never even once consciously registering it as a restaurant.

The food was unmemorable. I'm not even sure they had shad roe. But various aunts and uncles and cousins had materialized as word got out that BeBop was in the market for a meal, and that's one of my favorite memories of my grandmother. She brought people together like that, and she imbued places—even forgettable seafood restaurants with ridiculous crustaceans on the roof—with a sense of story. For someone like me—who'd spent his childhood running around like a lunatic trying to get *out* of his hometown—she was a link back to the place I'd managed so successfully to alienate myself from.

She died in February. She'd started having back pain around Thanksgiving and slept sitting in a chair for a few weeks. Then she didn't come to Christmas Eve dinner at Aunt Helen's and I knew it must be serious, and sometime after that she was diagnosed with the cancer that took her life.

There wasn't much they could do. She was ninety-one. She ate a baby aspirin every day and hadn't been to a doctor in years. She'd been in excellent health. All things considered, we said, she'd had a long and rich and full life.

I took the week off work and came down from New York to spend a few days with her, me and my goddamn Olympus voice recorder. The buses were full of Chinese gamblers from Queens going down to observe the Lunar New Year in the casinos. I bought a pumpkin cheesecake for Aunt Maureen and Uncle Dave (well, for Uncle Dave) and poked my head into BeBop's room and we chatted once a day. She fell asleep a lot and apologized for falling asleep, but she perked up a bit when we talked about Leeds Point.

We ordered Indian food one last time. I ate it. She didn't, but she said she enjoyed the smells. She made a compact feast out of a single meatball from Ventura's, formerly the Rugby Inn, where Uncle Maurice had walked that time in the blizzard. And I went back to New York knowing I'd never see her again.

THIRTY-NINE

A failed reconciliation, and why I feel rather like a shit

I reread Cynthia Lamb's Brigid's Charge, her novel about Deborah Leeds. I'd known that Lamb initially intended to write nonfiction, and I'd made the mistake the first time through of reading her novel as a kind of failed biography, which was unfair. Lamb's writing represents a great innovation in Jersey Devil literature in that it's the first treatment of the story—the only treatment of the story that I know of—that considers Mother Leeds as a human being, with basic human privileges.

In the book, Deborah's thirteenth pregnancy is a welcome one. She is happy when she learns she's carrying another child, and she wants to bear it. With that simple modification, the logic of original sin is instantly and permanently eliminated, and we are allowed to see the story as the echo of the domestic tragedy that it must have been.

Lamb writes in an openly feminist tradition. Her themes are reconciliation, continuity, secrecy and fate. The novel's central dilemma is between the *Old Religion*—Lamb's term for the occult or pre-Christian tradition that has coexisted uneasily beside, or beneath, Christianity for millennia—and the establishment Christianity of England and the American colonies. She deals with questions of reintegration—of male and female, of the body and the spirit, of the old religion and the new, of organized human society and amoral nature.

Her protagonists are feminist witches. Deborah is a healer and the heir to an ancient tradition passed down through her grandmother. Her project, or *charge*, is to attempt a reconciliation of the Old Religion with the Christian religion into which she was born. This task is best attempted in the New World, her grandmother says, where the necessary cultural space exists to operate. But out of this struggle, the grandmother predicts, Deborah's healing abilities will flow.

Fish permeate Lamb's novel, the cover of which is decorated with a brightly colored example of one. Deborah's arrival in the colonies is attended by an auspicious rainbow trout, held aloft by a young girl. The withered hand of a ship's cook, her first patient, is like a dead fish, which Deborah brings back to life. The air above the ship that carries Deborah across the Atlantic is filled with fish smells, which induce visions (by contrast the air above London smells of the "acrid vapors of tar"). In one scene, a woman catches a fish with a knife, throws the fish back, then kills herself with the knife and floats away downstream.

Fish are present throughout the novel in the embryonic human forms Deborah carries throughout her life during her thirteen pregnancies. When she is baptized, in a dream, a small fish leaps in celebration. The final step in the process of the healing of her antihero involves pigment collected from the Great Fish, the "first mother."

Lamb's plot ultimately turns on a case of mistaken identity involving a kind of fish. In a scene suffused with aquatic imagery, a physician administers smelling salts to a woman who's been overwhelmed, driving away the fish smells and the access to the larger mysteries she's on the verge of apprehending.

When I talked to Cynthia Lamb on the phone (we've never met), I asked her if she had been aware of a series of letters exchanged between Thomas Leeds and William Leeds, two brothers, exceptionally grouchy gentlemen who'd corresponded in the late 1730s. They were old and unwell, and the money was running out. Each somewhat morbid and preoccupied with his own mortality, they said they expected to die soon and were ready to do so.[127]

Amid the health complaints and general complaints in their letters, they bickered over a piece of gold that their mother had left them. William asked Thomas to send him the gold piece. Thomas agreed, but reluctantly.

They seemed to think the gold had magical significance, healing properties that their mother had told them about. Wil-

---

[127] The letters were published in John Demos' *Remarkable Providences* (1972)

liam said their mother worried that one day one of them might develop a "bad sore" and, in that case, the gold piece might "be of some benefit" to him.

"Our mother, when she gave that piece of gold to Jonathan, left a great *charge* that he and we should be careful of it," William said (emphasis mine).

Thomas, who didn't seem to disagree with this assessment of his mother's powers, nevertheless dismissed the request for the gold as one of his brother's "old tricks."

"That piece of gold is as much mine as the coat on my back," Thomas said. Still it seems he finally sent the gold to his brother.

When I talked to the historian John Demos, a specialist in colonial witchcraft, in whose anthology the letters were collected, he opened straight to the page and said there was "something spooky" in there.

William and Thomas seem to be the children of that first William Leeds (Daniel's brother) who emigrated at the end of the 1670s. The mother in question was a Dorothy or Dorothea Scilton of Essex, England. William (the second) and Dy had had five children in total, including a Jonathan, who died in 1718, and another son, Daniel, who is also sometimes mentioned in connection with the Jersey Devil story, since he is referred to in primary source documents as being "weak-minded" and "helpless."[128]

McCloy and Miller, in Phantom of the Pines, refer to "speculation" about this Daniel, pointing out that, "Before modern advances in medical services, physical or psychological abnormalities created extreme problems for any family in which they occurred," and that it was "theorized that a deformed child was born to the Leeds family, and that this unfortunate youngster was referred to as the 'Jersey Devil.' In those days, an abnormal child was often associated with the Devil."

I thought maybe Cynthia Lamb had read about Dorothea Leeds's "great charge," as William had called it, and that maybe

---

[128] Kintzel, Tree of Leeds; McCloy and Miller say they had six children.

these words had inspired her choice of book title, but when I asked her, she said it was a coincidence. She hadn't read the letters.

A lot of this story was like that. The Jersey Devil was a kind of relic that had been carried out of the past and dropped down into a culture in which it no longer belonged. When you heard the story, you couldn't tell if you were hearing echoes of particular events and people, or just artifacts of language from a different time, three centuries ago, when people compared their enemies to devils and believed that illnesses could be caused by sin.

You could find other artifacts if you were inclined to look for them. Japhet and Deborah Leeds, who BeBop said were the parents of Leeds Devil, had a grandson, Japhet, born in 1739, who was described (by the historian Francis Bazley Lee) as unmarried, "lame" and an "elder in the Leeds Point Mission." If you were looking for the roots of the Jersey Devil in "physical or psychological abnormalities" (McCloy and Miller's words), maybe he was your guy.

If you preferred the story of the Jersey Devil and the headless pirate, consider the following note from The WPA Guide to 1930s New Jersey, concerning the Christ Episcopal Church in Middletown, the Anglican stronghold in East Jersey.

"The church is still supported by pirate gold," the WPA Guide said, "the income from 'conscience money' left to this church and another in Shrewsbury by William Leeds, aide to Captain Kidd."

The body of this William Leeds (our Daniel's brother) was said to be buried at an Anglican church in Shrewsbury. "The parish history" of this church, the Guide continued, "began October 20, 1702, with the baptism of 24 persons, including William Leeds, a reformed member of Captain Kidd's crew."

Among the belongings Leeds bequeathed to the church was a chest, "a plain rectangular box 4 feet long and 2½ feet deep, which the church has exhibited at times. It has a hidden compartment—empty."

If you preferred the "patriotic" version of the Jersey Devil story (McCloy and Miller's word), in which a British soldier

175

curses Mother Leeds, there was Jeremiah Leeds' tale about the British captain who confiscated his cows, prompting him to join the militia, leave the Quakers and eventually flee to Absecon Island.

If you preferred cursed preachers, that was easy. Daniel Leeds had cursed half the preachers in three colonies.

As a piece of historical trivia, I doubted it would ever be possible to know where the Jersey Devil story really came from. The project itself might have been nonsensical. It was simply too complex a question, and the sources were too incomplete. I can say with certainty that I no longer cared, at least not in the way that I had at the beginning.

Pinning responsibility to a particular person or set of historical circumstances came to feel like a misguided and possibly obscene enterprise, a kind of grave robbery. The attempt to turn the folklore into history seemed more or less identical with the attempt to monetize the story, which would be to monetize a personal tragedy. One of the few things that it *was* possible to say with some confidence about Deborah Leeds was that she had been the mother of twelve children. Between 1704 and 1726, she had been pregnant, or post-partum, for roughly ten years of her life. If she had been tired and frustrated and sick of it all, who could really blame her?

In a way it was reassuring that so little was known about her life. Daniel Leeds had been such a public figure and so visible in the historical record. Japhet, his son, had been relatively private and much less visible. Deborah, Japhet's wife, was a woman of course and therefore more or less invisible.

With Japhet and Deborah almost all you had were the vital statistics. Japhet Leeds: yeoman, born October 1682 in Springfield. Or maybe it was February 1683. Either way it was around the time of his father's initial fight with Samuel Jennings. Deborah had been Deborah Smith before she married Japhet. Even her surname discouraged further inquiry.

There was some evidence that Japhet had been baptized into the Anglican Church around the time of his twenty-first birthday, but then he had married Deborah, a Quaker, by 1704, even as his father was actively working to subvert the election of three West Jersey Quakers to the colonial assembly.[129] The effect that Daniel's various controversies would have had on his son and his daughter-in-law is impossible to know. The effect Japhet's return to Quakerism and marriage to a Quaker woman would have had on Daniel: likewise blank.

I suppose it's possible that Daniel wasn't overly exercised. For a time he'd practiced a different religion than his own parents. He was nothing if not flexible, capable of surprising you. Japhet named one of his sons after Daniel (1716), well after all this mess had gone down, but also after Daniel's career was essentially over. And then there was Daniel's own last will and testament, which lists Japhet but names Felix and Philo executors. It felt more likely that there had been some kind of epic holy war.

A copy of a survey of the lands of Japhet Leeds (made on the fourth of September 1739 by Japhet himself) offered few clues to the location of the ruins of his house.[130] This was the document that BeBop and I had been looking for in 1999 when I first met Harry Leeds.

The survey did nothing to pin the family residence down to a particular ruin, offering, as landmarks, things like a certain dead pine tree, current whereabouts unknown. It said the land—eighteen acres—was situated on a branch of the Egg Harbor River, near the head of the river, in what was then Gloucester County.[131] In 1726, the house of Japhet and Deborah Leeds had been the location of one of three Quaker Meetings in the county.[132]

That same year, an itinerant Quaker preacher named Thomas Chalkley had traveled through this region, stopping at the house of Japhet and Deborah near the Little Egg Harbor River, where the local Weekly Meeting was held. Chalkley de-

---

[129] Kintzel says Japhet was baptized in February 1704.
[130] A copy of the survey was at the Atlantic County Historical Society
[131] The Egg Harbor River is still the Egg Harbor. But the Little Egg Harbor is now the Mullica. You hope these differences in nomenclature were the result of carelessness...
[132] Hall, citing the minutes of the Haddonfield Quarterly Meeting

scribed the visit in his journals, which were later published.[133]

"We swam our horses over Egg Harbor river," Chalkley wrote, "and went over ourselves in canoes, and afterwards had a meeting at Richard Summers', which was as large as could be expected, considering the people live at such a distance from each other."

Twenty years earlier, Chalkley had made a similar journey and a similar entry in his journal. Upon arriving in Egg Harbor, "some Backsliders and Apostates were displeased," he wrote. "One (in a very bitter Spirit) called us Cursed and Cruel Devils. Another wrote against us. To him I sent an Answer, from which he scandalized me in one of his Almanacks, and publicly belied me in Print; which lies I swept away with a Small Broom, printed in 1706, to which I never understood that he return'd any Answer, nor that he wrote against Friends afterwards, tho' he had made it his Practice for several Years."

Chalkley must have been talking about Daniel Leeds, whom he'd met somewhere near Leeds Point in 1706. Chalkley's visit with Japhet two decades later was a visible point of contact between Daniel and his son, but it was the only visible point of contact I could find, and Chalkley did not remark on its significance.

FORTY

An important caveat, and more Quaker refugees

During my phone call with her, Cynthia Lamb had informed me, gently, that our branch of the Leeds family had not lived in Leeds Point continuously for the two hundred and forty years between the Keithian controversy and the Great Depression. For a few generations, they were elsewhere.

---

[133] Thomas Chalkley, *Journal or Historical Account of the Life, Travels, and Christian Experiences of that Ancient, Faithful Servant of Jesus Christ, Thomas Chalkley, who departed this Life in the Island of Tortola, the fourth Day of the Ninth Month, 1741* (1751)

According to the historian John Hall, Japhet Leeds had willed Leeds Point and Further Island to his son John. John Leeds in turn had a son William, who married Mary Osborne, and among their offspring was Richard (born 1771) from whom BeBop's branch of the family was descended. But Richard Leeds, apparently, left Leeds Point.

Joyce Kintzel, the genealogist, notes that at a Quaker monthly meeting in Egg Harbor in 1794 it was reported that a Richard Leeds, "had gone out in his marriage and hath been precautioned beforehand and tenderly dealt with since doth not appear to be in a suitable disposition of mind to make satisfaction."[134]

At the next monthly meeting, one of the Quakers was assigned to inform Richard of his precarious status within the Society and to draw up a document of disownment. At the next monthly meeting, Richard was served with his disownment notice, and he in turn "signaled" that he wouldn't appeal the decision. He was kicked out of the Society of Friends, and seems to have left Leeds Point—another Quaker refugee.

Where Richard went I don't know. I didn't look very hard. His son Joel appears to be buried at the Cedar Grove Cemetery in Gloucester City, just across the river from Philadelphia, across the width of the state from Leeds Point. "Capt. Joel Leeds," his gravestone reads.

Joel Leeds appears to have married on Long Island. In the genealogies it says Thomas Chalkley Leeds (Joel and Amy's son) was born about 1826, also on Long Island. This is the Thomas Leeds who married Emaline and is the father of Charles Augustus Leeds, BeBop's grandfather, who built the house on Leeds Point Road and made Leeds Devil tracks in the snow and told his grandchildren they were related to Leeds Devil. But in the mean time, parts of three generations— Richard, Joel and Thomas—had all lived outside Leeds Point.

I never asked BeBop or Aunt Dottie where Charles had been born. They had not been raised as Quakers, so if I'd thought about it, I would have realized at some point their branch of the family had split with the Society of Friends. Per-

134 Quoted in Kintzel, Tree of Leeds

haps this break had come with Richard. By all appearances it *had* come with Richard. But whenever it came, their grandfather was apparently from a branch of the family that had left Leeds Point after being forced out of the local Quaker Meeting, a fact that might account for some of this touchiness concerning the other local branches of the family tree ("them Oceanville Leedses" and so forth).

Some of the family had remained Quakers. According to Francis Bazley Lee, the local historian, Japhet and Deborah had another son, Japhet, who was born at Leeds Point in 1710 and who married Rebecca Woodward. Among their children was a Samuel Leeds, born in 1754. Samuel was a farmer, prominent Quaker, and for many years a minister. He married Lovica Barber and they had children with familiar names—Japhet, Ann, Hannah and June—but also Barzillai and Henry.

Through Henry Leeds came another Samuel Leeds and then another Henry—Henry West Leeds, born at Cinnaminson, in Burlington County, on October 28, 1868. According to Lee, Henry Leeds went to the Friends' Boarding School at Westtown and in 1890 moved to Atlantic City where he opened Haddon Hall with J. Haines Lippincott.

"During the twenty years that Mr. Leeds has been connected with the house, he has established a most enviable reputation among people of culture and refinement," Lee wrote. The hotel was said to have the best collection of water colors of any seaside resort hotel in the country.

Lee said that, "Mr. Leeds" was "a member of the Society of Friends. In politics he is an ardent and enthusiastic Republican, and has held many positions both elective and appointive."

Today Haddon Hall, which had still been Haddon Hall when my mom started working there in the 1960s, is Resorts Casino Hotel and the new home of a Jimmy Buffett Margaritaville restaurant and casino complex.

FORTY-ONE

Harry Leeds revisited

The second time I met Harry Leeds we rendezvoused, at his request, at the Smithville Inn in Galloway, perhaps thirty-five feet due east of the western boundary of Leeds Point. It was a weekday, and the place was filled with old ladies and United States Marines. They were wearing their full dress blues, the Marines—some kind of wedding rehearsal apparently.

Harry and I met in the main foyer by the big fireplace. I arrived first and milled around awkwardly for a minute or two before finding a seat. Then Harry arrived and I stood awkwardly up just as he plopped himself comfortably down and started chatting up the old ladies. Within about fifteen seconds he was holding court, the old ladies laughing and carrying on.

That Harry Leeds, I thought. Always politicking. Always *on*.

It's possible that Harry remembered me, but I don't think so. Nearly ten years had elapsed since that first fateful encounter, and I hadn't spoken to him since. Someone at the Galloway Municipal Complex had given me his number, and I'd explained to him over the phone a little bit about my project, avoiding any specific reference to his documentary film work. I told him I was interested mostly in the Leeds family and in its long association with the Jersey Devil story. Maybe it was just me, but he seemed relieved by this.

We left the Inn and walked across Route Nine to where Harry's beige SUV—a little Bronco I think—was parked in a big field. He was smoking a KOOL Super Long cigarette, holding it between his middle and index fingers. There was something slightly diva-ish in the gesture, if it's possible to be at all diva-ish when you're a seventy-year-old ex-Marine with a pot belly who likes to joke about being the product of incest.

The inside of the Bronco smelled of cigarettes. Harry said he'd been traveling a lot back and forth to Delaware. A Wawa bag tied to the gear stick served as a trash bag.

He pulled out of the parking lot and headed south on

181

Route Nine, then west on Moss Mill Road, driving away from Leeds Point, further into Galloway proper, and we passed a stretch of woods where a stream had been dammed up, forming a little pond. Harry said it had been an old cranberry bog and that he'd picked cranberries there in his younger days, but I wasn't sure I was supposed to take this literally.

Another mile and Harry stopped the car on the roadside. We got out and he directed my attention into the screen of trees where the remains of some kind of building were visible. Someone had put a little fence up, chain-link. And this, Harry would have me understand, was the remains of the house where Harry's family believed that Mother Leeds had given birth to the Jersey Devil in 1735.

I knew—and Harry knew I knew—that he and his family believed no such thing. We were not looking at the ruins of an eighteenth-century structure, as the tangle of wires and shards of mass-produced glass plainly indicated. I'm not even convinced it was the remains of a house.

Harry seemed to sense my skepticism and changed tacks, speaking abstractedly about his usual routine when documentarians and camera crews came to him for help. He said he would typically take them to this spot from a different direction, walking through the woods along a path that ran beside the pond.

By now I was familiar enough with Harry's oeuvre to know this was the site he'd been taking film crews to for some years. Sometimes he would tell the story of his own personal encounter with the Jersey Devil, which had taken place "just at dark time" one day when he was a boy.

It was right here, he would say, right on this spot. "And the most prominent features of the devil was those piercing eyes, that were at ya!"

The place had everything, Harry said—the Pine Barrens, the cranberry bog, the earthen dam built by anonymous Piney hands and here, at the finish line, the ruins of the Jersey Devil house. Except it wasn't the Jersey Devil house. We weren't even in Leeds Point.

It was late in the day and it was getting dark. Harry said he

182

didn't know how much time I had. We got back in the car and he drove back toward Leeds Point, and he started talking, pointing out the scenes of various events from his childhood, rattling off the names of the people who had lived in this or that house.

We passed Lilly Lake, and Harry said he'd once had to pull a dead body out of the water there. We passed the house where Harry's grandmother, a Conover, had lived and the house of old Milt Hynser, who used to call BeBop "String Bean."

"Young Milt is an antique gun dealer," Harry said.

We passed another house. "Mayor Endicott lives here," he said. "This here is an old house, but these here are new. These are all new. Everett Doughty used to live in this old house right here. I mean Everett Armbruster. The only other houses back in those days were these here.

"The guy I was telling you about we pulled out of the lake used to live right here. Committed suicide. There was a Conover that lived right here.

"And this was an old house. This was an older house. This house here used to be a chicken farm when I was a kid. That's my son's house right there. That big one on the corner. That used to be a restaurant. Here's an old one. And this one here—my Uncle Jack owned that.

"All the towns are named after families," he said. "Higbeetown, Johnsontown, Smiths had Smithville. Leeds Point for the Leedses. Oceanville in them days was called Tanner Brook. Conovertown.

"Route Nine was the main route from here to New York. Wasn't no Parkway in those days.

"Atlantic City was called Leeds Plantation. Jeremiah Leeds, so he owned all the property over there, and he was married a couple different times. I guess one of his wives had a whorehouse over there. Chalkley Leeds was the first mayor."

Harry had turned off Route Nine and was now heading down Leeds Point Road toward the end of the point. "There's the Leeds Point Cemetery," he said. "Lot of old Leedses there." We passed the old post office, which used to double as a gas station and general store. "That there is where I got educated," he said. "Right in that old building right there."

Harry said he used to pick beans on a farm in what is now the wildlife refuge. We passed the big stone house at the end of Moss Mill Road, where Dan Sooy and Jesse Mathis had lived. "A lot of people think this is the house," Harry said.

Harry had somehow served in both the U.S. Marine Corps and in the Army. Depending on whom you talked to, he had either enlisted or been required to enlist, as a result of certain childhood adventures that brought him to the attention of the local judiciary.

Once in the military, he'd been sent to Vietnam where he was assigned to be the liaison to a film crew making documentaries in support of the war effort. It had been his first experience with public relations. I couldn't hear the name of the director, but Harry seemed to think he was important.

And indeed as we reached the marshes down at the bottom of Scotts Landing Road, Harry's vocabulary grew wonderfully cinematic, full of references to panning shots and vantage points and lighting effects. From this spot you could look out across the marshes toward Atlantic City, and then pan back toward the tree line where the mainland began. "I usually get them out here just before it gets dark. That way you see that sun coming through the leaves. It's really beautiful.

"Because I get crews coming in from all over the country," he continued, "primarily from California and New York. And they run on my schedule. I know the area and what they're looking for. I'll start them out here and come up and say, 'This is where the Pine Barrens starts and the meadows and where the Jersey Devil hung out and all that. So it's a nice scene."

When Harry got out of the military, he returned to South Jersey and bought the bar on the White Horse Pike and got into politics, and he stayed in politics at least part-time for twenty years.

"Hated it," he said.

"I got in a fight with everybody. I was here to serve the people, and you can't solve everybody's problems. I got elected five times here, and I never even run. They just throw my name on the ballot. I used to tell them, 'You know, I'm related to fifty percent of the people.'

"I was appointing a police officer one time whose name was Leeds. I got this guy in the audience saying—or, you know, guy and a lady both. Lady says, '*You believe in nepotism Leeds!*' and all this.

"I said, 'I'm related to—at that time—seventy-five percent of the people in town, 'cause my grandfather was quite a rounder. You might even be related to me.' They shut the hell up."

In the woods off Scotts Landing Road, behind the old stone house, Harry said, "My great-great grandfather lived over there, Jesse Leeds. I could barely remember coming up here, but I can remember."

We passed another house set back in the woods.

"My dad built that place."

"It's going to get confusing," he said. "My grandmother was a Leeds that married a Leeds. A Leeds from Leeds Point married a Leeds from Oceanville. People ask me, 'What's wrong with you, Leeds?' I say, 'I'm a inbred. What's your excuse?

"My whole family worked in the bays. Everybody worked in the bay, because that's how you ate. My father, my grandfathers, my great-great grandfathers—they were all bay men. They run rum before that, rumrunners. You pressed for time? We'll run out to the crick."

The restaurant, Oyster Creek, sits on a pile of seashells beside a little tidal stream about a mile out into the marshes. To get there, you drive down a long and straight road that is lined on either side with a thin screen of cedar trees.

As we made our way to the restaurant, Harry's mood seemed to grow increasingly confessional, so I decided to ask him *why* he did it, finally: why he took reporters around and told them we were afraid of the Jersey Devil, why he led them through this routine.

"Well, that's—the question is—why do I do it?" he said. "Why do I take the time. And I always talk from the legend, not from the thousand or so sightings. I leave it up to the reporters to do that…"[135]

He evaded for another minute or so, before trailing off without really answering my question. But he did mention another movie that he'd made, at the Down Jersey Folklife Center in Millville, but he mentioned it without any special emphasis, and I didn't even notice it until I listened to the tape again months later.

It was the culmination of ten years of reporting, but that's as close as I got to putting him on the spot.

FORTY-TWO

Harry doesn't eat crabs

Oyster Creek was closed. There were crab pots under the porch. The cats that used to haunt the place had been kicked out. "Board of health must have got to them or something," Harry said.

I said I didn't really have the patience to eat crabs.

"I'm not a crab-picker," he said. "If you ever pull a dead body out of the bay, you'll never eat crabs again."

"That's what they like?"

"Oh *man*. Them and eels. I used to love them. Once you see them damn eels squirming out of a body—No more for me."

FORTY-THREE

'Somebody worked overnight'

He took me to meet his father, Harry Senior, a little round-headed, elfish man in a New York Yankees baseball hat. It looked somehow distinctly more woolen than your typical baseball hat.

---

[135] This was not strictly accurate. Harry did claim to have seen the beast.

186

We showed up unannounced at the rancher-type house or apartment where Harry Senior lived off Route Nine in Oceanville, and where he was hanging out with his girlfriend, Marge.

Harry Junior wanted to see if his dad had the right medicines in the right quantities for the weekend or if a pharmacy run was necessary. "I got my bodyguard with me," Junior said as we walked in the door, meaning me.

Harry Senior was in his nineties. His health wasn't good. His hearing was nonexistent. But he seemed happy to have the company.

We sat there amid the wood paneling in the falling winter light and a mystery resolved itself. BeBop and Aunt Dottie had been childhood schoolmates of Harry *Senior*, whom they'd been confusing with his son all these years.

I told him that BeBop had died not long ago and he remembered her and seemed genuinely sorry to hear it, which endeared me to him instantly. Before long, it was tough to see why they'd thought of him as such a boogieman.

"You say Helen died?" he said. "I'm sorry to hear that. She was a real nice girl."

"Did you go to the one-room schoolhouse over here?" I asked.

A few seconds elapsed and Harry Senior said nothing.

Harry Junior raised his hands to his mouth and shouted.

"HE ASKED WHAT SCHOOLHOUSE DID YOU GO TO WHEN YOU STARTED OUT.

"YOU WENT RIGHT UP HERE, DIDN'T YA?"

Harry senior looked at his son. "Yeah," he said.

"Walked, snow rain and what. We had a lot of fun there, boy. My uncles, some of them went there. They were *ornery*. Had an old wooden stove outside. A, what ya call it, little *wooden thing* for a toilet..."

"An outhouse," Junior said.

"OUT HOUSE."

"Outhouse, yeah," Senior said.

"I'll take that and them days instead of this."

"Were you a fisherman?" I said.

"I clammed. I done everything," Senior said.

187

"He drove a coal truck," Junior said. "Sixteen dollars a week, wasn't it?"

"No. Fourteen dollars an hour," Senior said. "Four dollars an hour, I mean."

"*No*," Junior said. "You didn't make fourteen dollars a *day*. That's when you had to bag your coal and haul it," he said to me.

"Damn right, boy!" Senior said. "Hundred-pound bags. And carry them up three flights of stairs over in Atlantic [City]. Load 'em on, swing them up."

"He wonders why he's got a bad back," Marge said.

Harry Junior led us on a mental tour of the byways of Leeds Point and eastern Galloway Township, and though Harry Senior was very old, his memory failing, he gave a convincing account of where the various Leedses had lived.

"My golly," Marge kept saying. "I never realized there were so many Leedses around."

Marge's last name was Horner, she said, but she too was related to the Jersey Devil.

"My father had a gas station, Harry Horner's."

Harry Junior said that when he was a child the men would work in the bays, fishing during the day, and at night they would cut ditches in the marshes. The ditches, when they were completed, filled up with water and could be used to transport the day's shellfish catch from the bay to the clam houses on the mainland. The men would drag their catch in mesh bags, as they walked beside the ditches. If you had your own clam house, you could sell directly to the public or to retailers. Otherwise you left your catch in a sack in front of your house, and a wholesaler would purchase the clams from you to sell to retail markets in Absecon or Atlantic City, or Philadelphia even.

It was a half mile across the marshes from the mainland to the bay. The men would work half the night, cutting their ditches by hand, and then go home and sleep a few hours before getting up to go fishing and do it all again.

"I'd put those guys up against anyone for work," Junior said. "They were tough. They could gun too. Them guys were good gunners. They didn't miss."

Junior said it took the men "less than a few years" to finish the ditch-digging project.

"They done it at nighttime because the meadows would stiffen up—the mud would—and it would be easier. Grandpop and Jack had the same crick for a while until they got fighting. It was interesting I tell you."

During the Depression men from Leeds Point and Oceanville were paid to dig ditches in the salt marshes in Galloway, as they were all over New Jersey, as part of a scheme to dry out the marshes and rid the state of the notorious salt marsh mosquito, *Ochlerotatus sollicitans*, bane of tourism and agriculture. When the salt marshes were drained, the resulting soil would resemble in fertility the soils of Illinois or the Nile Valley, scientists had said.

"You say your grandfather was Charles Leeds?" Senior asked me.

"My great-great grandfather."

"I remember him—big, tall guy with a mustache."

Which was absolutely true.

Harry Senior seemed to think for a while.

"Two or three bunches of Leeds in there, in those lanes," he said.

"And you're related to the Jersey Devil like I am?"

"Yeah. Yup. I guess so. I *was*."

"So's Marge," Junior said.

"I don't know where so many Leedses come from," Senior said. "Somebody must have worked overnight."

Harry Leeds Senior told a story about an old blind man who used to walk around Leeds Point, led by his wife. The old man couldn't see a thing, Harry said, but he could get around when led by the arm. He sure could get around. Apparently the wife did all the talking, an idea that Senior found hilarious.

"Duck Feet?" Junior said.

"ARE YOU TALKING ABOUT DUCK FEET?"

Harry Junior said that as a kid he had worked picking beans and blueberries in different farms throughout Galloway. He and his father briefly debated the price for a pint of beans during the 1940s. Junior reminded Senior that he ran a team of

189

bean-pickers and was an authority on pricing. "I was in charge of the money," he said.

Senior seemed to find this idea irresistibly funny.

"Who *you?*" he said, and he laughed.

"How is New York?" Senior said, to me.

"Very loud," I said. "Very busy."

"That's like what we got around here," Senior said.

"Well, maybe I'll see you some time again. If you're ever down this way again, stop in. I like to talk about old people— not old *people* but the old *times*. I hate to see them gone. I've seen a lot of death."

Harry Senior wasn't a well man. He spoke in a low mumble that was almost impossible to understand. Listening to the tape was like looking at a Rorschach test. I couldn't tell if I was hearing things or making them up, but I think he really did make that joke about proliferation of Leeds in the region being the result of somebody's "working overnight."

Within a few months of the visit, Harry Senior had died. I happened across his grave one day when I stopped by the Oceanville cemetery. Beside it there was a little plinth with a beer can on it and a plaster statue of Bambi.

"Harry Leeds," it said. "The Deer Hunter."

FORTY-FOUR

Return to the Galloway Muni Complex

I went back to the Galloway Township Municipal Complex, this time to meet Ken Sooy, the Official Township Historian. Like Leeds, the name Sooy has a long history in South Jersey. McPhee, in his book about the Pine Barrens, says, "Sooy is a German name more common in the Pines than Smith." Ken Sooy said he must have been related somehow to Dan Sooy from Beck's book, but he didn't know how precisely.

Ken was a Galloway lifer and lived in the house where he grew up in Leeds Point. Like Harry, he'd made the rounds on the Jersey Devil documentary film circuit, and like BeBop, he seemed to want to strangle Harry Leeds, and for similarly sub-liminal reasons. Ken operated a landscaping business and nursery on his property in Leeds Point. He had big mutton chops and smelled like grass clippings. It was the busy season, he said, for the nursery, but he took the time to meet me.

I hadn't been back to the Galloway Municipal Complex since 1999, but little had changed—the same old-school TV set, the same VCR stand that looked like it had been lifted from the AV room at my high school, and apparently the same VCR. On the walls were maps, including one, an old Beers Map, that BeBop and I had gone to consult the first time I met Harry. There was a statue of the Jersey Devil, stark naked, on one of the shelves. On the map you could seen the outline of the Shourds property.

Ken said he thought that Mother Leeds was really a Shourds, a conclusion that he based, I think, on this map. "My research shows me that Mother Leeds was actually a Shourds," he said. "They would never have called a woman by her maiden name after thirteen kids—or twelve kids. It would have never happened. So she had to be married to a Leeds. And the house that all the evidence I have points to comes up as being a Shourds house, back on the old maps, so it indicates to me that a Leeds married a Shourds and lived in the Shourds house. That's the opinion I have."

"Do you have a specific couple in mind?" I said.

"No, I do not," he said. "Shourds would be the logical name of the woman that married the man. The other thing is the Shourds family practiced a little bit of herbalism, when they first came here, and to a bunch of Quakers, that might have stirred some *evil thoughts*."

The logic was the same that BeBop and I had followed. The oral tradition, as it had come down to him through family members, gave Ken the location of the ruins of the Jersey Devil house, and the map gave him the name of the old own-er. Rounding out the argument was the description of the site given to Henry Beck by Carrie Bowen. And the fact that Bow-en had called the mother of the Jersey Devil a Shourds.

Ken said he thought the story probably had its origins when a "deformed" child had been born in Leeds Point.

191

"What we really think happened, after doing a little bit of research—especially some history on how people treated different people at different times—we really believe that there was a deformed child born, probably a Down syndrome kid. If she truly had thirteen kids, I mean, it would be very good odds for a Down syndrome kid to be born."

The child would have been kept hidden away, but inevitably people would have seen or heard things. They would have imagined the rest. That was the theory anyway.

"My great-grandfather, who was born in 1866, said that up until cars came around, you could frequently—if the wind was blowing from the ocean—you could hear the breakers on Brigantine beach at night," Ken said. "If the sea was up a little bit, if the wind was blowing that way, especially in the summertime when you had the windows open. There was no noise pollution, no cars, no planes, no buses, no nothing. Any noise was amplified. We can't even comprehend what that noise was like, where there was no other noises."

Ken corroborated a feeling I'd had since my second meeting with Harry Leeds—namely that his reasons for taking me to that random ruin in Smithville weren't wholly cinematic. The spate of nonsense documentaries on The Discovery and History Channels etc. had inspired another round of unwanted tourism to Leeds Point. As a result, Harry had been banned from the real site, Ken said.

"The only reason he took them [film crews, and me] to the site he took them to, was because nobody would bother him," he said. "He wasn't allowed to go to the actual site. He had gotten into problems with the…with the family that lives on that site and they wouldn't allow him on their land."

Though Ken was a little reluctant himself to tell me where he thought the actual Jersey Devil house was located, he said he thought it was the site that Carrie Bowen had shown to Beck in Jersey Genesis.

Ken had known Carrie Bowen (whom he called "Mrs. Carrie Mathis Bowen") personally. She had been his math teacher in grade school, and had real esteem for her as an educator and a source for local folklore. "I had her for two years," in school,

Ken said, "and the woman—I never seen her tell a lie. And she was meticulous in the fact that, if you didn't dot an *i* on your paper, you got a zero. That's how she was—very meticulous—and she testified that that was the house where the legend had come from. I just believe she told the truth."

Aunt Dottie had also known Carrie Bowen but had a different impression. "She couldn't tell the truth" she said. "Schoolteacher, down in Pleasantville."

Aunt Dottie said that Bowen had the wrong house. She said she couldn't understand how anyone who'd lived in Leeds Point could fail to know the right spot. "We knew a different place that they always said—the old-timers did—that he was born in a completely different house to what that Carrie Bowen said it was."

That Carrie Bowen also claimed somehow to be related to the Leeds family, but she too had been on Grand-pop Charles' shit-list.

"He wouldn't have her related to the Leedses, because she couldn't tell the truth," Dottie said.

When I went back to Ken and told him my great-aunt disagreed with Bowen, he said, "Well, there's two possible sites, and there is debate. I've been to both of them. Either one is possible. They're within five hundred feet of each other, so I don't get too concerned."

Ken Sooy had known both Harry Senior and Harry Junior his whole life, and he too seemed to have had his share of run-ins with the Leeds gentlemen.

"Harry Jr. spent a lot of his life in the military," Ken said, "because he was basically *required* to *enlist* shall we say. Because of some kind of problems, *juvenile* problems, put it that way. Of course, that didn't come out in the elections."

In those days if you got in trouble you could choose to go into the military or go to reform school, and Harry chose the Marines. And it made a "good person" out of him, or a "decent person" anyway, Ken said. He married a military woman (Ellie) and had been away from Galloway for a number of years. After his stint in the Marines, Harry joined a different service branch. He joined the Army.

"Harry wasn't around here a whole lot from 'fifty-three or 'fifty-four," Ken said. "He wasn't around here for at least twenty years. When he did come back he got involved in politics very quickly. And after he got in politics he bought the bar, and he stayed involved in politics pretty much up until he died, at least in spirit. The last few years, the last few years he was sick. But he wasn't sick a long time."

FORTY-FIVE

Daniel Leeds' astrological toolkit

In Cynthia Lamb's Brigid's Charge, Deborah Leeds keeps her devotion to the Old Religion—to the heathen or countryside tradition of her maternal ancestors—a secret from her own husband and from most of her children. Lamb herself keeps open the question of whether the various reconciliations she imagines are in fact possible. But out of this one failed reconciliation—between the Old Religion and the Quaker Christianity of West Jersey—Lamb imagines that the Leeds Devil was born, and this struck me as a singularly apt metaphor for understanding the persistence of the Jersey Devil story in modern New Jersey.

The Quakers had always objected to Leeds' Almanac. Anyone who knew anything about the family knew that much. I even knew that the Quakers opposed the document due to its "heathenish" contents (a word used by Daniel and his contemporaries), which I took to mean Daniel's insistence on using the Gregorian calendar, with its familiar names—Thursday, Friday, March, June etc.—for the days of the week and the months of the year. The Quaker convention was to refer to the days and months numerically—First Month, Second Month, First Day, Second Day, etc.—since to do otherwise was to evoke gods of the old religions (Thor, Frigga, Mars etc.) whom the Quakers wished to suppress. But Leeds' Almanac *was* the old religion. Simply changing the names at the top of the page wasn't going to change that.

Daniel Leeds, as almanac-maker, was a practitioner of an occult belief system. The advice his almanacs gave—on planting, on medicine, on the killing of bedbugs, on the peeling of onions—was understood to proceed from his knowledge of the movements of the heavenly spheres. Daniel Leeds was an astrologer.

The Leeds Almanac was an astrological toolkit. It gave readers the data they needed to make their own astrological calculations. And astrology—along with the arts of geomancy, chiromancy, alchemy, metascopy, etc.—was part of the Old Religion, one of the heathen or pagan traditions that predated Christianity and that had existed, beside or beneath it, for seventeen hundred years.

During times of détente, when practiced by the right sort, such arts were not incompatible with membership in polite Christian society, but under different conditions, when practiced by persons of uncertain social standing, they were black magic, part of Satan's arsenal against humanity. They were a variety of witchcraft.

Daniel must have been at least as well known for his almanac-writing as he was for any of the religious or political controversies he took part in. The almanac is the one great constant across his career. He himself wrote almanacs for twenty-seven years, beginning with his first published work, the "Almanack for the YEAR of Christian Account 1687," published toward the end of 1686. The almanac franchise, established by Daniel and passed down to his children, continued for parts of six decades.

In the beginning they were simple documents, one or two pages of vertical columns, little more than calendars really. But as the years went on they got longer and more elaborate. Beside the entries for some days would be symbols corresponding with parts of the human body. Beside others would be little notations ("Remarka.days" for instance or "Purific.Of Mary"). Beside some days he made suitably vague weather predictions ("Windy weather" or "fore tells Snow") that I think BeBop, who liked to poke fun at the "weather guessers" would have gotten a kick out of.

By 1693, the almanac was up to fifty-one pages. The 1697 almanac ("By Daniel Leeds, Philomat.") was twenty-two pages. The 1706 almanac ("The American Almanack") was twenty-four pages. Across the tops of the calendars would appear the names of the months in their familiar Gregorian forms, but beside the familiar names (preceding them in fact) the months would be identified by number, according to Quaker custom. Thus: "The xi. Month, January," from the time when January was the eleventh month and New Year was observed in March.

After Leeds' split with the Quakers, the emphasis on *heathenish* elements seemed to increase in intensity. By 1693, January wasn't just *January* it was "Januarius" for *Roman Janus*, "their first Heathen King and God." April was referred to as Second Month but also as "Dripping April" or "*Zif.*" March was First Month but also "Blustering March" or "*Abib.*" Fourth Month was June ("Hot June") and also "Tamuz." Tenth Month was "Tebeth" and "Leaf-less December."

Some years the almanacs contained something called the Anatomy, a little human figure surrounded by signs of the zodiac, that was designed to assist readers in prescribing medicines based on astrological principles. Some editions contained Vulgar Notes—lists of days and numbers and letters that were believed to possess magical significance. The historian Richard Godbeer says Leeds Almanac itself was a "tabular equivalent of the Anatomy."[136] The whole document was a handbook on astrological medicine, among other occult arts.

Daniel Leeds was an advocate of judicial astrology, the notion that the movement of the heavens directly affected human affairs, including political affairs. When Harry Leeds had suggested, in 1999, that the Jersey Devil predicted wars, I thought it one of the more outlandish claims ever made about the beast. But the idea of the Jersey Devil as "harbinger" perhaps had its origins in the astrology of Leeds' almanacs three centuries earlier.[137]

---

[136] Godbeer, *The Devil's Dominion: Magic and Religion in Early New England* (1994)

[137] Or see for instance, J. Elfreth Watkins' description of Leeds Devil as a "harbinger" in 1899, or Caleb Pusey's "Satan's Harbinger" from 1700.

Daniel Leeds' book *Temple of Wisdom* (1688) was essentially an anthology of Old Religion philosophy, consisting mostly of writings by the German mystic Jacob Boehme and essays by Sir Francis Bacon. Leeds approvingly summarized astrological works by William Lilly and John Partridge. Jon Butler, the historian, says Daniel quoted works by Hermes Trismegistus (father of Hermeticism) and "trumpeted" Paracelsian medicine and "defended the general proposition" that eclipse affected world politics.[138]

The historian Arthur Versluis has suggested that Daniel's surveying may itself have been a kind of geomancy, another form of divination.[139] Versluis says Temple of Wisdom was probably the first Christian theosophical work in America.

Occult practices, including astrology, were more or less acceptable among polite society during the seventeenth century. Butler notes that William Lilly, the English astrologer, averaged more than two thousand occult consultations per year between 1645 and 1660. Lilly and his colleagues wrote books and almanacs that were "eagerly consumed by the reading public," Butler says. It wasn't just poor or illiterate folk, Butler says, but also "wealthy" and "prestigious" men who sought out such advice.[140] Lilly's clients came from the leading merchant and aristocratic families.

Almanac-making was a competitive enterprise. The actual charts and predictions of celestial events—eclipses and solstices etc.—were more or less fungible. Publishers sometimes bought them wholesale from third-party suppliers. Where the successful almanac-maker distinguished himself was in the ancillary matter, the introductions and conclusions, and here Leeds excelled. The historian Marion Barber Stowell says Leeds might have written the first true farmer's almanac in America, the first to be directed primarily at rural audiences, with agricultural reminders and advice on husbandry. Leeds included practical information on the location and schedules of courts and fairs. He continued to give information on the

---

[138] Butler, "Magic, Astrology and the Early American Religious Heritage," in *The American Historical Review*, April 1979

[139] Versluis, *The Esoteric Origins of the American Renaissance* (2001)

[140] Butler, Magic

meetings of the Quakers long after his split with the Society. His "Short Description of Highways" became a regular feature of later almanacs. He included aphorisms forty years before Franklin used them in *Poor Richard's.*[141]

The historian Peter Eisenstadt says the typical eighteenth-century almanac had a print run of four or five thousand copies. Nathaniel Ames, at his peak, printed fifty thousand to sixty thousand per year. I have no idea how many Leeds Almanacs were sold but Daniel probably did better than most. "No genre of print in eighteenth-century America had as wide or general circulation as the almanac," Eisenstadt says.[142] It's often said they outsold the Bible.

"The popularity of the almanacs was linked directly to their occult contents," Butler says. Daniel Leeds' occultism, in other words, was linked directly to his success as a writer and entrepreneur. Butler argues that some almanac-makers might not have subscribed to the occult philosophy their almanacs espoused, but merely included their Anatomies and Zodiacs to appeal to audiences. He cites Samuel Clough, the author of the *New York Almanac,* who wrote in one year's edition, "The Anatomy must still be in, Else the Almanack's not worth a pin."[143] These occult elements were exactly the parts of Leeds Almanacs that the Quakers wanted to expunge.

Whether Leeds invoked the ancient gods of the old religions for marketing purposes or spite or out of his own prior commitments (or all three), he invoked them to great effect. August was the month when "bright Phoebus," having warmed the northern hemisphere, retired "nimbly toward the Southern," and the refreshing "Gales of Zephyrus" began to "refrigerate the scorching Sun-Beams." In April the "Nymphs of the Woods in Comfort" welcomed "Aurora." In January ("the Rich mans Charge and the Poor mans Misery") the "Cold (like the Dayes)" increased but "qualified with the hopes and expectations of the approaching Spring." I spent one

---

[141] Stowell, "American Almanacs and Feuds," in *Early American Literature* (Winter, 1975)

[142] Eisenstadt, "Almanacs and the Disenchantment of Early America," in Pennsylvania History (Spring 1998)

[143] Quoted in Butler, Magic

astonished evening reading Leeds' romantic, agrarian poetry before realizing it was a wholesale plagiary of Hesiod.

When Daniel was not offering poetic reflections on the turning of the seasons, he gave practical advice on the killing of bedbugs, on when to bleed and purge, when to cut superfluous branches, when to advantageously geld sheep—all based on the heavenly progress of the spheres. "I am informed," he wrote, that weevils can be killed using salt. The practice of "bathing in rivers" in July, he observed, was "wholesome." The "peeling of Onions," at any time, he said, was "vexatious."

Leeds said America was a country that made poor men rich and rich men poor. If he himself had ever become rich, it would have likely been through almanac sales. The documents, for which he had a built-in audience every year, must have been a powerful platform for a controversialist. Compared to the dreary theological tracts of his rivals, Leeds Almanacs were riveting. Maybe the most offensive part of Leeds' success, to the Quakers, was that it drew them into the almanac business, where they had to go if only to compete with Leeds. But even this might have helped Daniel's popularity. Almanac feuds, too, would become a time-honored way to encourage sales.

In News of a Trumpet, Daniel's initial statement of faith, Leeds said his decision to publish in support of the Keithian cause and against the Quaker orthodoxy had been due to "a motion heavenly." In 1691, he wrote, "when Differences arose at Philadelphia between George Keith and others" his "Understanding and intellect" were "again enlarged…and I began to find a Call within me…Wherefore I set a Resolution to Search and Try things for myself, and not to believe on trust, because others did."

The significance of the phrase "motion heavenly" had been lost on me, but it had not been lost on Caleb Pusey, who threw the words back at Daniel in Satan's Harbinger, in a fling about Leeds and his "pretended motion heavenly." Daniel had been talking about his astrology of course. The two major controversies of his life, Daniel seemed to be saying—his support for Keith and his commitment to the almanac—had the same metaphysical source in his commitment to an occult belief system.

Whether we take him at his word, of course, is another question. But it had been the Quakers' attempt to suppress the almanac and to seek retribution against the Keithians that had led to the pamphlet wars, to Satan's Harbinger, to Daniel's flight to Leeds Point and all the rest.

But the world was changing. The power that magic and occult belief held on the society at large was on the wane. What had been acceptable and popular among educated and influential persons of the middle seventeenth century would become unacceptable and unpopular by the middle eighteenth. Leeds almanac would lose its influence with or without the Quakers.

The timing and causes of this phenomenon are naturally the subject of extensive debate among historians far more qualified than I. Eisenstadt writes that, "The hold of occultism on popular culture grew increasingly tenuous after 1700," but he notes that recent scholarship has emphasized the "continuing vigor" of magic, arguing that "popular magic, untouched by the currents of the Enlightenment, continued to flourish throughout the eighteenth century."[144]

Butler dates the decline of popular magic to 1720, the year of Daniel Leeds' death incidentally. Almanacs stopped predicting political events, he says. They stopped listing astrological signs along with their herbal recommendations, and they began to emphasize the natural properties of medicines rather than their celestial significance.[145] "Although basic astrological information still appeared in almanacs," he writes, "after about 1720 no almanac-makers promoted sophisticated occult ideas as Pennsylvania's Daniel Leeds [sic] and Jacob Taylor had done earlier."[146]

The causes of occultism's decline are likewise debated. Enlightenment philosophy and skepticism helped discredit belief in occult magic. New medical techniques limited its usefulness. Evangelical Christianity replaced its ritual forms. Opposition from establishment religion helped drive it underground.

---

[144] Eisenstadt, Almanacs and Disenchantment

[145] Butler, Magic

[146] Butler, Magic

Modern industry and economic life upset the cultural ecology in which it had flourished. Legal threats made it risky. Rising literacy consigned it to the undereducated and impoverished fringe. In an oft-cited passage from 1762, Nathaniel Low wrote that, "all who write fashionably at this Day, condemn [astrology]…as nothing but a mere whim, and all who pretend to knowledge of it, are derided and set as nought as nothing but a parcel of Fantasticks that are with their insipid Delusions endeavoring to impose on the Publick."[147] Whatever the reasons, if Daniel Leeds' children chose to remain in the family business, they faced much different career prospects than their father.

Both Eisenstadt and Butler agree that belief in magic would not have failed unilaterally across the society. Eisenstadt writes at some length on Max Weber's idea of *disenchantment*. Magic did not die out entirely, but its social strength was greatly diminished, even as individuals held on to their own particular beliefs. Butler says there's reason to think occult practices survived until the Revolution, but they did so idiosyncratically. He calls this shift from formal to informal, from acceptable to forbidden, from high caste to low class the "folklorization" of magic. What had been public and social became private, individual and fragmented. But belief in magic did not go away, it simply went *elsewhere*—away from the center of public life.

In another oft-cited passage, from 1770, Ezra Stiles said of occultism and pagan belief, "Something of it subsists among some Almanac makers and fortune tellers," but "in general the System is broken up, the Vessel of Sorcery ship-wreckt, and only some shattered planks and pieces disjoined floating and scattered on the Ocean of…human Activity and Bustle." He couldn't have picked a better metaphor if he had been writing about the Leedses themselves.

---

[147] Quoted in Eisenstadt, Almanacs and Disenchantment

FORTY-SIX

Revisiting Daniel

Historians have tended to see Daniel Leeds either as a small-time political functionary and petty criminal, or as a borderline madman and habitual purveyor of salacious nonsense. Religious and cultural historians, while acknowledging the influence of his almanacs, have tended to emphasize Daniel's general contentiousness and frequent feuds.

Patricia Bonomi, the Cornbury biographer, says Leeds was a "printer by trade [sic]" who practiced the "Grub Street style" and who raked Quaker history for subjects to shower with ridicule. With "a convert's zeal," she says, Leeds led "the effort to discredit Friends in New Jersey."[148]

Donald Kemmerer calls Leeds a "petty politician" and an "amenable" surveyor general who could be relied upon to disregard the law at the convenience of his political masters.[149] Edwin Tanner calls him an "especially subservient tool" of Governor Coxe and a henchman of Governor Cornbury.[150] John Pomfret says Leeds can't be trusted to count accurately the number of Quakers in the colonies owing to his dislike for the religious group.[151] Henry Cadbury calls Leeds "a violent opponent of orthodox Friends."[152]

Marion Barber Stowell, a historian of colonial almanac-making, says Leeds was innovative but contentious. "Daniel was outspoken, vindictive, and perhaps hypersensitive," she says, "yet he had a sense of humor."[153] Edward Cody says Leeds was a "fiery Keith supporter" who "accused just about

---

[148] Bonomi, The Lord Cornbury Scandal

[149] Kemmerer, Path

[150] Tanner, Province of New Jersey

[151] Pomfret, "West New Jersey: A Quaker Society 1675-1775," William and Mary Quarterly, October 1951

[152] Cadbury, "Quakerism and Uncanonical Lore," *The Harvard Theological Review* (July, 1947)

[153] "Almanacs and Feuds," in Early American Literature (Winter, 1975)

every leading Quaker of either fornication, adultery, drunkenness, thievery, blasphemy, homosexuality or a combination of these vices," and was "denounced" by Caleb Pusey for his dishonesty and gross perversions.[154]

But if Leeds was a subservient tool, I'm not sure whom for exactly. His fight with the Quakers spanned parts of four decades, nearly all his adult life. It predated Cornbury's arrival in the colonies by a decade (at least), and it continued for a decade after Keith returned to England (at least).

In fact Leeds' career can be seen as a sustained fight against one person, Samuel Jennings, with whom he might have had some personal beef dating back to his earliest years in the colony. In the early 1690s during the Keithian controversy, Jennings was the clerk of the Quarterly Meeting of Ministers in Philadelphia and a Magistrate in the city's court, putting him squarely in the sights of Keith's proposed reforms. When the Keithians questioned the propriety of Public Friends' serving simultaneously as magistrates in civil government, they were looking straight at Jennings.

Jennings, along with Thomas Lloyd, was one of the two victims of the libel allegedly perpetrated by the Keithians in the late summer of 1692. And Jennings behaved memorably at the subsequent trials and in his own later accounts of the dispute, leering at the defendants as their sentences were read out, throwing Keithian supporters out of the courtroom, and generally behaving like a petulant ass throughout the proceedings.

Daniel's fights at the Burlington Meetings in September and October 1694 concerned documents (the "Chesterfield Certificates") that had been drafted for the benefit of Jennings at the request of Jennings' own wife. Seven years later, Jennings was the star—the "most aspiring bird in the CAGE"—of Leeds' pamphlet, News of a Strumpet. And when Leeds worked to subvert the assembly election of 1704, he was working to keep Jennings and his party out of power. When the results of the election were finally enforced, and the three West Jersey Quakers (Lambert, Gardiner and Wright) finally took their seats, it was Jennings who ascended to the position of

---

[154] Cody, Price of Perfection

speaker of the assembly, a position he instantly used to attack Governor Cornbury and, indirectly, Leeds.

The conflict between Leeds and Jennings may have begun a decade before the Keithian controversy, in the early years of the colony, when Jennings sat on a committee designated to examine all documents circulated by Quakers, putting Leeds, as a professional writer, under his direct purview. When Leeds' Almanac of 1687 was confiscated, it might have been on Jennings' orders. When Leeds' book, Temple of Wisdom, was suppressed by the Philadelphia Meeting, it would probably have been on Jennings' authority.[155] When Leeds' remarriage to Dorothy Young—around the time of Japhet's birth—was challenged, Jennings may have been a key figure trying to block the marriage.

In the records of the Burlington Meeting (now at Haverford College in Pennsylvania) there is a reference to a serious altercation between Leeds and Jennings from as early as 1683.[156] Though I couldn't (or didn't) find out what this was about (maybe Daniel's decision to remarry after the death of his wife) the historian John Pomfret says six members of the meeting were required to arbitrate the dispute.[157]

Daniel's motives seemed neither petty nor criminal to me. In his sustained opposition to Jennings and his wing of the orthodox Quaker establishment in West Jersey and Pennsylvania, Daniel was on the side of free speech against religious censorship, on the side of due process against arbitrary incarceration, on the side of the sweat equity of the Nicolls patentees and other smallholders against the feudal prerogatives of the colonial proprietors, and on the side of the separation of powers against the consolidation of secular power under a preening and nakedly authoritarian religious elite.

"Strumpet" may have been a little nasty and Daniel's actions against the Quakers in 1704 might have been simply an-

---

[155] Cadbury, Quakerism and Uncanonical Lore, talks about suppression of the book by the Philadelphia Meeting
[156] Thanks to Ann Upton, the librarian there, for reading this to me over the phone.
[157] Pomfret, West New Jersey

tidemocratic, but overall I'd say Daniel was on the side of the good guys. All things considered, he seems like the kind of ancestor you might be proud of.

Jennings by contrast was consistently assholish and reactionary throughout his long career. His initial power grab may have come as early as 1681, when he called to order the first meeting of the assembly in West Jersey and made a number of assertions of power, including the appointment of himself as deputy governor, a post from which he was later removed. His attack on the Keithians in the fall of 1692—*after* the Yearly Meeting had already dismissed Keith—seems especially petty and vindictive. His contempt for the judicial process, and for those persons who presumed to criticize him, is apparent in both the Keithian accounts of the controversy and in Jennings' own attempts to defend himself in later writings. His dismissal of William Bradford as printer, for his "Baseness and Treachery" in printing the Keithian pamphlets, is but one petulant example. When Jon Butler, the historian, says the libel trials can only be seen as "an exercise in personal retribution," he is leveling an historical judgment on the Public Friends in general and Jennings in particular. And he is probably giving us a fine insight into Leeds' own perspective on the matter. Jennings had after all just arrested Daniel's friends, stripped them of their livelihoods and sent several of them, including Leeds himself and his family, into exile, all on grounds that they had ventured to criticize him and his colleagues on the court.

Jennings' attitude toward the democratic tendencies of his fellows was demonstrated during a soliloquy that he delivered at the libel trials on the wisdom of the law that was being used to persecute the Keithians. In the speech, he congratulated the government in passing legislation to ensure "the reputation of Magistrates from the contempt of others, foreseeing no doubt (and perhaps perceiving something of it then) that People by reason of their equality in other things, might be under greater temptations, to run into this evil there, than where the condition of the Magistrates had raised them above, and set them at a greater distance from the Common People."

There had always seemed something vaguely ahead-of-its-time,

205

even (God forbid) modern, about Daniel Leeds. Daniel was nothing if not mobile—geographically, confessionally, socially. He changed continents, changed religions (twice), changed jobs. He changed social classes too. He was listed in early land records as a yeoman but he later "graduated" (the Burlington County Court Book's word) to gentleman. In a part of the world (New Jersey) that would one day come to be synonymous with real estate subdivisions, Daniel, as surveyor general, did some of the original subdividing. He was religiously pragmatic and politically opportunistic. His stated wish to read things and see for himself rather than accept them on faith has a pleasant post-Enlightenment ring to it. He had an irreverent streak that contrasted refreshingly with Jennings' shrill preoccupation with status.

Jennings would write that the original sin of the Keithians had been their *unbounded ambition*. And of course Keith and Bradford and Leeds were ambitious, but in a way that seems totally conventional three centuries later. They wanted to write and speak without threats of censorship, imprisonment, forced apologies and judicial retaliation if they said something unpopular.

And they were, in a way, successful. Butler says the Keithian crisis "stimulated a renaissance in disciplinary and institutional creativity that changed the leadership of Delaware Valley Quakerism between 1695 and 1720." The Public Friends' victory in 1692 paradoxically "hastened the decay" of their own control over church government, he says. Not long after their triumph, the Quakers issued a statement of beliefs similar to the one Keith had advocated (though they didn't require signatures). By 1698, the Philadelphia Monthly Meeting had formed a separate "retired" meeting, where members could elect to sit in silence, free from the speeches of the Public Friends.[158]

Butler even argues a connection between the religious and social mobility of the Delaware Valley and the later, more widespread societal mobility—geographic, social, religious—associated with the nineteenth century. At the time of the

---

[158] Butler, Power, Authority, and the Origins

Keithian controversy, Chester County, Pennsylvania, the focus of Butler's writing, was characterized by a "striking mobility of spiritual commitment," Butler says.[159] Quakers became Keithians. Keithians became Baptists. Baptists became Keithians. Keithians became Anglicans. And so forth.

If this "denominational and sectarian" mobility was common in other times and places, Butler writes, then "perhaps the churning of America's nineteenth-century urban population, to take just one example, was but an industrial manifestation of broader and older processes of spiritual as well as physical movement which stemmed from many sources, including religious ones."

I'm not sure I understood it., but I think I liked that a lot.

FORTY-SEVEN

Ben Franklin, and Titan Leeds' Ghost

In 1732, Benjamin Franklin, writing as "Poor Richard" Saunders, announced in the preface to his *Almanac For the Year of Christ 1733* that Titan Leeds, the youngest son of Daniel Leeds and the inheritor of his father's famous almanac, was scheduled to die of unspecified causes at precisely 3:29 p.m. on the afternoon of October 17, 1733.

This news, while unfortunate for Titan, was not altogether unwelcome in the Saunders household, Poor Richard said. Mrs. Saunders had been pressuring him to find new sources of income, and a publisher had offered to cut him in on the profits should he produce an almanac, which up to now he had been very reluctant to do, out of respect for his "good Friend and Fellow-Student" Mr. Titan Leeds, "whose Interest I was extreamly unwilling to hurt."

Happily, this "Obstacle" would soon be removed. "Inexorable Death" had "prepared the mortal Dart." The "fatal Sis-

---

[159] Butler, "Into Pennsylvania's Spiritual Abyss: The Rise and Fall of the Later Keithians, 1693-1703," in *The Pennsylvania Magazine of History and Biography* (April, 1977)

ter" had "extended her destroying Shears" and soon Titan Leeds ("that ingenious Man") would be taken from us.

Richard said Titan was aware of the prediction and disagreed with it—not with the general conclusion but with the specific details. By Titan's own calculation, the departure date was October 26, not October 17. "This small difference between us we have disputed whenever we have met these nine Years past," Poor Richard deadpanned.

It was pitch perfect, it must be said, down to the Initial Caps.

By 1714, Daniel Leeds had retired from the almanac business and had handed the franchise down to his sons, Felix and Titan.[160] He was seventy-two years old and about to be tried for election fraud. Samuel Jennings, his longtime adversary, had been dead for six years. Maybe it was time.

In response to the provocation in Poor Richard's, Titan Leeds responded rather gracelessly, it must be said. In his own Leeds Almanac, Titan said that Poor Richard—this "conceited scribbler" this "precise Predicter who predicts to a Minute"—had "usurpt the Knowledge of the Almighty" and "manifested himself a Fool and a Lyar."

The appointed hour for his death had plainly come and gone, Titan said, yet here he was still plainly alive, full of righteous indignation, and able to expose the error of the upstart Poor Richard (to "publish the Folly and Ignorance of this presumptuous Author"). And so forth.

Somehow this only made things worse.

The next year Poor Richard announced that due to almanac sales, his wife was able to get a "Pot of her own" and a "pair of Shoes." Richard could not tell for certain whether Titan Leeds had in fact died, owing to a "Disorder" in his family that had prevented him from receiving Leeds' last Embrace, closing his Eyes, etc. But he could say that the 1734 edition of the Leeds Almanac had *not* been written by Titan, owing to the "very gross and unhandsome Manner" with which Poor Rich-

---

[160] You have to admire the cojones of a man who's harassed his whole career for his use of *heathenish* names, then calls his sons Felix, Philo and Titan.

ard had been treated in its pages. "Mr. Leeds was too well bred to use any Man so indecently and so scurrilously," Poor Richard said, "and moreover his Esteem and Affection for me was extraordinary."

The real fear was that someone was using Leeds' name to sell almanacs, an "unpardonable Injury to his Memory, and an Imposition on the Publick." And so forth.

In his Almanac of 1735, Richard/Franklin continued the joke. Richard said that although he had resolved to put the dispute behind him, he continued to receive messages from Titan Leeds, who, though deceased, carried on the controversy from beyond the grave. Richard said he "receiv'd much abuse from the Ghost of Titan Leeds, who pretends to be still living, and to write Almanacks in spight of me and my Predictions."

The Leeds' Almanac had declined sadly in quality in recent years, Richard said. No *living* person could have produced them. Therefore there could be no doubt that Titan Leeds was indeed "defunct and dead" as was required for the honor of astrology, that "Art professed both by him and his Father before him." Still, the abuse was hurtful. And "tho' I take it patiently, I take it very unkindly."

By 1738, Titan Leeds was in fact dead, but the Bradfords (William and Andrew) continued publishing his cash cow almanac—they had apparently pulled similar stunts in the past, which might have been why Titan was oversensitive—and, though Leeds Almanac eventually came to an end, Franklin kept on making fun of it.

In the 1740 edition of the almanac, Poor Richard wrote that he'd received another message from Titan Leeds—it had appeared in his hand while he slept in his study.[161] In it, Richard said, Titan predicted that his old Friend W.B. would remain sober for nine hours ("to the astonishment of all his Neighbours") and that John Jerman (another almanac-maker) would be "openly reconciled to the Church of Rome" and that the Bradfords would continue publishing Leeds Almanacs (despite Titan's death).

The Bradfords responded with their own note from the

---

[161] Sorry, his *Study*

grave, posing as the Ghost of Titan Leeds. "Dear Friend Saunders alias Franklin," they wrote. "I expect to have you with us before many Years, where you will find your friend Titan waiting for you."

It was not an especially original hoax—Franklin was copying a hoax that Jonathan Swift had carried out against the English astrologer John Partridge in 1708—but it was well executed. Titan's response was humorless, dogmatic, self-righteous and probably, poetically, fatal. In one stroke Franklin had increased the profile of his fledgling almanac, piggybacking off a much more established publication and making an important rival look ridiculous in the process. In fact he made the whole institution of judicial astrology—rival almanac-makers busily calculating the hours of one another's deaths—look ridiculous, which was at least part of his intention.[162] The real Richard Saunders, after all, had been an astrologer-physician who died in 1692.

The historian Marion Barber Stowell sees Franklin's hoax as extremely clever marketing. In launching Poor Richard's, Franklin was entering a competitive field—seven rival almanacs in Philadelphia alone—and Leeds' naiveté granted him a public relations coup.[163] "With Leeds' (probably) unwitting help," Stowell writes, "Ben Franklin launched his successful series of Poor Richard almanacs."

Peter Eisenstadt goes even further, saying Franklin's attitude toward astrology—at least as expressed in the almanacs—was ambiguous, and that he was not above hinting at the validity of occult belief to increase his marketing appeal. "At his slyest," Eisenstadt says, "Franklin criticized other almanac makers for doing what he himself did so well—providing a mixed message about the validity of astrology." It was a marketing lesson that would remain useful two hundred and fifty years later.

---

[162] Stowell, "American Almanacs and Feuds," in Early American Literature (Winter, 1975)

[163] William Pencak says five rivals; "Politics and Ideology in Poor Richard's Almanack," in Pennsylvania Magazine of History and Biography (1992)

Franklin published Poor Richard's Almanac from 1732 to 1758. He sold thousands of copies each year. It made him his fortune, and he added his voice, in this way and in others, to the Enlightenment currents that helped push occult almanacs, and belief in magic in general, to the periphery. He did what the Quakers failed to do, kill Leeds' Almanac. Leeds' romantic, agrarian poetry was replaced by Franklin's folksy, preachy home economics, the Old Religion pushed aside by Industry, Frugality and Common Sense.

And he added the phrase *Leeds Ghost* to the lexicon in the process.

Someone said once that magic has no church.[164] A corollary might be that it has no church records. The Leeds family may have gone back to Quakerism (some of them) but they had not gone back to Burlington. They remained in Leeds Point, on the periphery, away from the center of the political and economic life of the colony. They became fishermen, farmers, bay men. No more pamphlet wars or dramatic conversion experiences. The family's story too had become *folklorized* maybe. But if they had been more public, or at least inclined to diary-keeping, they might have left history. Instead they left folklore, which is more durable if, perhaps, less satisfying.

Daniel Leeds, George Keith, Ben Franklin, Samuel Jennings—theirs were the temporal struggles of men close to the seat of power and they are forgotten. But walk into any Wawa in South Jersey and you can hear echoes of Mother Leeds.

FORTY-EIGHT

A walk in the woods with the Devil Hunters

One rainy night in the winter of 2003, I went into the woods with Laura Leuter and the Devil Hunters to look for the Jersey Devil. Like losing one's virginity, and carried out in a similar spirit, this had had to happen at some point, I figured. Why

---

not with these people?

My notes from this encounter were lost in a fire. Or in a flood. Or they were devoured by insects. Or maybe I was just too depressed to keep them.

I remember we met, at Leut's request, at JD's Pub & Grille in Smithville (*that* JD), a favorite Devil Hunter watering hole. There were four or five Hunters in attendance that night, I want to say—Belle, an aspiring actress, and Charley, a cheerful young man with a mustache and maybe Shawn or Mike (Devil Hunters who've since retired)—but honestly I can't remember.

Leut sat in the middle and held court for the duration of the meal. She was definitely the group's Alpha member, the most talkative, the most authoritative, the most conversant in the Jersey Devil literature. She had been listed on the group's website as the "president" but has since been re-designated "director," I see.

We talked about the group's founding, about Leut's childhood interest in the story, which had blossomed during young adulthood into this organization, a professional research organization, dedicated to searching for the big monster in the Pine Barrens.

To be honest, I had expected them to be crazy. If I haven't been clear on this point, I don't think that the Jersey Devil is a real creature. I think it's an interesting folk story. I think the idea of looking for big monsters in the woods of South Jersey is a childish and possibly deranged idea. I think looking for unclassified megafauna anywhere within one hundred miles of the Boston-Atlanta Metropolitan Axis is childish and possibly deranged. I assumed all my life that all the people I associated with felt basically the same way I did about this kind of thing. Yet here we were.

The tentative plan had been to eat dinner in the pub and then maybe go for a walk in the woods. Leut said she wasn't entirely optimistic about the prospects of a hunt that night, given the inclement weather and the lack of adequate preparations. Also, someone had driven all the way down from Bayonne and it was kind of late. But we'd see.

We sat there in the pub and kind of eyed each other. I remember the menus had little pictures of monsters holding beer steins on them. I felt like I was being evaluated according to some obscure criteria. I felt like I was on a first date.

I spent some time trying to work up the sand to ask them the question: What did they really think? Did they think it was out there? As in, right now? What did they think it was doing, out there right now? And did they really think they were going to catch it one day?

Yes, apparently. Apparently they did think some of those things because we eventually went out and looked for it, but I'm still not sure *how* they thought those things, what they told themselves for any of it to make sense.

If I ever had gotten around to asking them, my notes were lost in that damned flood.

When I met them, the Devil Hunters had already filmed a documentary for a show on the Fox Family Channel called *Scariest Places on Earth*. Leut and two other Devil Hunters— Mike and Shawn—had gone out into the woods in Leeds Point with the film crew to shoot the footage. Harry Leeds made an appearance. The show's presenter wore a very sharp, Agent Scully-ish pantsuit, I remember.

After that, Leut appeared live one year with Jersey Devil author Ray Miller Jr. on the Comcast Network on Halloween night. The Devil Hunters appeared on The Learning Channel (*Monster Hunters*) and The Travel Channel (*Weird Travels*). They would go on to make appearances on *History Hunters* and *Hometown Tales* (both cable-access shows) and on The Discovery Kids Channel's *Mystery Hunters*, hosted by famed mystery hunter Christina Broccolini. Finally there would be the epic History Channel episode of MonsterQuest, featuring an investigation into an alleged sighting of the Jersey Devil in Egg Harbor Township in 2004. But those last few were still in the future.

Still, it must have occurred to me at some point that they were not crazy. They were merely *successful*—as a social group at least, if not as natural philosophers. They had been on TV and in the newspapers. Multiple times. Their ideas were sought out and broadcast, locally and nationally. They had performed and opined and they enjoyed a definite status, within certain circles anyway. And after all *I* had requested this meeting. I needed them more than they needed me apparently.

At some point the mood shifted perceptibly. I had told them about some of my research—about Deborah and Japhet and Daniel and Satan's Harbinger and all that. Maybe I had established my bona fides as a fellow researcher. Maybe they thought I'd been generous and wanted to reciprocate. Maybe they realized that, if anything, I was even deeper into the Jersey Devil game than they were, and they wanted to help me out. Whatever the reason, a decision seemed to have been made. Despite the light February rain, we would drive up Moss Mill Road to the end of Leeds Point for a perfunctory Devil Hunt. After that, it was just a nice night out at a restaurant with a good burger followed by a walk in the woods.

Supper ended. The check came. We split it. Here I must note that among those present at the table, I was the lone twenty-seven-year-old loser who was living at home with his parents, whose green Dodge minivan he'd had to borrow to get to JD's Pub & Grille that night.

Leut again tempered expectations, pointing out that Leeds Point was not exactly prime monster-hunting territory, what with so many suburban ranch houses nearby. It wasn't Batsto or New Gretna, much less the deep Pines, but it was still a location of some importance and surprisingly spooky.

We drove north up Route Nine then east down Moss Mill Road. We passed the Leeds Point Cemetery, where so many Leedses were buried. We passed a Wawa and a CVS, passed Harry Horner's old gas station, passed Harry Senior's old apartment, passed the old house of Duck Feet, passed the old pear farm (now part of the wildlife refuge) passed Anderson's General Store and the big Leeds House on the corner where Jesse Mathis and Dan Sooy lived.

Past the long-gone homestead of Daniel Leeds. Past the ruins of the house where Japhet and Deborah Leeds hosted the local Quaker Meeting. Past the house that Charles Leeds had built and where BeBop had grown up. Down the road that Charles Leeds rode his bike on every day to go fishing in the bay. All these places slid by, unremarked upon, in the rain.

At the end of Scott's Landing Road, where the woods ran out and stopped, was a sandy parking lot. In the daytime, people parked their cars there while they launched their boats into the creek. But now, in the middle of the night in the dead of winter, it was empty. We left the cars and walked into the underbrush.

In other words, we did what teenagers have been doing in this part of South Jersey since the beginning of time. Except we had walkie-talkies. And one of the Devil Hunters had a minor meltdown and wouldn't get out of the car.

We were sufficiently far out toward the end of the point that no one could hear us tromping around in the bushes, I don't think. I doubt we ever really got close to the ruins of the Shourds House, but perhaps that was intentional. Not that it really mattered. Carrie Bowen's Shourds House wasn't the real Jersey Devil house, not as far as BeBop and Aunt Dottie were concerned anyway. And all of this land had probably belonged to Daniel Leeds at one time.

No one would ever be able to say with any real meaning where Daniel lived or where his children or grandchildren had lived, or where precisely whatever domestic tragedy had unfolded out here many generations ago had actually taken place. I was pretty sure I no longer cared.

We happened upon the remains of some old building. It might once have been the foundation of a house, but it seemed more like the kind of cement platform you'd put your shed on. We stood in the woods, rain dripping softly off the tree branches, and looked down at the ruins with great complacency. It didn't seem particularly old. But the Devil Hunters seemed to think it was noteworthy—not a relic of the True Cross but an object of some importance nonetheless.

Meanwhile, Belle, the Devil Hunter in the car, had been sending increasingly frantic messages over the walkie-talkie. She was getting really freaked out actually, she said. Oh my God, she thought she heard something guys. Oh my God, really, what the hell was that, guys. Etc.

Maybe we really should be getting back to her, we thought. Enough standing around in the rain.

We made our way back through the woods to the parking lot and said goodbye to one another. The Devil Hunters got back into their jeep. I got back into my parents' minivan. Thus safely reestablished in our automobiles, Leeds Plantation reverted to its familiar suburban condition—carriages into pumpkins. And about twenty-five minutes later I was home.

FORTY-NINE

Bad productions

The Devil Hunters had been burned a little bit by The Scariest Places on Earth. They'd gone out on a hunt with the team of filmmakers, and it had been made to seem as if Leut had seen something monsterish and supernatural in the woods of Leeds Point, which of course she hadn't.

Leut said they spent two days shooting in total. The footage mostly showed the Hunters walking around in the woods with their surveillance equipment, looking tense. Leut wore a headset like a clerk at Old Navy. At one point they happened upon the slaughtered remains of an animal in the woods. This was presented as a discovery of genuine importance. Something had slaughtered an animal in the woods. This animal, right here, in the *woods*. Here were its remains. What could account for such an act? It was almost unknown to science.

Leut said the Fox producers treated them to dinner at the Smithville Inn, where they ate in the exclusive Leeds Room and were given free wine on the house. "The food was awesome! We did a little research, found out some cool stuff," she later wrote.[165]

In the end, the segment was thirteen minutes long and aired on both The SciFi Channel and on ABC's Family Channel around Halloween. Zelda Rubinstein—the four-foot-tall clairvoyant from the original Poltergeist movie—provided creepy voiceover services. Ken Sooy, in a camouflage hat, made a brief cameo. An unidentified man with a tremendous

[165] On the Devil Hunters' website

mullet appeared on camera and suggested that he'd been groped by the monster. Etc.

Leut and Co. were shown being introduced to Harry Leeds, who served as Indian Guide and took them to the site of the Jersey Devil house (one of the houses), pointing out the ruins in the woods and fulfilling a childhood dream for Leut.

"This is something I've been looking for since I was *like* seven years old," she said.

The sun went down. The night-vision goggles came out—grainy, black-and-green footage of the young researchers wandering about in the forest at night. It was all very Blair Witchian.

As the segment approached its climax, something—what kind of *thing*?!—was spotted down a gravel road, and there were lots of react shots of Devil Hunters looking perplexed.

"It looks like a big eyeball," Harry said.

Leut ran off, announcing her intention to "put a stop" to the shenanigans, and there, amid much superimposed snarling and the shaking of handheld cameras, the scene ended, and we abruptly smash cut to the interior of a Devil Hunter vehicle, backlit by the morning sun rising over Leeds Point.

"To this day Laura refuses to talk about what she saw that night in the Pine Barrens," Zelda said—a classic non-denial denial worthy of Blair Witch.

Everyone looked ridiculous of course, with the possible exception of Harry, whose persona seemed so self-consciously *constructed* that it's possible he was a co-conspirator. But probably you had to know him.

Ken Sooy too had had his share of bad experiences with the TV people. Ken had been involved in three documentaries over the years, traveling around with the directors and film crews, and he had a negative opinion of the process in general, he said. "It has come down to where it's nothing but different towns want it to look like it is from there for tourism reasons," he said. "And the writers of the videos of course naturally want to make it appear to be supernatural."

Appeals to facts and evidence—Ken's forte—were met with resentment, confusion or indifference. "They don't care what research shows."

The kicker for him had come not long before I met him, when a film crew arranged to spend the night on Ken's property in Leeds Point, where he owns about fifteen acres. Ken said the filmmakers had planned to spend the night outdoors camping, "to see if they heard any strange noises" (Ken's words), but when they got to Galloway they decided instead to rent an airplane for a flyover of the Pine Barrens.

The resulting documentary was predictably terrible. "One of the worst renditions of the story I ever saw," Ken said. It had made him "sick."

"They didn't even do a good job of making it a superstitious story." He'd watched it with friends and they laughed and laughed throughout.

Ken said he still got requests from media types, but he'd basically sworn of television work. He'd taken to responding by saying that he would participate only if he had some control over the final content. So far there had been no takers.

FIFTY

I meet a Piney

In a rented car that looked like an ice-cube tray, a Kia I think, I drove north and east from my childhood home in Egg Harbor Township, with no particular destination in mind, but with a general idea of making it to Chatsworth, McPhee's Capital of the Pines.

I headed up the White Horse Pike toward Egg Harbor City, passing Harry's old bar (Muskett's Tavern), passing an Agassiz Street, passing a lineup of defunct jitneys on the roadside, passing any number of Wawas and Super Wawas, passing the airport in Pomona where the 177th Fighter Interceptor Group of the New Jersey Air National Guard (the Jersey Devils) is based. Late-afternoon thunderclouds were piling up over the Pines.

Just beyond Egg Harbor City, I picked up Route 563 and headed toward Chatsworth, no idea what I was looking for, just happy to be off that damned casino bus. I stopped at a cranberry processing center and tried to chat up one of the workers, but without much success. There was a truck parked a few feet away and it had a Mexican fútbol bumper sticker (UNAM Pumas). I thought about Whimsy's observation about who works in the old Pine Barrens' industries these days.

Just below the town of Sweetwater, I crossed the Mullica River, very definitely in the Pine Barrens now, and drove along a little two-lane road. On either side were gun clubs, motorcycle clubs, the odd kayak-rental shop. The cranberry farmers appeared to be watering their bogs.

I stopped briefly in Beck's forgotten town of Speedwell. When Beck made his journey, sometime in the 1930s, the road was "dreary," he said. "It winds and twists through charred stumps and stunted trees."[166]

There had been an Indian schoolhouse of unknown provenance in Speedwell, Beck said, but by the time of his visit it had fallen into disrepair, "just another ruin of the pinelands, with here and there a wheel or wagon part in the clearing, to recall its last activity." When I was there, Speedwell seemed less like a ruin than a neatly tended lawn beneath stately pines.

In Chatsworth, I sat on an ersatz wrought-iron bench beside a hot dog stand and considered my fate. Like everywhere else in the Pines on this summer day, Chatsworth felt quiet and sunstruck. The only activity was at the hotdog stand and its affiliated Sno-Kone stand, which were being operated by an extremely efficient woman in a "Piney Power" tee-shirt who was chatting between customers on a blackberry in a bubble-gum case. A very persistent fly kept banging into my head.

Buzby's General Store (where McPhee had passed the time) was across the street, closed. It appeared to be for-sale. Long ago it had been converted to a gift shop ("The Cheshire Cat at Buzby's") where they sold books and artisanal cranberry marmalade and things of that nature. A copy of Weird New Jersey (the book) was visible through the window.

The woman running Hot Diggidy Dog ("Serving Down-

---

town Chatsworth for over 30 Years") said that no Buzbys had owned the store for years. She had a steady stream of customers at her stand, mostly men in pickup trucks. They wore tee-shirts commemorating fishing tournaments they'd fished in, just like people do down where I grew up. People would stop and talk as they ate their hot dogs, mostly about Little League baseball, it seemed like. The owner, Robyn, said Chatsworth was a convenient place to stop for people taking the back road down to the beach.

"Do you get a lot of Jersey Devil people?"

"More people for the snakes," she said. "Birdwatchers too."

"Are there any Pineys left?"

"There are absolutely Pineys," she said. "People come here for the simple life, even if they're not Pineys."

Three miles north of Chatsworth, I picked up Route Seventy-Two (Barnegat Road on my map) and pointed the ice-cube due east. Aunt Dottie had said I should go to Barnegat someday. "Do yourself a treat," she said. "I'm serious."

So, I drove east on Barnegat Road through the Pines, crossing over Route Nine, crossing under the Garden State Parkway, crossing over various bays and marshes as I entered Long Beach Island, at the northern end of which stood the Barnegat Lighthouse.

I'd been to LBI precisely once in my life, but this felt like familiar territory, a long and narrow barrier island, straight roads, million dollar beach homes blocks away from seaside motels. It was 8.67 miles of intermittent traffic, through Surf City, Harvey Cedars, Loveladies, to the tip of Barnegat.

When I got there, the lighthouse was closed. But I hadn't really wanted to climb to the top anyway. I wanted to walk out to the end of the jetty that runs beside it into the sea.

On the jetty, dragonflies were swarming among the rocks, flitting about my feet as I walked. The stone structure protruded a few hundred yards into the ocean, marking the narrow inlet that separated LBI from the next island north (Barnegat Bay Island). And there, sitting on the jetty and dangling his feet into the inlet, I met the first Piney I'd ever met in my life.

He was wearing a wetsuit, holding a speargun and applying sunscreen. I asked him if he'd heard of the Jersey Devil, and of course he had (I hadn't yet determined that he was a Piney). I asked if he knew anyone who was related to the monster, and he said no. I asked what the Jersey Devil was and I thought I heard him say something about it being a Piney.

"Are *you* a Piney?" I said.

"Oh, yeah. I'm definitely a Piney," he said. "I went out in the Pine Barrens since I was three and a half years old. Alls I did was hunt—turtles [unclear] and go in the woods and hunt everything. Cut firewood for most of my life. Actually still do trees in the winter."

He was a fair-complected man, and the layer of sunscreen was thick on his face.

We sat there for a minute with the dragonflies and the water and the tide ripping through inlet.

"What kind of fish?" I asked.

Triggerfish, or striper, he said. "Anything that's in size." But he didn't seem optimistic. When the water was turbulent, it made the visibility underwater bad, and it was hard to see the fish. Today the tide looked bad.

I said goodbye and carried on out to the mouth of the inlet.

On the way back he asked me if the current looked strong at the end of the jetty, but I really had no sense of what that meant.

FIFTY-ONE

New Jersey Devil

I have been thinking about windowsills lately, thresholds and doorways. As the ancients knew, such boundaries—liminal spaces—were the ideal habitat of ghosts. On Halloween, one of the *hinges* of the year, the boundary between the spirit world and the world of human activity thinned out and became permeable, and the dead could move back and forth. On such nights, it was said, there was a phantom in every doorway.[167]

The Leeds family ghosts seemed to exist across many boundaries too, social and otherwise. The Jersey Devil was a story old people told to young people, locals told to outsiders, persons of one social class told to or about persons of another social class. A classic picture of the Jersey Devil—maybe *the* classic picture of the Jersey Devil—was the view of the monster through an open window. As Henry Beck had imagined it, the Leeds child had been kept locked in the house, "sheltered mercifully from the curious who came to peep in at the windows." But this partial view did nothing to diminish curiosity. People saw *something* and imagined the rest.

"Wouldn't you have sidled by of an evening," Beck asked, "on one imaginary errand or another, to see what you could see?" Maybe in such ways a domestic tragedy was turned into a supernatural monster of nightmare and then into a comic icon, a folk symbol of regional pride, sold on the side of a coffee cup in an antique shop.

The Pine Barrens themselves seemed like a kind of liminal space. Sparsely inhabited, poorly understood, they were nevertheless perpetually traversed by the people who lived on either side of them. And from Pine Rats to the Kallikaks to the Jersey Devil itself, the woods too had been filled with their share of monsters. The written history of the legend—from Mayers to Beck to McPhee—was produced by men who traveled into the Pines from the cities or towns on their periphery. Maybe it was a kind of reversal of this situation that I felt when I moved away from South Jersey. I'd never really had much reason to talk about the Jersey Devil before I left home.

New Jersey itself could be seen as a kind of liminal space, defined more by what was on either side of it than by what it itself contained. Ben Franklin himself had famously, allegedly, called New Jersey a barrel tapped at both ends. Objects moved through it easily and in either direction. New Jerseyans have sometimes been described as amphibian, spending their nights at home and their days across the water in New York City or

---

[167] I'm obviously talking out my ass, but see e.g. Bettina Arnold, "Halloween Customs in the Celtic World" (online)

Philadelphia.

The geographer Charles Stansfield calls New Jersey a "transitional state" with a "corridor" function.[168] Michael Aaron Rockland and Angus Gillespie, in their book *Looking for America on the New Jersey Turnpike*, call it a "centrifugal state."[169] Strong forces work to pull it apart, they perceive. The writer and critic Luc Sante, in an essay in *The Nation* (2003) compared New Jersey to his native Belgium, a "neutral conjunction" between two domineering neighbors, "constantly run over by armies surging or retreating from one center of power to the other."[170]

New Jerseyans themselves are frequently derided as *bridge-and-tunnel*. The classic New Jersey question—What *exit* are you?—is asked of people even down in Atlantic County, forty miles from the Turnpike. At the level of language even, the state's residents sounded like parts of the transportation grid. There was an old commercial that used to run more or less continuously on New Jersey 101.5, a statewide radio station. "Not New York," the voice said. "*Not* Philadelphia—proud to be New Jersey." Even in statements of regional pride, we thought of ourselves as the nonspace between two big cities.

The classic New Jersey stereotype was the image of the state as seen through the window of a car on the New Jersey Turnpike, and like all partial views, this too was a distortion, a caricature, creating the impression of knowledge where there was in fact only superficial familiarity.

Perhaps because so many people were familiar with the New Jersey stereotype—so many people had driven down the Turnpike—it has been a standing invitation to rebuttal, and since 1859, at least, writers and journalists have done an excellent business in contrasting the imagined perception of New Jersey with the on-the-ground reality. And this seems to me to be the imaginative space in which the history of the Jersey Devil has played itself out.

W. F. Mayers began his 1859 essay on the Pine Barrens by

---

[168] *A Geography of New Jersey: The City in the Garden* (1983)

[169] Rockland and Angus, *Looking for America on the New Jersey Turnpike* (1989)

[170] "On Mediocrity's Cutting Edge," The Nation, June 23, 2003

imagining a bird that has flown from the Battery at the southern end of Manhattan, fifty miles pineward, to find himself "hovering over a region of country as little like the civilized emporium just quitted as it is well possible to conceive." McPhee begins his 1968 book with a description of the view from the fire tower atop Bear Swamp Hill in Burlington County, a view that extends in unbroken forests of pine and oak and cedar to the horizon in every direction.

To me, New Jersey's identity problem was a problem of the suburbs. The New Jersey I grew up in was the suburbs. New Jersey itself was the archetypal suburban state. It was one of the most depressing things about being from New Jersey, I thought. Even our identity problems weren't particular to New Jersey. They were the same identity problems that suburban kids had everywhere.

I don't *think* this was just my imagination.

Rockland and Gillespie call New Jersey "the ultimate suburban state." Sante says that New Jersey, with its "accommodating temperate flatness," was "virtually designed to be a suburb."

The idea seemed to be that, while other places might have suburbs, and in greater profusion, none had them in the same unrelieved intensity as New Jersey. California had sprawl but it also had the Mojave Desert and Telegraph Hill. Massachusetts had strip malls but also Faneuil Hall and the Berkshires. New Jersey's rural districts, by contrast, were relatively unimportant anomalies. There were probably agribusiness spreads in Texas larger than the whole state, Sante said. Likewise, its cities were nearly all "beset, aggrieved, half-ruined" (also Sante's description). Newark was an "untidy dormitory for the poor" (Rockland and Gillespie's words). Atlantic City was "nothing but a line of casinos walling off a morass of slums" (also Rockland and Gillespie). "The rest," Sante said, was "mostly suburb."

Sante's essay was essentially a seventeen-hundred-word rant against the "suburban style" of New Jersey, which he said was in no way confined to the narrow strip of land between the Delaware and the Atlantic, but was rather the blandly familiar, chirpily militant corporate consumerism of middle-class persons everywhere.

"When you come upon a grouping of large tract houses, or of low-rise apartments masquerading as large tract houses, that is heralded by a signboard bearing a title ('Lark's Crest Estates'; 'The Village at Hunter's Ridge'), you are seeing New Jersey, even if you happen to be in Colorado," he said.

In the suburbs, the physical past was almost entirely invisible. And without visible history, no identity was possible. That seemed to be the logic anyway.

Sante sees New Jersey-style suburbanization as a kind of original sin. At some point, at some imprecise time in the past, the precursors of today's New Jerseyans (the "rural aldermen and freeholders" of yesterday) had sold out for some fleeting profit, had "happily submitted their townships to the shredder," trading their "placid neighborly four-corners and pastoral outlands to the shopping-mall and condo-complex bulldozers in exchange for golfing vacations in Bermuda."

One result of this "accommodation," Sante says, was the "eradication of historical identity." Thus "bereft of history," he says, New Jersey's identity was "pretty thin."

As a narrative of actual places and events, it was of course quaintly bullshitical, but as the articulation of a basic anxiety behind the suburban condition, it was a masterwork. Everywhere I went in New Jersey I felt like I saw the symptoms of this disease, the basic deracination of the suburban condition—Leut and her late-night archaeology expeditions, the Kingdom of Lucerne and their musketry and fiber arts, Boo and his bedroom full of bricks, maybe even Mike from Obscura and his stuffed-alligator desk lamp. Everywhere people seemed to be looking for authenticity and identity in some connection to history and a shared sense of the past. The last place that they would expect to find such things, it seemed, was in the suburbs.

Leut and Co. spent a fair bit of time rooting around New Jersey looking for actual physical artifacts of the past but they seemed to be in denial that they were standing in suburbia while doing so.

When I asked Donn Shearer what was interesting and "culturally valid" about our part of South Jersey, he said it was the northern and southern bay men and the loggers from the Pine Barrens, people he grew up calling "stump-jumpers."

These were the "people who practiced the rural industries that made the state in the first place," he said.

When I asked if it was an accident that those were precisely the non-suburban elements of the culture—the old timers who practiced the traditional industries tied to the land—he said he disagreed with the premise of my question. South Jersey wasn't the suburbs at all.

"South Jersey," he said "is the South."[171]

But of course I hadn't had to look to Donn or Leut or anyone else. All those interminable bus rides and hours spent playing folkroulette in Wawa parking lots had been my equivalent of the same thing, my attempt to find traces of history in the culture and landscape all around me.

It was a peculiar feature of the Jersey Devil that the one thing it was never permitted to be was suburban. But there was a kind of logic to it. In his book *The Folklore and Folklife of New Jersey*, in his section on the "Jersey Joke," the folklorist David Steven Cohen laments the negative public image of New Jersey, which he says is connected to but not identical with the "derogatory stereotype of decaying cities, polluting industries, and sprawling suburbs."

"The Jersey joke reflects a serious problem in the way New Jersey is perceived by the rest of the country," Cohen says.

Against this negative stereotype, were are invited to set the state's rich folk tradition. The purpose of his book, Cohen says, is "to use folklore to fight folklore," to "refute the derogatory stereotype and correct the identity problem by showing the richness and diversity of New Jersey's folk heritage."

As part of that rich, folk heritage, the Jersey Devil has been conscripted into the fight against New Jersey's bad image. Suburbia was the problem the Jersey Devil was supposed to correct.

---

[171] "No it's not," a nearby Lucernian had said.

FIFTY-TWO

Sante's list of acceptable Jerseyana

New Jersey's suburbs seemed to me the borderland where the contemporary Jersey Devil was born, the haunted liminal space of class and ambition that sustained the story in its modern iterations. Sante's New Jersey-style suburbia is a place fraught with questions of social class and ambition. The suburbs he describes are alternately a "parking lot for middle-class transients" and a "laboratory for testing upgrades and streamlinings of middle-class life."

The New Jerseyan that Sante describes is "generally seen as the embodiment of upwardly mobile rootlessness and material self-satisfaction," and naturally such rootlessness, particularly when connected to multinational corporate capitalism, is inimical to authentic culture. Regardless of his actual origins, the New Jerseyan has likely "shed every trace of accent or custom" on the cultural "climb," he says.

Here again Sante seemed less concerned with describing actual places or people than with articulating popular anxieties and stereotypes, but they were stereotypes I could relate to. They're the ones, I think, all this Jersey Devil nonsense was a reaction against. Conventional, middle-class ambition was at the root of what was supposedly wrong with a place like New Jersey—with any suburb anywhere. Affiliating one's self or one's town with folklore, with Pineys, with bay men—with the Jersey Devil—was a way of distancing one's self from that original sin, a way of seeming authentic.

If it seems far-fetched that the Jersey Devil should have anything to do with social class and ambition, consider that this story has been concerned with those things from the start.[172]

The Keithian controversy has been seen by some historians (Gary Nash, at least) in terms of class conflict and ambition. Daniel Leeds had belonged, at least initially, to the yeo-

---

[172] I may agree, it is far-fetched but work with me.

man class, one of the lower classes of colonial society, but "typically men of skill and drive" (Nash's words).[173] His opponents during the crisis—Samuel Jennings and Caleb Pusey—had been men of higher social standing. Pusey was one of a "small number of more substantial men among the initial immigrants" to Pennsylvania, Nash says.

Jennings himself had said the sin of the Keithians had been their unbounded ambition. In their project against the Public Friends and Pennsylvania magistrates, the Keithians had been supported, Nash says, by a "whole stratum of lesser merchants, shopkeepers, and master artisans—upward moving individuals, not a few of whom would enter the circle of mercantile leadership in the next decade."

These men, Nash says, "found that Keith's program provided a means for challenging the Lloydian 'greats,' who were resented for their narrow control of provincial life." Out of this challenge, at least one Leeds Devil—maybe *the* Leeds Devil—had been created.

A century and a half later, when Mayers went into the Pines, the social mobility and demographic churning—prefigured by the Keithians—had established itself more broadly in the national character.[174] Now it was the Pineys who were out of step. The Pine Rats that Mayers described were members of an alien social class, notable for their striking absence of ambition. These were the people who preferred to stay in the forest, happy in their applejack and berry-picking, instead of following the jobs and industries out of the Pines.

J. Elfreth Watkins, writing about the Leeds Devil in the 1890s, described the Pineys as "genial" but "unprogressive." No "manufacturing town, no internal improvements of any kind, are to be found in their region," he said. Pineys were "kindly disposed" and "warm-hearted to strangers" but "without stimulus to hard work." And in this atmosphere of course—again haunted by problems of class and ambition—another Leeds Devil was born.

Was it any wonder, Watkins asked, that the Piney should

---

[173] Nash, Quakers and Politics
[174] Butler, recall, makes the point about churning.

"adhere to the extravagant superstitions of the fanatical days of witchcraft?"

By the time John McPhee went into the Pines, in the 1960s, the yardstick had flipped again. New Jersey was on its way to becoming the great suburb of the western world. People moved around a lot. They changed jobs, changed counties, changed states. Landscapes had been bulldozed and houses built all within the lifetimes of the oldest residents. In the resort towns of the coast, even the homes it seemed were owned by New Yorkers or Pennsylvanians who visited them only for three warm months each year.

But even in New Jersey, a suburban wonderland as old and hyper-developed as any on the planet, enclaves of local culture and history persisted and these were now seized upon by people who seemed profoundly uneasy with the culture they were creating for themselves. The Jersey Devil, which a century earlier had been a symbol of darkness, ignorance and superstition, now seemed to offer a sense of history and authenticity to a New Jersey that was haunted by something else.

Toward the end of his essay, Luc Sante gave his readers a kind of list of acceptable Jerseyana—examples of aesthetically superior objects, places and people that readers might associate themselves with if they wished to stand out as authentic against the uniform landscape of strip malls and McMansions that otherwise dominated the scene. The list contained tomato fields and cranberry bogs and dive bars ("rogue" bars Sante calls them) and immigrant grocers and old Italian men tending to backyard fig trees and roadside diners covered with sheet metal—a list of Stuff White People Like, basically.

But you kind of felt like Harry Leeds and the Jersey Devil would have fit right in there.

FIFTY-THREE

A message from Harry Leeds' Ghost

Harry Leeds died in January 2011. I hadn't talked to him in a while. After he took me to visit his father that day, he kind of stopped returning my calls. I think he'd been travelling for work. At least that's what he told me.

I'd taken the casino bus down one day and my mom came to pick me up at the bus station, and on the ride home she told me about Harry. It had been in the papers, but I'd missed it. I'd only met him twice—by any objective measure I didn't know him at all—but I'd been chasing this story around for so long, inspired by him, that he felt like a big part of my life.

The obituary in the Press of Atlantic City described Harry as "an ex-Marine, former Galloway Township mayor and ceaseless promoter of the Jersey Devil." It called him "piney aristocracy," and said he was descended from Daniel Leeds. And it reprinted a quote that he'd given the paper about the Jersey Devil in 1995. "The myth is that he was a bad guy," Harry had said. "He was a decent guy who liked to help people."

Around this time I emailed a few old high school friends that I'd tracked down on Facebook, and I solicited some general thoughts on the Jersey Devil. Really only one person got back to me, Fred—we were linebackers together one year on the football team—but he was the person you'd want to hear back from, if you had to pick one.

I'd said something foolish about being interested in the Jersey Devil's role in South Jersey culture in particular and its implications for the American Dream in general, and Fred had responded with an unsurprisingly incisive message.

He said he'd been told the story by one of his brothers as a kid, how a member of the Leeds family had been locked away in the attic, the door opened only at feeding time, until the unhappy thirteenth child had escaped into the woods, later to

230

become known as the Jersey Devil.

Though Fred was "briefly concerned" at the "prospect of being attacked by the devil," he quickly realized even at that young age that "the story was ridiculous on several levels," and soon the fear receded into the background, as indeed the story itself had done.

"Eventually, I only really talked about the Devil with people who did not live in South Jersey."

Amen to that, I thought.

He continued.

"The area that I associate most directly with the devil—the eastern part of the Pine Barrens—doesn't really have a lot going on. It's some distance from Philly and New York, or even Camden and Newark. And it must have felt even farther away from those places before the construction of the A.C. Expressway and the Parkway. So, the people in the area were, and to some extent still are, kind of outsiders. Yet, since the mid eighteen hundreds, cosmopolitan folks from the far off cities have converged on Atlantic City and the surrounding beaches, initially in the summers and eventually pretty much year-round.

"While I think the locals are more than content with their position as outsiders, they likely have always had something of an inferiority complex and were—and to some extent still are—mocked by their intruders. In times when larger portions of the population believed in the supernatural, the Jersey Devil likely allowed locals to give the outsiders a scare, perhaps even causing their kids to have nightmares and thereby ruining their trip.

"Also, because the Devil belonged solely to the locals, it helped them nurture their independent identity. I think this remains true to some extent.

"Ask a Piney how it feels not to have the Yankees or the Eagles, Wall Street or the Museum of Art, and he'll say, 'Fuck you. We have the Jersey Devil.' And he'll mean it—not the 'We have the Jersey Devil,' but the 'Fuck you.'

"I have no idea whether any of this is true, historically or psychologically. But I think to some extent it explains the role of the devil in my life."

For one hundred and fifty years, reporters from New York and Philadelphia had been coming to South Jersey to write about the Jersey Devil, alternately demonizing or fetishizing the people they met here. For the last twenty years or so, a lot of those reporters had spoken to Harry Leeds.

"We have the Jersey Devil," Harry had told them. And maybe he'd meant it. Not the "We have the Jersey Devil," but the "Fuck you."

It was an idea.

Before he died, Harry had given me a DVD of some TV show he'd done. I'd assumed it was another one of his Monster-Quests, which in a sense it was, but with an instructive difference.

When I finally got around to watching it, I realized it was a video of a talk that Harry had given at the Wheaton Arts Down Jersey Folklife Center in Millville. This was the event Harry had mentioned—quickly, almost mumbling the words—when I tried to ask him *Why He Did It* that day as we drove out to Oyster Creek. It was only later when I went back and listened to my voice recording that I'd connected the two events and realized this was Harry's answer to my question.

The Folklife Center had been opening an exhibit on the Jersey Devil, curated by a folklore expert with a PhD from the University of Pennsylvania who began his presentation by saying that when he'd first moved to South Jersey to take this job, he knew nothing about the Jersey Devil. But he'd gotten up to speed pretty quickly, presumably. Now it seemed he knew all about it, because the Folklife Center had collected a great many images of the Jersey Devil for our viewing pleasure. He's since moved on to the American Folklife Center at the Library of Congress in Washington D.C.

By the looks of things on the video, there had been a pretty decent crowd that night at the Folklife Center, including a number of leading Jersey Devil lights. McCloy and Miller were there signing copies of their books. So was Tony DiGerolamo, the creator of a comic book based on the Jersey Devil, and Jim Albertson, a folk musician, who performed two songs about the Jersey Devil—one "incredibly bad" and the other "incredibly good" (his words).

A biologist, Kelly Cohen, also made a presentation. Cohen had brought along a big bird in a cage, a sandhill crane apparently. There's a theory that migrating sandhill cranes, passing through South Jersey, might have caused the great Jersey Devil scare of January 1909, and Cohen was there to demonstrate a sandhill crane. This one was four-feet tall with a seven-foot wingspan, and it thrashed about the museum as Cohen led us through the imaginative exercise of mistaking a sandhill crane for the Jersey Devil, which was not hard to do.

"He might get a little nervous," she said, "but he is used to public presentation." Someone suggested shutting the fire door "just in case he escapes."

"He's an excitable bird," Cohen said.

It was tough to tell if he officially had top billing, but the de facto marquee presenter appeared to be Harry Leeds. He did after all have a way of stealing scenes.

Harry had dropped his Elks-Lodge-type jacket and VFW hat in favor of a dapper black sport jacket and gray polo shirt, and he looked kind of like a hillbilly Sonny Crocket as he spoke thoughtfully and eloquently on the subject of the "Perception of the Jersey Devil in the Leeds Family," while pan pipes played in the background.

He was gracious and charming and informative and self-deprecating, and perfectly, candidly, self-conscious about his role in the story's perpetuation. This was Harry performing before a hometown audience. Millville isn't exactly Galloway or Egg Harbor—it's on the other side of the Pines—but it's close enough.

"What's the Jersey Devil like?" someone said.

"Ask my wife of forty-seven years," Harry said. "She thinks she's married to him."

Within minutes, they were eating out of his hand.

As he'd done the first time I met him, Harry put in a videotape. There was the requisite struggle with the VCR, and the audience fidgeted. Finally one of the other presenters, Albertson I think, ran up and fixed the VCR and saved the day.

"I'm not technically qualified for this job," Harry said.

Double entendre? Who could say?

The movie started. I was now watching a video of a video. How *meta*, I thought. Just like Harry.

"What I try do on this first short film that I will show you is—it's me passing own the legend to my grandson, who is the thirteenth descendant," Harry said.

The film started.

"We have seven films that we've put together and they're out in the airwaves all over the world," Harry said.

I couldn't quite tell for sure, but it looked like The Scariest Places on Earth that Harry had done with Leut in about 2002. At one point the Devil Hunters appeared with their walkie-talkies. Then Harry himself appeared with some helpful advice for tourists.

"You do not go into the Pine Barrens at night alone," he said, and the audience in the museum laughed and laughed.

It had never been the first-order lie—Harry's fable that he believed in the Jersey Devil, that he'd had met the monster as a child and that he'd had grown up among people who lived in fear of the beast. This was not what had impressed me so deeply about the man. It was the way he had conjured an entire persona—the archetypal Ancient Piney Local, always so instrumental to the story's survival—that I think I found so awe-inspiring. But it was only after a decade of dicking around in libraries and historical societies that I'd come to appreciate this.

In the end, I'd found it impossible not to like Harry, despite my grandmother's feelings for the man. He was a genuine shit-kicker in the grand old tradition, a fellow of undeniable charisma and social charm. I felt like South Jersey would miss him.

"This next film is a delight," Harry, in real life now, said. He'd totally taken over the emceeing duties from the folklorists.

The next film started. It *was* a delight.

The Devil Hunters were back, this time on The Travel Channel. Harry had taken them to the defunct cranberry bog in Smithville. "Oh wow, excellent!" Leut said. "This is straight out of *like* every Jersey Devil picture ever drawn!"

Charley was there, in the movie, looking dubious about the supposed age of the ruins that Harry had taken them to.

"They evidence they gathered was more than they hoped for," the narrator said.

McCloy and Miller appeared.

"McCloy and Miller look great on TV, don't they?" Harry said.

On the TV, McCloy had just suggested that the Jersey Devil had possibly eaten Mother Leeds.

And the audience in the Folklife Center laughed and laughed again.

FIFTY-FOUR

BeBop's Jersey Devil

Somewhere near the end of this absurd journey I went out to Leeds Point to see the hole in the ground—the ruins of the place where *they always said* the Jersey Devil was born.

I'd been talking to Aunt Dottie on the phone. Sometimes I'd call her with specific questions and sometimes I'd just want to chat. She was ninety-four years old. She was lucid and funny, but she hadn't lived in Leeds Point for eighty years. She hadn't set foot in the town in over a decade. Sometimes her memory wasn't great.

For whatever reason on this day she started talking about the ruins of the house in the woods—giving me precise directions to the site. Her voice had taken on this funny quality, as if she were describing something plainly visible before her mind's eye—a precise distance from a particular bend in the road, so many feet from another landmark, on a particular side of the road—so I decided to go out there to have a look.

It was not, for the record, the house that Harry had been taking camera crews to before he was banned. Nor, for that matter, was it the *only* site that Dottie and BeBop had described to me over the years. But I drove out to Leeds Point and followed Aunt Dottie's directions and there it was, exactly where she said it would be—a little hole in the ground, more of an indentation really. There were vegetables growing out of it and others crawling back down into it, old bricks crumbling around the periphery.

It was a quiet evening in the late spring, the sun was setting above the little suburban lanes—Pheasant Meadow Drive, Falcon Crest Court, etc.—and the wings of insects caught the light rays as it set. I looked down at this little indentation in the ground and felt a chill across the back of my neck.

As it happens, I *don't* think Harry Leeds' performance at the Wheaton Arts Down Jersey Folklife Center should be the last word on the Jersey Devil. Harry may have been more candid than he was on The Discovery Channel, but his routine seemed a product of the same basic conceit: that a Piney can have an authentic culture but a suburban housewife from Northfield or Absecon cannot.

Harry may or may not have been a real Piney. I don't pretend to know. I know that he spent much of his adult life in the military, and that he was the mayor of a suburban New Jersey township. But I do know that he played a Piney on TV, and the Jersey Devil was part of this persona.

My grandmother's approach I think was more sincere. Be-Bop and Aunt Dottie knew that their hometown had a history. Their family had been a part of it for three hundred years. Maybe they avoided the symptoms of the suburban disease in part because they hadn't moved to the suburbs. They'd just stayed in place while the suburbs developed around them. I know they never pretended to be Pineys or anything other than what they really were.

But of course I never had to meet Harry Leeds to find someone acting a part. When I left South Jersey, when I went off to college and then to live in New York, I entered my own kind of haunted liminal space of social class and ambition. When I started dropping the family fire-breathing monster into conversations, I was really trying to suggest that I wasn't just another middle-class suburban kid from New Jersey. I was from the *other* New Jersey of acceptable tomato fields and authentic cranberry bogs and rogue bars and slow-moving Piney rivers. My ambitions are of the charming, acceptable kind, affirming to the national character, rather than of the crass, middle class of shampooed lawns and oversized houses and manicured automobiles, I was saying. Be not afraid.

But I wasn't really from that other New Jersey. I grew up in Brookside Farms.

I think BeBop and Aunt Dottie helped me get comfortable with that fact, to realize that you could be from the suburbs and feel attached to an authentic history and culture. It was a shame that it had taken something so rare and fantastic as the Jersey Devil to achieve this basic sense, but it wasn't the Jersey Devil that provided it. It was all the other stuff I found while looking for the Jersey Devil with my grandmother.

EPILOGUE

Deborah Kallikak lived out her days at the Training School in Vineland. Though she had been offered her freedom once she was past breeding age and no longer considered a threat to the Republic, she elected to remain at the institution, which was after all the only home she had ever known.

By 1949, Goddard and Kite's research had long since been discredited and (at least partially) recanted, but the consequences of their work lingered. Goddard himself had gone off to California. The new superintendant of the institution was a man named George Thornton. In a note that appeared in a newsletter on psychiatric disorders, published by the American Association on Mental Deficiency, Deborah was quoted as saying, "Mr. Thornton and I are growing old together."

About the same time, she told a social worker, "I guess after all I'm where I belong, I don't like this feebleminded part but anyhow I'm not i-idic [idiotic?] like some of the poor things you see around here."[175]

In his 1981 book The Mismeasure of Man the natural historian Stephen Jay Gould accused Goddard and Kite not only

---

[175] Quoted in Tullner, Imaginary Birth and Slow Death

of a zealous and near-genocidal scientism but also of a simple journalistic fraud. Gould said that while looking at a volume of Goddard and Kite's book, he noticed that photographs of some Kallikaks had been crudely altered. In one photograph Deborah Kallikak, a "beautiful" woman (Gould's word), was shown sitting in a rocking chair and wearing an elegant white dress, a cat stretched out across her lap. But beside this were other photos of the un-rehabilitated *kakos* sitting in obvious poverty in front of their countryside shacks.

But the book was now nearly seventy years old, and the ink had faded. Gould could see that dark lines had been drawn across the eyes and mouths of the free kakos to make them look more depraved and sinister. "It is now clear that all the photos of noninstitutionalized kakos were altered by inserting heavy dark lines to give eyes and mouths their diabolical appearance," Gould wrote.

Gould said his colleague Steven Selden showed the photos to James Wallace, the director of photographic services at the Smithsonian Institution, who confirmed the crude "skullduggery."

"There can be no doubt that the photographs of the Kallikak family members have been retouched," Wallace wrote. "By contemporary standards, this retouching is extremely crude and obvious. It should be remembered, however, that at the time of the original publication of the book, our society was far less visually sophisticated."

Goddard was not one of Gould's scientific heroes, in case we missed it, and he dedicated his book to his own immigrant grandparents, "Grammy and Papa Joe, who came, struggled, and prospered, Mr. Goddard notwithstanding."

Lord Cornbury, the governor whose various frauds Daniel Leeds had suffered through his association with, was undergoing an image makeover too, it seemed. The historian Patricia Bonomi, whose 1998 book *The Lord Cornbury Scandal: The Politics of Reputation in British America* led the revision of Cornbury, argues that Cornbury was an effective and loyal governor who was the victim, first, of the rumor-mongering of his political opponents during his lifetime and later of the credulity of

Whig historians determined to believe the worst about a decadent royal governor.

Bonomi said the politics of the Cornbury era had been characterized by "intense ardor and unbounded ferocity." Without a sanctioned system of political parties and with few legitimate outlets for criticism, "a climate of conspiracy, slander, and general foul play" were pervasive. "Gutter politics" triumphed in the public square.

In that context, maybe Leeds' News of a Strumpet hadn't been so deranged after all.

Daniel Weeks, a historian who wrote a book on Saltar and Bowne—the collectors of the so-called Blind Tax that had been used to bribe Cornbury—said he too thought there was a revision of the governor's reputation going on. Weeks said he thought Cornbury had been the victim of a deliberate slander by contemporaries, including Lewis Morris.

Cornbury had been under orders from the home government to strengthen the colonial militia, a project in which he faced obstruction from the Quakers. He said the case could be made that New Jersey's smallholders—landowners who were not proprietors—were being "oppressed and abused and their economic interests were being subverted by a very strong and corrupt proprietary power headed by Lewis Morris." The reason Cornbury got in trouble, Weeks said, was because he tried to do something about this.

"I think there was a big publicity campaign in New Jersey and in New York to ridicule Cornbury and bring him into disrepute during his own time," Weeks said. "When you look under the surface of that, you can't find any evidence."

The case for Cornbury's transvestitism had apparently always been flimsy, having been based on claims that originated decades after his death, or in letters written by his enemies.[176] The famous portrait at the New York Historical Society, allegedly depicting the governor in drag, was no longer identified as Cornbury at all. When I went up to the historical society on Central Park West, the curator who showed me around had been a graduate student under Bonomi. She said there had

---

[176] Bonomi

been resistance on the part of at least one of the trustees to taking down the little ID tag that had identified the woman as Cornbury. The transvestite governor had been a museum superstar, she said, and people were sad to see her go.

At the time of this writing, the good people of the Kingdom of Lucerne were off to attend the first annual New Jersey Pirates and Privateers Weekend at the Ocean County Fairgrounds in Berkeley Township.

Joe Fulginiti (aka Gray Beard) had passed away sadly after a battle with pancreatic cancer. But Donn Shearer could still be seen brandishing a sword and swinging from the rigging of various ships along the coast, including the Dark Star, a fifty-foot pirate ship replica that took people on tours out of Wildwood. He cuts quite a figure, it must be said.

Mike Schum, who'd made those excellent comments about the bones in the pond in Millville, had bought a shop that specializes in role-playing games—Aetherstorm Gaming. They host tournaments in North Cape May. There was a nice write-up in the Press of A.C.

Mike Zohn and his partners from Obscura Antiques and Oddities had their own show ("Oddities") on The Discovery Channel and The Science Channel. They were finishing the fourth series.

Lord Whimsy's book, The Affected Provincial's Companion, had been published in Germany (*Handbuch für den wahrhaftigen Dandy*) with a drawing of a lobster on the cover. An option to turn the English version of the book into a movie had been purchased by Johnny Depp's production company, Whimsy announced. He seemed at least as pleased about the lobster.

Leut and Co. had gone into semi-retirement. When I asked her for a last interview, she kind of politely declined saying she had a family now and a full-time job. The Hunters still made the odd foray into the woods and sometimes updated their website though. Whatever it is they're looking for, I hope they find it.

Harry Leeds' influence could still be felt across Galloway and South Jersey. One day, while wandering around Smithville, I stepped into an antiques shop that does a good business in Jersey Devil tchotchkes. The proprietor, a man named Marshall, said Harry used to bring the film crews by his place when he was alive. After the shows aired, there would often be a bump in sales. After one show, a life-size carving of the Jersey Devil that had sat out in front of the shop was sold for a considerable sum.

Marshall said there was still a steady stream of documentarians, college kids mostly, who would come down to make movies for school. "They're in these programs," he said. "They want to make a video. So they come all the way down here from Seton Hall or wherever—two good-looking girls and two guys—and can we make a movie?

"That's modern folklore."

And Galloway Township never did adopt the Jersey Devil as the Official Township Mascot. There was something comforting in this, I thought. I assumed the mascot had been the idea of real estate agents or the spouses of orthodontists, but of course it had been Harry's idea all along.

Official explanations on why the initiative failed vary. Meg Worthington, who was a member of the township council at the time the idea was proposed, told me there had been resistance to having a devil affiliated publicly with the town.

"People just weren't thrilled about having a devil as their mascot," she said. "Galloway had a large Christian community [at the time]. Today it's much more diverse. I guess people are kind of conservative socially, and I guess they just thought, 'Hey, this has gone too far. We really don't want the devil being our primary mascot.' And I can see what they're talking about."

There had also been resistance from the township's police officers, apparently, who'd felt that having a little turnip-headed monster in a bow tie on the sides of the squad cars would make them look "ridiculous" (Meg's word).

"They lashed out as well," Meg said. "They thought it demeaned them, hurt their credibility."

Ken Sooy, who agreed with Meg about the Christian community, said there was also a copyright problem.

"They copied a picture to put on the police cars," Ken said. "They had the decals made, or the plastic stick-ons, and they violated somebody's copyright, because they didn't get permission from the guy who owned the picture, stupidly.

"The main problem was the churches though."

If there were objections to putting a sick or abused child on tee-shirts and township letterhead, the religious lobby did not voice these concerns.

Ken seemed to think that the copyright holder, Robert Sheetz—whose brother, Ed (now deceased), drew the image of the "Original Jersey Devil" (Ed's words) that is sold on tee-shirts and postcards across South Jersey—would have happily agreed to partner with the township, but when I spoke to Robert, I got a different impression.

Robert confirmed that the family had sued Galloway for copyright infringement. When I asked if he would have allowed the township to use the copyrighted image if they had asked permission, and if there had been some kind of compensation agreement, he said he didn't think so.

"We've already had so many dealings with this drawing—three lawsuits that we've already filed over the years, and numerous times we've refused to let people use it for various reasons, because we are very protective of it. We don't wish to have anyone using it, whereby we haven't given any permission."

He continued.

"Just because the Leeds family feels as though that—going back years—that their ancestors were responsible for this in the beginning, does not necessarily mean that they have a right of any kind for this particular drawing. Do you follow me?"

"I just wanted to know if Galloway violated your copyright," I said.

"Galloway has no right to use our copy of the Jersey Devil. If they want to have a Jersey Devil for any reason, then they can draw up their own version of it.

"If you want any more information, go to one of your relatives in Galloway Township—anybody by the name of Leeds. According to them, they're all related."

I kind of got the feeling if I'd stayed on the phone much longer he would have sued me.

There were any number of reasons why I thought the Jersey Devil shouldn't be anything's Official Mascot, but I liked that it had been this combination of religion and commerce that had kept the monster where it belonged.

Then a thought presented.

"Ha ha! The Christians! Suppressing the heathenish tendencies of a member of the Leeds family! Just like Daniel's almanac in 1687!"

And there was something comforting in that too.

Thanks to the editorial crew: McFadden, Hernantelope, Tropsie(s), Choome, Jungstar and Vahjonsovich.

Thanks to Mr. Phipps for snarky re-write advice and Edwina for correcting faux-English diction.

Thanks to El and Tom for putting up with my garbage.

Thanks mom and dad for everything else in the entire world.